DATE DUE

OCT 2 1 2003	
NOV 0 4 2003	

BRODART   Cat. No. 23-221

The Psychology of Eating

The Psychology of Eating
From Healthy to Disordered Behavior

Jane Ogden

Blackwell
Publishing

350 Main Street, Malden, MA 02148–5018, USA
108 Cowley Road, Oxford OX4 1JF, UK
550 Swanston Street, Carlton South, Melbourne, Victoria 3053, Australia
Kurfürstendamm 57, 10707 Berlin, Germany

First published 2003 by Blackwell Publishers Ltd, a Blackwell Publishing
company

Library of Congress Cataloging-in-Publication Data

Ogden, Jane, 1966–
    The psychology of eating : from healthy to disordered behavior / Jane
Ogden.
        p. cm.
Includes bibliographical references and index.
    ISBN 0–631–23373–3 (hbk : alk. paper) — ISBN 0–631–23374–1 (pbk :
alk. paper)
    1. Eating disorders.   2. Appetite disorders.   3. Food habits.   I.
Title.
        RC552.E18   O47   2003
        616.85′26—dc21
                                                                2002004858

A catalogue record for this title is available from the British Library.

Set in 10/12 Sabon
by Graphicraft Limited, Hong Kong
Printed and bound in the United Kingdom
by MPG Books, Bodmin, Cornwall

For further information on
Blackwell Publishing, visit our website:
http://www.blackwellpublishing.com

Contents

Figures

Foreword

The study of eating covers a range of areas from food choice, weight concern, and eating-related problems such as obesity to eating disorders. My own work has concentrated on dieting and its place in the treatment of obesity. Obesity has long been decried as a serious medical disorder. For example, a government-sponsored conference in the United States in the early 1980s concluded that anyone who was as little as 5 lbs heavier than "ideal" weight should be considered to be obese. It was recommended that anyone suffering from such "obesity" should be aggressively treated with calorie-restricted diets. Many in the medical profession have long seen obesity as the primary health threat facing Western societies (and their definition of obesity, as the US National Institute of Health conference indicates, includes more than half of the adult population). Obesity has been accused of causing heart disease, diabetes, elevated blood pressure, and a whole host of other medical maladies that may contribute to elevated mortality. More ominously, the incidence of obesity has been rising steadily since the 1960s. Dieting, then, seems on the face of it to be a solution to a widespread health threat.

What those condemning the harmful effects of obesity often fail to notice is the strong association between overweight and repeated, often chronic, attempts at weight loss through caloric restriction, or dieting. Approximately 25 years ago, I attended a scientific conference focused on eating behavior and obesity. I presented my newly published research on what appeared to be paradoxical overeating in restrained eaters (or chronic dieters), and suggested that weight-loss dieting might not only fail to be helpful to obese patients, but could actually be harmful. A doctor in the audience jumped up and angrily accused me of killing people by encouraging them not to diet. He insisted that dieting was the only "cure" for the "disease" of obesity, a disease that would surely kill anyone so afflicted.

In fact, several researchers, including Ruben Andres and Paul Ernsberger among others, have demonstrated that for many disorders attributed to obesity, dieting and weight fluctuations are more likely to be the culprits than is merely being overweight. A more sinister association that also gets little attention from the obesity field is that between the increase in the incidence of dieting over the past four decades and the corresponding increase in the incidence of obesity. The growth in obesity is usually cited as a reason for imposing more diets on the overweight; the fact that it is just as likely that the proliferation of diets and weight-loss programs is *causing* increased obesity is rarely acknowledged. In fact, the multi-billion-dollar diet industry relies on the failure of its products to produce weight loss to maintain its profitability. The fact that diets may promote obesity may simply be a fortuitous side-effect, from their point of view.

Before the mid-1970s, research on dieting focused exclusively on how to make people eat less and lose weight. Occasionally the issue of how to maintain weight loss was addressed, but in general, the only query was how much weight could the person lose. The question of *whether* someone who was overweight (by whatever definition) should try to lose weight never arose. Since that time, there has been steadily increasing attention to the impact of repeated weight loss attempts on the person and on society. Research on dieting has shifted to an examination of what restrictive dieting does to various aspects of behavior, emotion, and self-image, as well as to its personal and societal costs. Psychologists, sociologists, nutritionists, physiologists, and medical specialists have all contributed to the growing literature examining the various effects of restricting one's caloric intake in order to lose weight. Societal, family, and individual factors influencing the decision to diet are being investigated to broaden our understanding of who diets and why. The contribution of these same factors, as well as dieting and body dissatisfaction, to eating disorders such as anorexia nervosa and bulimia nervosa is also coming under closer scrutiny. Instead of a general recommendation that everyone should diet and lose weight, prescriptions for self-improvement now emphasize healthy eating and exercise; lifestyle changes have replaced self-starvation.

The growth of the dieting research establishment may not be as prodigious as that of the diet industry itself, but the sheer variety of disciplines wherein dieting is now an accepted topic of investigation militates against anyone being able to be conversant with all aspects of the literature. In *The Psychology of Eating*, Jane Ogden brings together research on dieting from these diverse domains. She examines the full spectrum of healthy eating and food choice, through the body dissatisfaction pervasive among women in Western culture and contributing to the epidemic of weight-loss attempts, and on to obesity and clinically disordered eating and their treatments. In this volume, Ogden reviews and cogently discusses the prevailing theoretical approaches to the understanding of weight-loss dieting and its associated maladies, and carefully examines the contributions and shortcomings of each theory. Although it is probably no longer possible to be exhaustive in reviewing this line of work, Jane Ogden, a long-time, well-regarded contributor to this field herself, has managed successfully to bring together the principal issues and domains concerning the interrelated areas of dieting, obesity, body image, and eating disorders. In addition, she presents an integrated scrutiny of the major themes and motifs running through the field. This sort of overview of such a wide-ranging area is difficult to perform, but this volume does an excellent job, providing a much-needed synthesis for those who study and treat those with disordered eating and body image. This is also an outstanding introduction for anyone entering the field. For researchers, practitioners, and those simply interested in understanding the complexities of eating and related issues, this book provides a valuable resource.

Janet Polivy
Toronto, Canada

Acknowledgments

This book is the product of many years of research, supervision, teaching, and conferences. I am therefore grateful to all my students who have enthusiastically engaged with my lectures on eating behavior and have wanted to carry out studies in this area. They have often been challenging and have offered new interpretations and new questions for study. I am also grateful to my colleagues who have supported my research interests and have been prepared to discuss ideas and projects. I am particularly grateful to David Armstrong for all his interest, insights, and support.

chapter one

Introduction

Obesity and overweight are on the increase, eating disorders are becoming more common, and many people diet to lose weight. In parallel, diet-related subjects are in vogue and over the past few years there has been an explosion of interest in any aspect of diet, from healthy eating through to eating disorders. The popular press offers features on diet, bookstores sell books on healthy eating, and television producers broadcast documentaries on people who are overweight, underweight, have a solution to weight, or need a solution to their weight. The academic and research literature has also proliferated. Diet provides the focus for dieticians, nutritionists, endocrinologists, geneticists, psychiatrists, and a range of psychologists from social, biological, health, and clinical psychology perspectives. There are journals dedicated to the subject of diet, specialist books produced, and conferences held to provide a forum for discussion. This book aims to provide a detailed map of this expanding area.

This chapter covers:

- The aim of this book
- The focus of this book
- The structure of this book
- Further reading

The Aim of this Book

The literature on diet is vast and is contributed to by individuals with a range of different interests. Some are interested in healthy eating, others are concerned with eating-related problems, and most produce work which is focused on their one area. Work is specialized to enable detailed research and theoretical development. As a result the relationships between different aspects of diet-related work become unclear. For example, healthy eating provides a context for understanding obesity, but these two literatures are often kept separate. Food choice offers a context for understanding eating disorders, but the paths of these areas rarely cross. Dieting and body dissatisfaction are relevant to understanding eating disorders, obesity, and food choice but are only sometimes studied by the same people and written about in the same papers and same books.

This book aims to provide a detailed map of the diet literature and to cover the spectrum of eating behavior, from healthy eating through body dissatisfaction and dieting to obesity and eating disorders. In doing so, it aims to show how these different areas are related to each other and to draw out some common themes which run through this immense body of work.

The Focus of this Book

Diet is studied from a range of different disciplinary and theoretical perspectives, and a comprehensive understanding of diet cannot be achieved without these different literatures. This book therefore includes literature from a range of approaches such as nutrition, physiology, psychiatry, and sociology. But the primary focus of the book is psychology. In particular, this book draws on mainstream psychology in the form of developmental, cognitive, clinical, social, and health psychology. It integrates this approach with that from the psychotherapeutic literature which is often based on clinical experience and informed by feminist or psychoanalytic perspectives. This book therefore offers "the psychology of eating" in the broadest sense and illustrates how a wealth of perspectives have been used to analyze this complex area of work.

The Structure of this Book

The structure of the book is illustrated in figure 1.1. Chapter 2 focuses on healthy eating and describes what is currently considered to be a healthy diet, how diet influences health both as a cause of morbidity and mortality, and how diet is used as a treatment once a diagnosis has been made. It then explores who has a healthy diet and describes large-scale surveys which have assessed children's diets, the diets of young adults, and the diets of the elderly. This chapter draws on both the medical and nutrition literatures. Next, chapter 3 explores the research on food choice. This chapter focuses on three main theoretical approaches from psychology, and assesses the contribution of developmental theories, with their

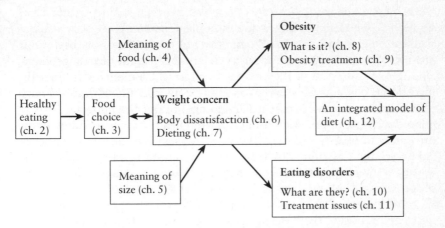

Figure 1.1   From healthy to disordered eating: A spectrum of diet

emphasis on exposure, social learning, and associative learning, and cognitive theories, with their focus on social cognition models. It also describes psychophysiological approaches in terms of the role of drugs and neurochemicals on hunger and satiety, the impact of chemical senses on food choice, the impact of food on mood and cognitions, and the role of stress in determining either under- or overeating. It is argued that, although useful as a means to explain healthy eating, these approaches to food choice only implicitly include the complex meanings associated with both food and body size. In line with this, chapters 4 and 5 address the meanings of food and the meanings of size respectively. Chapter 4 draws on the sociological and anthropological literatures which have examined the meaning of food and integrates these with writings of psychotherapists. Chapter 5 examines the meaning of size in terms of the impact of the media and the associations with thinness and obesity, and examines both the social psychology and feminist approaches. As a result of these meanings, food choice is complex and many individuals develop weight concern. One form of weight concern is body dissatisfaction; chapter 6 examines what body dissatisfaction is, how it is measured, and what causes it. Body dissatisfaction often leads to dieting, which is the focus of chapter 7. This chapter describes why body dissatisfaction leads to dieting. It explores the consequences of attempted food restriction and specifically examines the relationship between dieting and overeating and the role of boundaries, mood, cognitions, self-awareness, and denial. These two chapters on weight concern mainly focus on psychological research, with an emphasis on experimental and cross-sectional work. Weight concern illustrates the point at which healthy eating starts to become problematic. It is a common phenomenon and one which has unpleasant consequences for the majority of those who show both body dissatisfaction and dieting. Obesity is another eating-related problem, and this is addressed in the next two chapters. Chapter 8 describes the prevalence, consequences, and causes of obesity, and argues that, although diet plays an important part in its etiology, eating behavior needs to be placed within a multidimensional causal model. Chapter 9 addresses the treatment of obesity and explores the effectiveness of dietary treatments, addresses the question of whether obesity should be treated at all, and explores alternative treatments including exercise, drugs, and surgery. Anorexia and bulimia nervosa are also diet-related problems and these form the focus of chapters 10 and 11. Chapter 10 explores the prevalence and causes of these eating disorders; chapter 11 examines the treatment approaches which have been developed and tested. The chapters on obesity and eating disorders describe the psychological, epidemiological, nutritional, and psychiatric perspectives on these problems. Throughout the book many themes recur across disparate aspects of diet and from different literatures. The final chapter (chapter 12) first provides a summary of the book. It then highlights these common themes and offers an integrated model of diet.

Further Reading

This book provides a comprehensive overview of the literature on diet from healthy to disordered eating. Below is a guide to journals and books for further reading on the subject.

Journals

There are many journals which publish work in the area of diet. The following are some of the major specialist journals:

International Journal of Eating Disorders
International Journal of Obesity
Appetite
European Eating Disorders Review
Obesity Research
European Journal of Clinical Nutrition
American Journal of Clinical Nutrition

Journal of the American College of Nutrition
British Journal of Nutrition
Nutrition Review

These journals can be accessed on-line through databases such as Pubmed, Medline, and Psychinfo.

Books

There are numerous popular and academic books on aspects of diet. The following are some key books which are a useful source of information.

Healthy eating

Truswell, A.S. 1999: *ABC of Nutrition*, 3rd edition. London: BMJ Books.

Food choice

Capaldi, E. (ed.) 1996: *Why We Eat What We Eat. The Psychology of Eating*. Washington, DC: American Psychological Society.
Gilbert, S. 1986: *Pathology of eating*. London: Routledge.
Mela, D.J. and Rogers, P.J. 1997: *Food, Eating and Obesity: The Psychobiological Basis of Appetite and Weight Control*. London: Chapman and Hall.
Shepherd, R. (ed.) 1989: *Handbook of the Psychophysiology of Human Eating*. London: Wiley.

Weight concern

Grogan, S. 1999: *Body Image: Understanding Body Dissatisfaction in Men, Women and Children*. London: Routledge.
Ogden, J. 1992: *Fat Chance! The Myth of Dieting Explained*. London: Routledge.
Polivy, J. and Herman, C.P. 1983: *Breaking the Diet Habit*. New York: Basic Books.
Thompson, J.K. 1990: *Body Image Disturbance: Assessment and Treatment*. Elmsford, NY: Pergamon.

Obesity

Allison, D.B. (ed.) 1995: *Handbook of Assessment Methods for Eating Behaviours and Weight Related Problems: Measures Theory and Research*. Newbury Park, CA: Sage.

Brownell, K.D. and Foreyt, J.P. (eds) 1986: *Handbook of Eating Disorders: Physiology, Psychology and Treatment of Obesity, Anorexia and Bulimia*. New York: Basic Books.
NHS Centre for Reviews and Dissemination, University of York 1997: *Systematic Review of Interventions in the Treatment and Prevention of Obesity*. York, UK.
Obesity 1999: *The Report of the British Nutrition Foundation Task Force*. Oxford: Blackwell Science.

Eating disorders

Allison, D.B. (ed.) 1995: *Handbook of Assessment Methods for Eating Behaviors and Weight Related Problems: Measures Theory and Research*. Newbury Park, CA: Sage.
Brownell, K.D. and Foreyt, J.P. (eds) 1986: *Handbook of Eating Disorders: Physiology, Psychology and Treatment of Obesity, Anorexia, and Bulimia*. New York: Basic Books.
Brownell, K.D. and Fairburn, C.G. (eds) 1995: *Eating Disorders and Obesity*. New York: Guilford Press.
Fallon, P., Katzman, M.A., and Wooley, S.C. (eds) 1994: *Feminist Perspectives on Eating Disorders*. New York: Guilford Press.
Gordon R.A. 2000: *Eating disorders: Anatomy of a Social Epidemic*, 2nd edition. Oxford: Blackwell.
Hsu, L.K.G. 1990: *Eating Disorders*. New York: Guilford Press.
Stunkard, A.J. and Stellar, E. (eds) 1984: *Eating and Its Disorders*. Research publications, Association for Research in Nervous and Mental Disease, Vol. 62. New York: Raven Press.
Szmukler, G., Dare C. and Treasure, J. (eds) 1995: *Handbook of Eating Disorders: Theory, Treatment and Research*. London: Wiley.

Classic texts

Bruch, H. 1974: *Eating Disorders: Obesity, Anorexia and the Person Within*. New York: Basic Books.
Keys, A., Brozek, J., Henscel, A., Mickelson, O., and Taylor, H.L. 1950: *The Biology of Human Starvation*. Minneapolis, MN: University of Minnesota Press.
Orbach, S. 1986; 2nd edn 1993: *Hunger Strike: The Anorectic's Struggle as a Metaphor for Our Age*. London: Faber and Faber.
Orbach, S. 1978: *Fat is a Feminist Issue . . . How to Lose Weight Permanently – Without Dieting*. London: Arrow Books.

chapter two

Healthy Eating

This chapter explores what constitutes a healthy diet, with a focus on the five main food groups. It then describes the role of diet in health in terms of contributing towards illnesses such as coronary heart disease, cancer, and diabetes, protecting the body against such illnesses, and being part of interventions to improve health once a diagnosis has been made. Finally it examines the results of large-scale surveys which have described the diets of children, young adults, and the elderly.

This chapter covers:

- What is healthy eating?
- The role of diet in contributing to illness
- The role of diet in treating illness
- Who has a healthy diet?

What is Healthy Eating?

The nature of a good diet has changed dramatically over the years. In 1824 *The Family Oracle of Good Health* published in the UK recommended that young ladies should eat the following at breakfast: "plain biscuit (not bread), broiled beef steaks or mutton chops, under done without any fat and half a pint of bottled ale, the genuine Scots ale is the best," or if this was too strong it suggested "one small breakfast cup . . . of good strong tea or of coffee – weak tea or coffee is always bad for the nerves as well as the complexion." Dinner is later described as similar to breakfast, with "no vegetables, boiled meat, no made dishes being permitted much less fruit, sweet things or pastry . . . the steaks and chops must always be the chief part of your food." Similarly in the 1840s Dr Kitchener recommended in his diet book a lunch of "a bit of roasted poultry, a basin of good beef tea, eggs poached . . . a sandwich – stale bread – and half a pint of good home brewed beer" (cited in Burnett,

1989). In the US at this time, diets were based around the staples of corn, rye, oats, and barley for making bread, the use of molasses as a cheap sweetener, and a quantity of salt pork which could survive the warmer weather in the absence of refrigeration. Blood pudding was also a source of meat; it was made from hog or occasionally beef blood and chopped pork, seasoned and stuffed into a casing which was eaten with butter crackers to provide a meal for the workers (McIntosh, 1995). What constituted a healthy diet in the nineteenth century was very different from current recommendations.

Concerns about the nation's diet in the UK came to a head following recruitment attempts during the Boer War at the beginning of the twentieth century, when 38 percent of volunteers were rejected due to malnutrition and poor health. This resulted in the establishment of the Inter Departmental Committee on Physical Deterioration, and the passing of the Education Act in 1906 and the Medical Inspection Act in 1907, introducing free school meals and free medical and dental checks for children. The government also introduced parent education classes to inform mothers about the nature of a healthy diet. In the US, the Great Depression of the 1930s resulted in Roosevelt's New Deal programs, the establishment of food subsidies, and the distribution of surplus agricultural products to families and schools. Refrigeration and canned foods also became more available at this time. Greater improvements in the diets of many Western countries, however, mainly came about as a result of the rations imposed during both the world wars. These rations resulted in a reduction in the consumption of sweet foods and an increase in the place of carbohydrate in the diet. In addition, the need to provide the armed forces with safe and healthy food stimulated research into food technology and established dietary standards.

Since this time there has been a proliferation of the literature on healthy eating. A visit to any bookstore will reveal shelves of books proclaiming diets to improve health through weight management, or salt reduction, or a Mediterranean approach to eating, or the consumption of fiber. There is, however, a consensus among nutritionists nowadays as to what constitutes a healthy diet (Department of Health, 1991). Food can be considered in terms of its basic constituents: carbohydrate, protein, alcohol, and fat. Descriptions of healthy eating tend to describe food in terms of broader food groups and make recommendations as to the relative consumption of each of these groups as follows. Current recommendations are illustrated in figure 2.1; these are:

- **Fruit and vegetables:** A wide variety of fruit and vegetables should be eaten, and preferably five or more servings should be eaten per day (National Heart Forum, 1997).

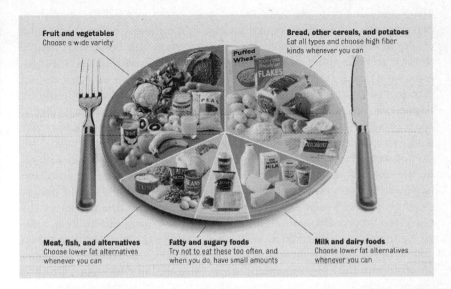

Fruit and vegetables
Choose a wide variety

Bread, other cereals, and potatoes
Eat all types and choose high fiber
kinds whenever you can

Meat, fish, and alternatives
Choose lower fat alternatives
whenever you can

Fatty and sugary foods
Try not to eat these too often, and
when you do, have small amounts

Milk and dairy foods
Choose lower fat alternatives
whenever you can

Figure 2.1   Healthy eating (*Source*: The balance of good health, reprinted by permission of the Health Education Authority 1994)

- **Bread, pasta, other cereals, and potatoes:** Plenty of complex carbohydrate foods should be eaten, preferably those high in fiber.
- **Meat, fish, and alternatives:** Moderate amounts of meat, fish, and alternatives should be eaten and it is recommended that the low-fat varieties are chosen.
- **Milk and dairy products:** These should be eaten in moderation, and the low-fat alternatives should be chosen where possible.
- **Fatty and sugary foods:** Food such as potato chips, candy, and sugary drinks should be consumed infrequently and in small amounts.

Other recommendations for a healthy diet include a moderate intake of alcohol (a maximum of 3–4 units per day for men and 2–3 units per day for women), the consumption of fluoridated water where possible, a limited salt intake of 6 g per day, eating unsaturated fats from olive oil and oily fish rather than saturated fats from butter and margarine, and consuming complex carbohydrates (e.g. bread and pasta) rather than simple carbohydrates (e.g. sugar). It is also recommended that men aged between 19 and 59 consume about 2,550 calories per day and that similarly aged women consume about 1,920 calories per day, although this depends on body size and degree of physical activity (Department of Health, 1995).

Recommendations for children are less restrictive for fatty foods and dairy products, and it is suggested that parents should not restrict the fat intake of children aged under two. By five years old, however, children should be consuming a diet similar to that recommended for adults, indicating that a child's fat intake should be gradually reduced between the ages of two and five. Prentice and Paul (2000) argued that the fat requirements for children can be judged in terms of sufficient fat in the diet to provide fuel for energy, to give an adequate supply of essential fatty acids, and to allow the adequate absorption of fat-soluble minerals. Children therefore need more fat than adults, and for younger children breast milk is an essential source of fat, particularly in developing countries where weaning foods tend to be low in fat. Children also require more dairy products than adults to meet their greater need for calcium.

Current recommendations for healthy eating in adults therefore describe a balanced and varied diet which is high in fruit and vegetables and complex carbohydrates and low in fat. Children's diets should approximate this, but can be higher in fat and dairy products. Healthy eating is considered important as it impacts on health in two main ways. First, a healthy diet can be protective against the development of illness, while an unhealthy diet may contribute towards disease. Second, a healthy diet can help manage or treat an illness once a diagnosis has been made. Over recent years there has been a proliferation of research into the association between diet and health. Much of this remains controversial, and even the most generally accepted "facts" have not been left uncontested. What is presented here reflects the state of research at this time.

The Role of Diet in Contributing to Illness

An individual's health is influenced by a multitude of factors including their genetic makeup, their behavior, and their environment. Diet plays a central role and can contribute directly towards health. It can also impact on health through an interaction with a genetic predisposition. The effect of both over- and underweight on health and diseases such as coronary heart disease, hypertension, and cancer is discussed in chapters 8 and 10. The impact of the actual composition of a person's diet is described here.

Diet and coronary heart disease

Before the beginning of the twentieth century, coronary heart disease was a rare condition. Its incidence increased steadily in Western countries from 1925 to 1977 except for a dip during World War II. Since this time its incidence has fallen dramatically in the US and Australia and has fallen by about 25 percent in the UK (World Health Organization, 1994). In contrast, Eastern European countries including Russia, Hungary, and the Czech Republic have experienced an increase in coronary mortalities in recent years. At this time, coronary heart disease remains the single largest cause of death in the US and the UK. Although biological factors play a part in coronary heart disease, diet is probably the fundamental factor. This is clearly shown by incidence of the disease in immigrant groups. For example, coronary mortalities are very rare in Japan, but Japanese groups who move to the West quickly show the pattern of mortality of their new environment (Syme et al., 1975). Coronary heart disease usually involves three stages: 1) the development of atherosclerosis (narrowing of the arteries), 2) a thrombosis superimposed on the atherosclerotic plaque (a blood clot), and the impact of this, which can be sudden death, heart attack, angina, or no symptoms; this depends on 3) the state of the myocardium. Each of these three stages is influenced by different components of the diet.

Atherosclerosis

The material that accumulates in the arteries causing atherosclerosis is cholesterol ester. Cholesterol ester exists in the plasma of the blood and is higher in individuals with a genetic condition called familial hypercholesterolemia. Half of the cholesterol in the blood is biosynthesized by the liver and half comes from the diet. Diet influences blood levels of cholesterol in two ways. First, blood cholesterol can be raised by saturated fat found in animal fat and in boiled, plunged, or expresso coffee (not instant or filtered). Secondly, blood cholesterol levels can be reduced by polyunsaturated fats found in plant oils, by soluble types of fiber such as pectin found in fruit and vegetables and by oat fiber found in vegetables, oatmeal, and oat bran, and by soya protein (Truswell, 1999).

Thrombosis

A blood clot is caused by an increase in the coagulation factors in the blood including Factor VIII, fibrinogen, and platelets. Under normal healthy conditions a blood clot is essential to stop unwanted bleeding. If there is already a degree of narrowing of the arteries this can cause a coronary event. Thrombosis is influenced by diet in the following ways:

a fatty meal can increase Factor VIII, smoking and obesity are associated with increased fibrinogen, alcohol is associated with decreased fibrinogen, and fish oil (found in sardines, herring, mackerel, or salmon) has been shown to reduce platelet aggregation (Truswell, 1999).

The state of the myocardium

The general healthiness of the myocardium may determine how an individual responds to having a thrombosis. An overall healthy diet consisting of a balance between the five food groups is associated with the health of the myocardium.

Diet and blood pressure

Essential hypertension (raised blood pressure) is one of the main risk factors for coronary heart disease and is linked with heart attacks, angina, and strokes. It is more common in older people and is related to diet in the following ways:

Salt

Salt is the component of diet best known to affect blood pressure, and the Intersalt study (Intersalt Cooperative Research Group, 1988) explored the relationship between salt and blood pressure in 10,000 people from 52 different communities in 30 countries around the world. The results showed a correlation between 24-hour urinary sodium and the rise in blood pressure with age. However, correlations between salt intake and blood pressure are difficult to confirm due to methodological problems such as the variation in daily salt intake and differences in individual sensitivity to salt. As a means to reduce hypertension, health regulatory bodies recommend a salt intake of less than 6 g per day, which is much less than that currently consumed by most people. Avoiding salt is difficult, however, as most of the salt consumed is not that added at the table (9 percent) or in cooking (6 percent) but used in the processing of food (58.7 percent). For example, salted peanuts contain less salt than bread per 100 g. Furthermore, many canned foods such as baked beans and breakfast cereals have their high salt content masked by the sugar added. Salt is also necessary, particularly in poorer countries where diarrhea is common, as it helps the body to rehydrate itself. In fact Britain imposed an extortionately high salt tax when it governed

India, as salt was not only a useful flavor enhancer but also an essential part of the diet and therefore guaranteed a high level of revenue.

Alcohol

Alcohol consumption has several negative effects on health. For example, alcoholism increases the chance of liver cirrhosis, cancers (e.g. pancreas and liver), memory deficits, and self-harm through accidents (Smith and Kraus, 1988). Alcohol also increases the chances of hypertension; heavy drinkers have higher blood pressure than light drinkers and abstainers, and this has been shown to fall dramatically if their alcoholic beer is replaced by low-alcohol beer. Alcohol may, however, also have a positive effect on health. In a longitudinal study, Friedman and Kimball (1986) reported that light and moderate drinkers (between 1 and 2 units per day) had lower morbidity and mortality rates than both nondrinkers and heavy drinkers. They argued that alcohol consumption reduces coronary heart disease via the following mechanisms: 1) a reduction in the production of catecholamines when stressed, 2) the protection of blood vessels from cholesterol, 3) a reduction in blood pressure, 4) self-therapy, and as 5) a short-term coping strategy. The results from the General Household Survey (1992) also showed some benefits of alcohol consumption, with the reported prevalence of ill health being higher among nondrinkers than among drinkers.

Micronutrients

Several components of the diet have been hypothesized to lower blood pressure but evidence is still in the preliminary stages. For example, potassium found in foods such as potatoes, pulses, and dried fruits, calcium found in hard water, long-chain fatty acids found in fish oils, and magnesium found in foods such as bran, wholegrain cereals, and vegetables have been shown to reduce blood pressure.

Diet and cancer

Diet is believed to account for more variation in the incidence of all cancers than any other factor, even smoking (Doll and Peto, 1981). How diet affects cancer is unclear. One theory is that all foodstuffs contain natural non-nutrients which can trigger cancer. Such factors have been shown to cause mutations in a laboratory bacterial culture, but there is no evidence that they can do the same in human beings. A second theory claims that a poor diet weakens the body's defense mechanisms. The cancers most clearly related to diet are those of the esophagus, stomach, and large intestine. There is also a possible link with breast cancer.

Esophageal cancer

The rates of esophageal cancer vary enormously around the world and are at their highest in China, Iran, and South Africa. The strongest dietary factor in the development of esophageal cancer is alcohol, particularly when the alcohol is derived from apples, and this often works in association with the impact of smoking. Other dietary factors which have been hypothesized to be associated with esophageal cancer include vitamin deficiencies and moldy food.

Stomach cancer

The incidence of stomach cancer has halved in the past 25 years in Britain but is at its highest in Japan. The epidemiological data suggest that salt, and pickled and salted foods trigger stomach cancer, while fruits and vegetables, the refrigeration of foods, and vitamin C intake are protective.

Large intestine cancer

Cancer of the large bowel is the second largest cause of death from cancer in Britain and is ten times more common in Britain and the US than in developing countries. Rates in Scotland have been among the highest in the world. Evidence suggests that wheat fiber and vegetables may be protective, while animal fat and meat (particularly if well cooked) and some types of beer are associated with its causation.

Breast cancer

Breast cancer is the largest cause of death in women in Britain, with the majority of cases occurring in women who are post-menopausal. Possible dietary links with breast cancer include high fat intake and weight gain as predictive, and wheat fiber and soya as protective (Truswell, 1999).

Diet and diabetes mellitus

There are two types of diabetes. Type 1 diabetes always requires insulin and is also called childhood onset diabetes. Some evidence has pointed towards a role for genetic factors, and research has also indicated that it is more common in those children who were not exclusively breastfed for the first three to four months of life (Truswell, 1999). Type 2 diabetes tends to develop later on in life and can be managed by diet alone. This form of diabetes shows a clearer relationship with diet. Type 2 diabetes seems to be mainly a complication of being overweight and the risk of developing it is greater in those who show weight around the abdomen rather than on the thighs or buttocks (Ohlson et al., 1985; see chapter 8 below). It is generally assumed that Type 2 diabetes is associated with diets high in sugar. Evidence for this association is poor, and high fat intake seems to be its main dietary predictor, with high fiber and high carbohydrate intakes being protective. Interestingly, moderate drinking as opposed to abstaining is associated with a reduced risk of Type 2 diabetes.

Diet and gallstones and urinary tract stones

Gallstones are more likely to occur in women and certain ethnic groups. Obesity and dieting with rapid weight loss can increase the risk of gallstones, while moderate alcohol intake and vegetarian and high fiber diets are protective. Urinary tract stones can be made of either calcium or oxalate. Calcium stones are related to diets rich in protein, sodium, simple carbohydrates, vitamin D, calcium, alcohol, curry, and spicy foods and low in cereal fiber and water. Oxalate stones are related to diets rich in foods containing oxalates such as spinach, rhubarb, beetroot, and tea, and diets low in water.

The Role of Diet in Treating Illness

This chapter has focused on the association between diet and the onset of a disease. Research has also examined whether changes in diet can improve health after the diagnosis of a problem. Obesity treatment is explored in chapter 9 and the treatment of eating disorders is examined in chapter 11. There is no evidence for the impact of dietary change on cancer; therefore this chapter will examine the impact of dietary change on coronary heart disease and diabetes.

Coronary heart disease

Patients diagnosed with angina or heart disease, or who have had a heart attack, are recommended to change their lifestyle, with particular emphasis on stopping smoking, increasing their physical activity, and adopting a healthy diet. The effectiveness of such rehabilitation interventions has been assessed using randomized control trials. For example, van Elderen, Maes, and van den Broek (1994) developed a health education and counseling program for patients with cardiovascular disease after hospitalization, with weekly follow-ups by telephone. Thirty CHD sufferers and their partners were offered the intervention and were compared to a group of 30 control patients who received standard medical care only. The results showed that after two months, the patients who had received health education and counseling reported a greater increase in physical activity and a greater decrease in unhealthy eating habits. In addition, among those subjects in the experimental condition (receiving health education and counseling), those whose partners had also participated in the program showed greater improvements in their activity and diet and, in addition, showed a decrease in their smoking behavior. At 12 months, subjects who had participated in the health education and counseling program maintained their improved eating behavior. The authors concluded that although this study involved only a small number of patients, the results provide some support for including health education in rehabilitation programs. In 1999, Dusseldorp et al. carried out a meta-analysis of 37 studies examining the effects of psychoeducational programs (health education and stress management) for coronary heart disease patients. The results indicated that such programs produced a 34 percent reduction in cardiac mortality, a 29 percent reduction in recurrence of heart attack, and significant positive effects on blood pressure, cholesterol, body weight, smoking behavior, physical exercise, and eating habits. However, the educational programs had no effects on whether the patient had subsequent surgery, or on their mood. Therefore changing diet as part of a complex series of lifestyle changes seems to result in improved health both in the short and longer term.

Diabetes mellitus

Dietary change is central to the management of both Type 1 and Type 2 diabetes. At times this aims to produce weight loss, as a 10 percent decrease in weight has been shown to result in improved glucose metabolism (Blackburn and Kanders, 1987; Wing et al., 1987). Dietary interventions are also used to improve the self-management of diabetes, and aim to encourage diabetic patients to adhere to a more healthy diet. Patients with Type 1 diabetes should receive individualized dietary advice from their health professionals. More general advice can be given to those with Type 2 diabetes. In 1998, Nuttall and Chasuk reviewed the literature on dietary management and diabetes and described the following as "general principles" of the nutritional management of Type 2 diabetes:

- Dietary recommendations for diabetes patients should reflect those for healthy eating aimed at the general population.
- These recommendations should be flexible and target the individual needs of each patient.
- Sugar does not need to be restricted more than for a healthy diet.
- Readily digestible starches raise the blood glucose more than sugars.
- The benefits of weight loss on glycemic control will occur within two or three months.
- Patients should not be criticized for failing to lose weight, and weight cycling should be avoided.

Dietary interventions for diabetes take the form of either primary care or hospital-based educational input involving either one-to-one contact, lectures, or group discussions. Dietary advice is often given alongside other general health advice, as those with diabetes are at increased risk of coronary heart disease. Much research has addressed the effectiveness of these interventions. For example, Beeney and Dunn (1990) evaluated the impact of five hospital-based diabetes education programs in Australia on 558 patients, and reported that although the educational interventions resulted in improved diabetes knowledge, this did not correlate with improved metabolic control. In an attempt to improve the effectiveness of educational input for diabetes, Wing and colleagues have varied interventions for diabetes in terms of a range of factors. For example, they have altered the intensity of the intervention, the length of follow-up, the type of interventions used (e.g. very low calorie diet versus usual care) and whether the intervention is targeted at individuals with diabetes or those at risk due to familial history (e.g. Wing, 1993; Wing et al., 2001). Evaluations of such interventions indicate that although they may improve knowledge, change beliefs, and create some change in diet, weight, and even metabolic control in the short term, attrition rates are high and levels mostly return to baseline in the longer term. This pessimistic picture is similar to that for obesity described in chapter 9, and indicates that improving diabetes self-care is a difficult task. Recently there has been an interest in developing interventions for diabetes which are tailored to the individual and draw upon the theoretical perspectives described by the Stages of Change model (Prochaska and DiClemente, 1984) and social cognition theories (e.g. Ajzen and Fishbein, 1970; Ajzen, 1985). Such an approach involves brief but intensive one-to-one interventions and focuses on the motivation and self-efficacy of the individual (Clark and Hampson, 2001). Analysis of the effectiveness of this approach remains in its early stages.

In summary, at the point of writing this book there are clear recommendations concerning what constitutes a healthy diet. Whether these recommendations remain consistent over the next few years remains to be seen. There is also a substantial literature exploring the impact of diet on health, and the evidence suggests that apart from weight per se having an effect on the health status of the individual, the separate components of a diet are also important in terms of causing ill health, being protective, and also promoting better health once a diagnosis has been made. In the light of this literature the question "Who has a healthy diet?" has been asked.

Who Has a Healthy Diet?

Ideally there would be one international survey of food intake which accessed a representative sample of males and females of all ages, cultures, religions, and geographical locations and used the same definitions of food as a means to describe the content of people's diet across the world. This has not been done, and probably never will be. However, what has been done are surveys of different age groups, in different countries, using different measures. This overview will explore children's diets, the healthy eating practices of young adults, and eating in the elderly, and provides a series of snapshots into the diets of these different groups. Most of the available data come from the Western hemisphere. Diets in the developing world will also be considered with reference to malnutrition in children.

Children's diets

Understanding children's diets is important not only in terms of the health of the child but also in terms of health later on in life, as there is some evidence that dietary habits acquired in childhood persist through to adulthood. For example, Steptoe, Pollard, and Wardle (1995) showed that adults prefer to eat foods that they ate as children, and longitudinal studies of food intake such as the Minnesota Heart Study (Kelder et al., 1994) indicated that children who select the least healthy options at baseline continue to do so throughout the study. Further, the Bogalusa Heart Study (Nicklas, 1995) compared the dietary intake of ten-year-olds with that of young adults and found similarities with respect to protein, total fat, dietary cholesterol, and sodium. There is also some evidence for the impact of childhood nutrition on adult health. For example, Hales et al. (1991) reported an association between poor fetal and infant growth and impaired glucose tolerance at age 64. Likewise, adult atherosclerosis which begins in childhood (Moller et al., 1994) has been shown to relate to serum lipid levels in the child (Newman et al., 1986; Berenson et al., 1998). Barker (e.g. 1992) has specifically examined the role of both childhood and *in utero* nutrition on the development of adult illnesses and has provided evidence for his "Fetal Origins Hypothesis." In particular, his research indicates that early nutrition may relate to illnesses such as hypertension, ischemic heart disease, stroke, and chronic bronchitis. Researchers have therefore examined the question "What do children eat?"

The Western hemisphere

Many children's diets in the West are unsatisfactory. For example, the Bogalusa Heart Study in the US showed that the majority of 10-year-olds exceeded the American Heart Association dietary recommendations for total fat, saturated fat, and dietary cholesterol (Nicklas, 1995). A survey in the UK in 1989 showed a similar picture, with 75 percent of children aged 10 to 11 exceeding the recommended target level for percentage of energy derived from fat (Buttriss, 1995). Likewise, Wardle (1995) reported that 9–11-year-old British children showed inadequate intakes of fruit and vegetables, consuming less that half the recommended daily intake on average, and that only 5 percent of children studied exceeded the recommended intake.

One large-scale survey in the US provided a more detailed view on children's diets. For this study data were collected from over 7,000 children aged 5 and under, and nearly 11,000 aged 19 and under, in the years 1994–1996 and 1998 (US Department of Agriculture, 1999). In terms of overall healthiness the data indicated that for those aged 5 and under, 46.2 percent consumed the recommended amount of food energy, 96.6 percent consumed the recommended amount of protein, 30.6 percent consumed the recommended amount of total fat, and 86.5 percent consumed the recommended amount of cholesterol. This suggests that the majority of children have healthy diets in terms of protein, but only a minority have healthy diets in terms of fat and overall calorie consumption. For essential vitamins and nutrients, only 52 percent showed a healthy consumption of calcium, and 60.9 percent consumed iron at the recommended levels. For those aged between 5 and 19 the results showed a similar pattern, with the majority having a healthy diet in terms of protein but not in terms of other dietary components. The data also provided insights into what food was eaten and where, and indicated that over 80 percent of both the under-5s and those between 5 and 19 were eating snacks which contributed about 20 percent of their total calorie intake. In sum, the data on children's diets indicate that children's diets in both the US and UK do not match the recommendations for a healthy diet, particularly in terms of their fat content and consumption of fruit and vegetables.

Malnutrition

Dietary recommendations aimed at Western countries in the main emphasize a reduction in food intake and the avoidance of overweight. For the majority of the developing world, however, undereating remains a problem resulting in physical and cognitive difficulties and poor resistance to illness due to lowered intakes of both energy and micronutrients. Recent data from the World Health Organization examining the prevalence of malnourished children indicate that 174 million children under the age of five in the developing world show low weight for age, and that 230 million are stunted in their growth. Further, the WHO estimates that 54 percent of childhood mortality is caused by malnutrition, particularly related to a deficit of protein and energy consumption. Such malnutrition is highest in South Asia, where it is estimated to be five times higher than in the Western hemisphere, followed by Africa, then Latin America. Prentice and Paul (2000) explored the dietary needs of children in the developing world. They suggested that a common problem is the low energy content of the foods used to wean children, and that this can lead to growth faltering and ultimate malnutrition. In particular they studied children's diets in Gambia and concluded that breast milk is an essential source of fat for children, and is often the main source of fat until the child is two years old. Problems occur, however, when children are weaned onto low-fat adult food. They also concluded that although these lowered energy diets can sustain health in the absence of illness, they are insufficient to provide "catch up" growth if the child is ill with infections such as diarrhea. Malnutrition is therefore a problem for developing countries. The WHO states that malnutrition also occurs in virtually all countries, as even when the majority of a country's population has access to sufficient food a minority can still be deprived.

Eating in young adults

Many eating habits are established in childhood. They are then further crystallized in the first years of independence when individuals become responsible for their own food choices and food preparation. Research has therefore explored the diets of young adults. One large-scale study at the beginning of the 1990s examined the eating behavior of 16,000 male and female students aged between 18 and 24 from 21 European countries (Wardle et al., 1997). During classes, students completed self-report measures of their food intake, resulting in a 90 percent response rate, and were asked about five aspects of their dietary behavior. Overall, the results showed that 39 percent tried to avoid fat, 41 percent tried to eat fiber, 53.5 percent ate fruit daily, 54 percent limited their consumption of red meat, and 68 percent limited salt (see figure 2.2). These results

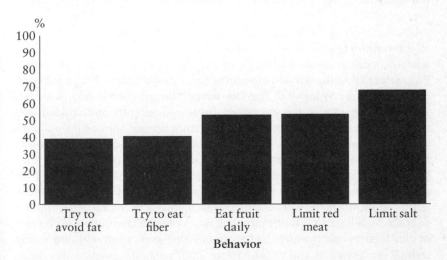

Figure 2.2 Healthy eating in young adults (*Source:* after J. Wardle, A. Steptoe, F. Bellisle, B. Davou, K. Reschke, R. Lappalainen, and M. Fredrikson, Health dietary practices among European students, *Health Psychology*, 16 (1997), reprinted by permission of American Psychological Association, Washington DC)

suggest that the prevalence of these fairly basic healthy eating practices was low in this large sample of young adults. In terms of gender differences the results showed that more women than men stated that they tried to avoid fat and cholesterol, tried to eat more fiber, avoided red meat, and were more likely to eat fruit daily; men and women were similar in their use of salt. Thus, the women in this sample reported more healthy eating practices than the men. The results also provided insights into the different dietary practice across the different European countries. Overall, there was most variability between countries in terms of eating fiber, red meat, fruit, and salt. Fat consumption seemed to vary the least. Those in countries such as Sweden, Norway, the Netherlands, and Denmark ate the most fiber, while those in Italy, Hungary, Poland, and Belgium ate the least. Students in Mediterranean countries such as Italy, Portugal, and Spain ate the most fruit and those in England and Scotland ate the least. Further, the young adults in Belgium and Portugal made fewest attempts to limit red meat, while those in Greece, Austria, Norway, and Iceland made more attempts. Finally, salt consumption was highest in Poland and Portugal and lowest in Sweden, Finland, and Iceland. In sum, this survey indicates that the diets of young adults across Europe could be improved, although women generally have healthier diets than men, and that young adults in some countries have adopted some, although not all, of the recommended healthy dietary practices.

The elderly

It is estimated that there are currently 580 million individuals aged over 60 in the world today and that the proportion of elderly people in the West is higher than it has ever been. This is due to three factors. First, there is a cohort effect, with many children being born over 60 years ago who have now become the elderly population. Second, there are fewer children being born now, resulting in a large percentage of the population being elderly; third, life expectancy has increased such that more people live to an older age. Several studies have explored the diets of this elderly population. Overall, this research indicates that energy intake declines in old age and that malnutrition in the elderly is associated with dementia, depression, social isolation, institutionalization, and loneliness (Schlettwein-Gsell et al., 1991).

One large-scale study took place in 1988–9 and collected dietary information from 2,586 elderly people aged between 70 and 75 living in 19 small towns in 12 countries across Europe (de Groot, van Staveren, and Hautvast, 1991). The study used a questionnaire and collected data concerning all aspects of food intake as well as demographic, mobility, and health factors. Follow-up data were then collected in 1993. Although participation was somewhat selective, as the more healthy were more willing to participate, the results provide some insights into dietary habits across Europe. Overall, the results showed that participants varied in terms of the frequency of their meals, with participants in eastern towns eating three times a day on average, while those in Dutch and German-speaking towns ate six or more times a day. They varied in terms of the frequency of cooked meals, with high numbers of both men (15 percent) and women (13 percent) not having a cooked meal every day. They also varied in terms of consuming home-produced foods, with about 90 percent always eating at home, but 10 to 30 percent in Swiss towns eating regularly at restaurants and 30 percent of the elderly in Greece and Poland regularly eating in the homes of their children. Further, they could be classified according to the use of specific diets, with a large number following low-salt diets or a diet prescribed by the doctor (Schlettwein-Gsell et al., 1991). As to whether the participants had a healthy diet, the results showed that the majority of the sample were healthy in terms of the prevalence of anemia and blood albumin (as a marker for nutritional status) (Dirren et al., 1991) and blood lipid levels (Kafatos et al., 1991). In terms of energy intakes, the data indicated that women in seven countries had energy intakes lower than required, but that the majority were consuming the correct amount of protein. For levels of fat and carbohydrate intake the results showed that southern Europe was healthier than northern Europe, but that in terms of alcohol and vitamin A, northern European countries were healthier than those in the south (Schlettwein-Gsell et al., 1991). Overall, 19 percent of men and 26 percent of women had an inadequate nutrient intake (de Groot and van Staveren, 2000). These baseline data therefore indicated that the diet of the majority of this elderly population was satisfactory but that both gender and geographical differences existed which the authors argued could provide a basis for identifying risk profiles for future interventions (de Groot, van Staveren, and Hautvast, 1991). At the five-year follow-up the data were analyzed to explore the predictors of survival. The results for Danish and Greek cohorts suggested that an increased probability of survival was related to the consumption of a traditional Mediterranean diet rich in cereals, vegetables, fruit, lean meat, and olive oil (Trichopoulou et al., 1995; Osler and Schroll, 1997).

In another study of the elderly, the National Diet and Nutrition Survey examined the eating habits of nearly 2,000 men and women aged over 65 years in the UK (Bates, Prentice, and Finch, 1999). The results showed that nutrient intakes were generally satisfactory but that this population showed deficient intakes of vitamin D, magnesium, potassium, and copper. These deficiencies were greater for the older elderly, those living in institutions, those of lower social class, and those who lived in the northern regions of the UK. In terms of gender differences the results showed that women ate more butter, full-fat milk, cakes, apples, pears, and bananas, while the men consumed more eggs, sugar, certain meat products, beer, and lager. The authors concluded that there were no overall differences between men and women in terms of the healthiness of their diets, as men had better diets in some respects and women in others.

In a further study of the elderly in the US, 474 non-institutionalized individuals with ages from 65 to 98 were interviewed about their food intake in the previous 24 hours (Ryan, Craig, and Fin, 1992). The data were analysed to explore their diets in terms of food-group intake and vitamin consumption. The results showed that a large percentage showed intakes of energy and nutrients which were below the recommended amounts. In addition, a large minority of men and women had poor intakes of vitamin E, calcium, and zinc, and a large minority of men also had poor intakes of vitamin A.

Overall, research exploring the diets of the elderly indicates that although many younger and non-institutionalized members of this group have satisfactory diets, many, particularly the older elderly, report diets which are deficient in vitamins, too low in energy, and have poor nutrient content.

Conclusion

Recommendations for a healthy diet have changed much over the years but it is currently believed to consist of five food groups consumed in differing proportions. In particular, a healthy adult diet should be high in complex carbohydrates, fruit and vegetables and low in fat. Children's diets can be higher in fat and dairy products. Diet affects health through an individual's weight but also by its role in the development of illnesses such as heart disease, cancer, and diabetes. Much research has addressed the role of diet in health and although at times controversial, studies suggest that foods such as fruits and vegetables, oily fish, and oat fiber can be protective, while salt and saturated fats can increase the risk of poor health. Diet also has a role to play in treating illness once diagnosed, particularly coronary heart disease and diabetes. Although interventions to improve diet can be successful in the short term, many individuals return to baseline levels of self-care at follow-up. Research has also explored how healthy people's diets are. This chapter reviewed a selection of studies which suggest that the diets of children, young adults, and the elderly are deficient in a variety of ways. These studies have focused on diets in developed countries where the problem is mainly one of overconsumption. Research shows that for developing countries the situation is the opposite, with malnutrition being a common problem.

Towards an integrated model of diet

At present there exists a consensus among health professionals as to what people should eat. But many people do not eat in line with these recommendations. Research has therefore addressed the factors involved in food choice. This is the focus of the next chapter.

chapter three

Food Choice

This chapter asks "Why do people eat what they eat?" Much research has addressed the complex factors involved in food choice. This chapter explores three main psychological perspectives. First it examines developmental models of food choice with their focus on exposure, social learning, and associative learning. Second, it examines research which has drawn upon cognitive theories, with their emphasis on motivation, and social cognition models. Finally it explores the psychophysiological perspectives. In particular it assesses the role of drugs and neurochemicals on hunger and satiety, the impact of chemical senses on food choice, and the role of stress in determining either under- or overeating.

This chapter covers:

- Developmental models of food choice
- Cognitive models of food choice
- Psychophysiological models of food choice

There is consistent evidence that newborn babies innately prefer certain foods. In studies using facial expressions and sucking behavior as an index of preference, babies have been shown to prefer sweet-tasting substances (Desor, Maller, and Turner, 1973) and salt (Denton, 1982), and to reject bitter tastes (Geldard, 1972). Beauchamp and Moran (1982) reported, however, that six-month-old babies who were accustomed to drinking sweetened water drank more sweetened water than those babies who were not. It seems that even the apparently inherent preference for sweet tastes may be modified by familiarity. Furthermore, given the enormous cultural diversity on food preferences, it is generally accepted that food choice following birth is more complex than simply a matter of innate preferences. This has been clearly argued by Rozin, who stated that "there is no doubt that the best predictor of the food preferences, habits and attitudes of any particular human would be information about his ethnic group . . . rather than any biological measure that one might imagine" (Rozin, 1982).

Food choice is the result of a complicated set of processes which have been categorized in a range of different ways. Early research (Yudkin, 1956) argued that food choice was influenced by physical factors (e.g. geography, season, economics, and food technology), social factors (e.g. religion, class, education, and advertising), and psychological factors (e.g. hereditary, allergy, and nutritional needs). Shepherd (1989) described the factors influencing food choice as either external (the type of food, the social and cultural context) or internal to the individual (personality, sensory factors, cognitions). One large-scale survey of food choice conceptualized the factors that influence food choice as nine different motivations (Steptoe, Pollard, and Wardle, 1995). These were sensory appeal, the costs to health, convenience of purchasing and of preparation, weight control, familiarity of the food, mood regulation, the natural content of the food, and ethical concerns about manufacture and country of origin. This chapter focuses on psychological influences, and describes this literature in terms of the core theoretical approaches which have been used to explore food choice. These are the developmental processes, the role of cognitions, and psychophysiological factors (See figure 3.1).

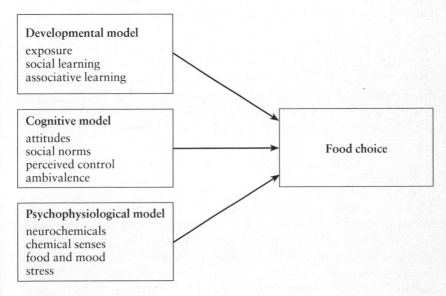

Figure 3.1 Food choice

Developmental Models of Food Choice

A developmental approach to food choice emphasizes the importance of learning and experience and focuses on the development of food preferences in childhood. An early pioneer of this research was Davis (1928, 1939), who carried out studies of infants and young children living in a pediatrics ward in the US for several months. The work was conducted at a time when current feeding policies endorsed a very restricted feeding regimen, and Davis was interested to examine infants' responses to a self-selected diet. She explored whether there was an "instinctive means of handling . . . the problem of optimal nutrition" (Davis, 1928). The children were offered a variety of 10 to 12 healthy foods prepared without sugar, salt, or seasoning and were free to eat whatever they chose. Her detailed reports from this study showed that the children were able to select a diet consistent with growth and health and were free from any feeding problems. The results from this study generated a theory of "the wisdom of the body," which emphasized the body's innate food preferences. In line with this, Davis concluded from her data that children have an innate regulatory mechanism and are able to select a healthy diet. She also, however, emphasized that they could only do so as long as healthy food was available, and argued that the children's food preferences changed over time and were modified by experience. Birch, who has extensively studied the developmental aspects of food choice, interpreted Davis's data to suggest that what was innate was the "ability to learn about the consequences of eating [and] to learn to associate food cues with the consequences of ingestion in order to control food intake" (Birch, 1989, p. 181). Birch therefore emphasized the role of learning and described a developmental systems perspective (e.g. Birch, 1999). In line with this analysis, the development of food preferences can be understood in terms of exposure, social learning, and associative learning.

Exposure

Human beings need to consume a variety of foods in order to have a balanced diet, and yet show a fear and avoidance of novel foodstuffs, known as "neophobia." This has been called the "omnivore's paradox" (Rozin, 1976). Young children will show neophobic responses to food but must come to accept and eat foods which may originally appear as threatening. Research has shown that mere exposure to novel foods can change children's preferences. For example, Birch and Marlin (1982) gave two-year-old children novel foods over a six-week 'period. One food was presented 20 times, one 10 times, one 5 times, while one remained novel. The results showed a direct relationship between exposure and food preference, and indicated that a minimum of about 8 to 10 exposures was necessary before preferences began to shift significantly. Neophobia has been shown to be greater in males than females (both adults and children), to run in families (Hursti and Sjoden, 1997), and to be minimal in infants who are being weaned onto solid foods but greater in toddlers and pre-school children (Birch et al., 1998).

One hypothesized explanation for the impact of exposure is the "learned safety" view (Kalat and Rozin, 1973), which suggests that preference increases because eating the food has not resulted in any negative consequences. This suggestion has been supported by studies which exposed children either to just the sight of food or to both the sight and taste of food. The results showed that looking at novel foods was not sufficient to increase preference and that tasting was necessary (Birch et al., 1987). It would seem, however, that these negative consequences must occur within a short period of time after tasting the food, as telling children that a novel food is "good for you" has no impact on neophobia, whereas telling them that it will taste good does have (Pliner and Leowen, 1997). The exposure hypothesis is also supported by evidence indicating that neophobia reduces with age (Birch, 1989).

Social learning

Social learning describes the impact of observing other peoples' behavior on one's own behavior and is sometimes referred to as "modeling" or "observational learning." An early study explored the impact of "social suggestion" on children's food choices, arranging to have children observe a series of role models making food choices different to their own (Duncker, 1938). The models chosen were other children, an unknown adult, and a fictional hero. The results showed a greater change in the child's food preference if the model was an older child, a friend, or the fictional hero. The unknown adult had no impact on food preferences. In another study, peer modeling was used to change children's preference for vegetables (Birch, 1980). The target children were placed at lunch for four consecutive days next to other children who preferred a different vegetable (peas vs carrots). By the end of the study the children showed a shift in their vegetable preference which persisted at a follow-up assessment several weeks later. The impact of social learning has also been shown in an intervention study designed to change children's eating

Figure 3.2　Social eating

behavior using video-based peer modeling (Lowe, Dowey, and Horne, 1998). This series of studies used video material of "food dudes," – older children enthusiastically consuming refused food – which was shown to children with a history of food refusal. The results showed that exposure to the "food dudes" significantly changed the children's food preferences and specifically increased their consumption of fruit and vegetables. Food preferences, therefore, change through watching others eat (see figure 3.2).

Parental attitudes to food and food choices are also central to the process of social learning. In line with this, Wardle (1995) contended that "Parental attitudes must certainly affect their children indirectly through the foods purchased for and served in the household, . . . influencing the children's exposure and . . . their habits and preferences." Some evidence indicates that parents do influence their children's eating behavior. For example, Klesges et al. (1991) showed that children selected different foods when they were being watched by their parents than when they were not. Olivera et al. (1992) reported a correlation between mothers' and children's food intakes for most nutrients in preschool children, and suggested targeting parents to try to improve children's diets. Likewise, Contento et al. (1993) found a relationship between mothers' health motivation and the quality of children's diets. Parental behavior and attitudes are therefore central to the process of social learning, with research highlighting a positive association between parents' and children's diets.

There is, however, some evidence that mothers and children are not always in line with each other. For example, Wardle (1995) reported that mothers rated health as more important for their children than for themselves. Alderson and Ogden (1999) similarly reported that whereas mothers were more motivated by calories, cost, time, and availability for themselves, they rated nutrition and long-term health as more important for their children. In addition, mothers may also differentiate between themselves and their children in their choices of food. For example, Alderson and Ogden (1999) indicated that mothers fed their children more of the less healthy dairy products, breads, cereals, and potatoes, and fewer of the healthy equivalents to these foods, than they ate themselves. Furthermore, this differentiation was greater in dieting mothers, suggesting that mothers who restrain their own food intake may feed their children more of the foods that they are denying themselves. A relationship between maternal dieting and food choice is also supported by a study of 197 families with pre-pubescent girls by Birch and Fisher (2000). This study concluded that the best predictors of the daughter's eating behavior were the mother's level of dietary restraint and her perceptions of the risk of her daughter becoming overweight. In sum, parental behaviors and attitudes may influence those of their children through the mechanisms of social learning. This association, however, may not always be straightforward, with parents differentiating between themselves and their children in terms of both food-related motivations and food choice.

The role of social learning is also shown by the impact of television and food advertising. For example, after Eyton's *The F Plan Diet*, which recommended a high fiber diet, was launched with a great deal of media attention in 1982, sales of bran-based cereals rose by 30 percent, wholewheat bread sales rose by 10 percent, wholewheat pasta by 70 percent, and baked beans by 8 percent. Similarly, when Edwina Curry, then junior health minister in the UK, said on television in December 1988 that "most of the egg production in this country, sadly, is now infected with salmonella," egg sales fell by 50 percent and by 1989 were still only at 75 percent of their previous levels (Mintel, 1990). Similarly, massive publicity about the health risks of beef in the UK between May and August 1990 resulted in a 20 percent reduction in beef sales. One study examined the public's reactions to media coverage of "food scares" such as salmonella, listeria, and BSE and compared it to their reactions to coverage of the impact of food on coronary heart disease. The study used interviews, focus groups, and an analysis of the content and style of media presentations (Macintyre et al., 1998). The authors concluded that the media have a major impact upon what people eat and how they think about foods. They also argued that the media can set the agenda for public discussion. The authors stated, however, that the public do not just passively respond to the media "but that they exercise judgement and discretion in how much they incorporate media messages about health and safety into their diets" (p. 249). Further, they argued that food choices are limited by personal circumstances such as age, gender, income, and family structure, and that people actively negotiate their understanding of food within both the micro context (such as their immediate social networks) and the macro social contexts (such as the food production and information production systems). The media are therefore an important source for social learning. This study suggests, however, that individuals learn from the media by placing the information being provided within the broader context of their lives.

In summary, social learning factors are central to choices about food. These include significant others in the immediate environment, particularly parents and the media, who offer new information, present role models, and illustrate behavior and attitudes which can be observed and incorporated into the individual's own behavioral repertoire.

Associative learning

Associative learning refers to the impact of contingent factors on behavior. At times these contingent factors can be considered reinforcers, in line with operant conditioning. In terms of food choice, research has explored the impact of pairing food cues with aspects of the environment. In particular, food has been paired with a reward, used as the reward, and paired with physiological consequences.

Rewarding food choice

Some research has examined the effect of rewarding food choice, as in "If you eat your vegetables I will be pleased with you." For example, Birch, Zimmerman, and Hind (1980) gave children food in association with positive adult attention compared with more neutral situations. This was shown to increase food preference. Similarly, the recent intervention study described above which used videos to change eating behavior reported that rewarding vegetable consumption increased that behavior (Lowe, Dowey, and Horne, 1998). Rewarding food choice seems to improve food preferences.

Food as the reward

Other research has explored the impact of using food as a reward. For these studies, gaining access to the food is contingent upon another behavior, as in "If you are well behaved you can have a cookie." Birch, Zimmerman, and Hind (1980) presented children with foods either as a reward, as a snack, or in a non-social situation (the control). The results showed that food acceptance increased if the foods were presented as a reward, but that the more neutral conditions had no effect. This suggests that using food as a reward increases the preference for that food.

The relationship between food and rewards, however, appears to be more complicated than this. In one study, children were offered their preferred fruit juice as a means to be allowed to play in an attractive play area (Birch et al., 1982). The results showed that using the juice as a means to get the reward reduced the preference for the juice. Similarly, Lepper et al. (1982) told children stories about children eating imaginary foods called "hupe" and "hule," in which the child in the story could only eat one if they had finished the other. The results showed that the food which was used as the reward became the least preferred one, and this has been supported by similar studies (Birch, Marlin, and Rotter, 1984; Newman and Taylor, 1992). These examples are analogous to saying "If you eat your vegetables you can eat your dessert." Although parents use this approach to encourage their children to eat vegetables, the evidence indicates that this may be increasing their children's preference for pudding even further, as pairing two foods results in the "reward" food being seen as more positive than the "access" food. As Birch (1999) concluded, "Although these practices can induce children to eat more vegetables in the short run, evidence from our research suggests that in the long run parental control attempts may have negative effects on the quality of children's diets by reducing their preferences for those foods" (p. 51).

Not all researchers, however, agree with this conclusion. Dowey (1996) reviewed the literature examining food and rewards and argued that the conflicting evidence may relate to methodological differences between studies, and that studies designed to change food preference should be conducted in real-life situations, should measure outcomes over time and not just at one time-point, should involve clear instructions to the children, and should measure actual food intake, not just the child's stated preference. The recent intervention study described above incorporated these methodological considerations into its design (Lowe, Dowey, and Horne, 1998) and concluded that food preferences could be improved by offering rewards for food consumption as long as the "symbolic context" of reward delivery was positive and did not indicate that "eating the target foods was a low value activity" (p. 78). As long as the child cannot think "I am being offered a reward to eat my vegetables, therefore vegetables must be an intrinsically negative thing," then rewards may work.

The association between food and rewards highlights a role for parental control over food choice. Some research has addressed the impact of control, as studies indicate that parents often believe that restricting children's access to food and forbidding them to eat certain foods are good strategies to improve food preferences (Casey and Rozin, 1989). Birch (1999) reviewed the evidence for the impact of imposing any form of parental control over food intake, and argued that it is not only the use of foods as rewards which can have a negative effect on children's food preferences, but also attempts to limit a child's access to foods. She concluded from her review that "child feeding strategies that restrict children's access to snack foods actually make the restricted foods more attractive" (p. 52). For example, when food is made freely available children will choose more of the restricted than the unrestricted foods, particularly when the mother is not present (Fisher and Birch, 1999; Fisher et al., 2000).

Food and physiological consequences

Studies have also explored the association between food cues and physiological responses to food intake. There is a wealth of literature illustrating the acquisition of food aversions following negative gastrointestinal consequences (e.g. Garcia, Hankisn, and Rusiniak, 1974). For example, an aversion to shellfish can be triggered after one case of stomach upset following the consumption of mussels. Research has also explored pairing food cues with the sense of satiety which follows their consumption. One early study of infants showed that by about 40 days of age infants adjusted their consumption of milk depending upon the calorific density of the drink they were given (Formon, 1974). Similarly, children can adjust their food intake according to the flavor of foods if certain flavors have been consistently paired with a given calorific density (Birch and Deysher, 1986).

Problems with a developmental model

A developmental approach to food choice provides detailed evidence on how food preferences are acquired in childhood. This perspective emphasizes the role of learning and places the individual within an environment which is rich in cues and reinforcers. Such an analysis also allows for a moderate interaction between learning and physiology. However, there are some problems with this perspective, as follows:

- Much of the research carried out within this perspective has taken place within the laboratory as a means to provide a controlled environment. Although this methodology enables alternative explanations to be excluded, the extent to which the results would generalize to a more naturalistic setting remains unclear.
- A developmental model explores the meaning of food in terms of food as a reward, food as a means to gain a reward, food as status, food as pleasant, and food as aversive. However, food has a much more diverse set of meanings which are not incorporated into this model. For example, food can mean power, sexuality, religion, and culture. Such complex meanings are not incorporated into a developmental perspective.
- Once eaten, food is incorporated into the body and can change body size. This is also loaded with a complex set of meanings such as attractiveness, control, lethargy, and success. A developmental model does not address the meanings of the body.
- A developmental model includes a role for cognitions, as some of the meanings of food including reward and aversion are considered to motivate behavior. These cognitions remain implicit, however, and are not explicitly described.

In summary, developmental models of food choice highlight a central role for learning. From this perspective, food choice is influenced by exposure, which can reduce neophobia, social learning through the observation of important others, and associative learning, as food cues can be paired with aspects of the environment and the physiological consequences of eating.

Cognitive Models of Food Choice

A cognitive approach to food choice focuses on an individual's cognitions and has explored the extent to which cognitions predict and explain behavior. Some research has highlighted a weak link between a person's beliefs about their ability to control their health and dietary behavior (e.g. Bennet et al., 1995). Similarly, one large-scale study of dietary practice across Europe reported an association between beliefs about the importance of specific dietary practices and the implementation of these practices (Wardle et al., 1997). Most research using a cognitive approach has, however, drawn on social cognition models. Several models have been developed, including the Health Belief Model (HBM: Becker and Rosenstock, 1984), the Protection Motivation Theory (PMT: Rogers, 1985), the Theory of Reasoned Action (TRA: Fishbein and Ajzen, 1975), the Theory of Planned Behavior (TPB: Ajzen, 1985), and the Health Action Process Approach (HAPA: Schwarzer, 1992). These models vary in terms of whether they use behavioral intentions or actual behavior as their outcome variable and the combination of cognitions that they include. In general, however, the models incorporate the attitude to a given behavior, risk perception, perceptions of severity of the problem, the costs and benefits of a given behavior, self-efficacy, past behavior, and social norms; they are described in detail in texts such as Ogden (2000b) and Conner and Norman (1996). These models have been applied to eating behavior both as a means to predict food choice and as central to interventions to change food choice. This chapter will focus on research using the TRA and TPB, as these have most commonly been applied to aspects of food choice (see figures 3.3 and 3.4).

Some research using a social cognitive approach to food choice has focused on predicting the intentions to consume specific foods. For

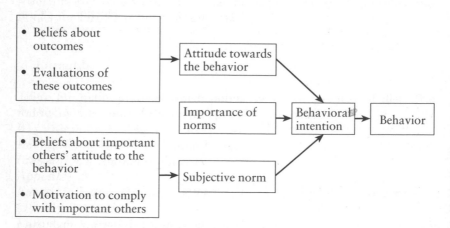

Figure 3.3   The basics of the Theory of Reasoned Action

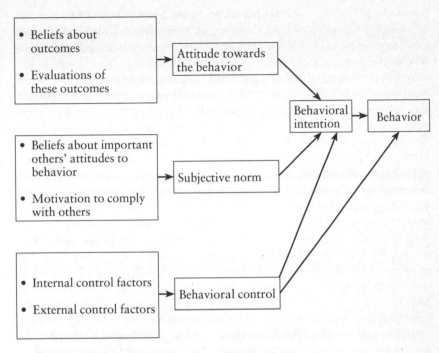

Figure 3.4   The basics of the Theory of Planned Behavior

example, research has explored the extent to which cognitions relate to the intentions to eat cookies and wholemeal bread (Sparks, Hedderley, and Shepherd, 1992), skimmed milk (Raats, Shepherd, and Sparks, 1995), and organic vegetables (Sparks and Shepherd, 1992). Much research suggests that behavioral intentions are not particularly good predictors of behavior per se, which has generated work exploring the intention–behavior gap (Gollwitzer, 1993; Sutton, 1998). Therefore, studies have also used the TRA and the TPB to explore the cognitive predictors of actual behavior. For example, Shepherd and Stockley (1985) used the TRA to predict fat intake, and reported that attitude was a better predictor than subjective norms. Similarly, attitude has also been found to be the best predictor of table salt use (Shepherd and Farleigh, 1986a), eating in fast-food restaurants (Axelson, Brinberg, and Durand, 1983), the frequency of consuming low-fat milk (Shepherd, 1988), and healthy eating conceptualized as high levels of fiber and fruit and vegetables and low levels of fat (Povey et al., 2000). Research has also pointed to the role of perceived behavioral control in predicting behavior, particularly in relation to weight loss (Schifter and Ajzen, 1985) and healthy eating

(Povey et al., 2000). The social-norms component of these models has consistently failed to predict eating behavior.

Some studies have explored the impact of adding extra variables to the standard framework described within the social cognition models. For example, Shepherd and Stockley (1987) examined the predictors of fat intake and included a measure of nutritional knowledge, but found that this was not associated with either their measure of attitudes or their participants' behavior. Povey et al. (2000) included additional measures of descriptive norms (e.g. "To what extent do you think the following groups eat a healthy diet?"), and of perceived social support (e.g. "To what extent do you think the following groups would be supportive if you tried to eat a healthy diet?") but found that these variables did not add anything to the core cognitions of the TPB. Research has also examined the impact of accessing the individual's hedonic responses to food with a focus on beliefs about the sensory properties of the food concerned. The results, however, have been contradictory in this area. For example, Tuorila-Ollikainen, Lahteenmaki, and Salovaara (1986) asked participants to rate their beliefs about low-salt bread both before and after tasting some bread, and reported that the post-tasting hedonic ratings predicted eating behavior above their measure of attitudes. In contrast, Tuorila (1987) asked participants to rate milk which varied in its fat content for its hedonic properties and reported that these ratings of the sensory aspects of the food did not add anything to the basic cognitive model. Shepherd (1989) provided a review of these studies and suggested that the hedonic responses to food may be more important if the food is novel than if it is familiar.

The attitudinal research described so far conceptualizes individuals as holding either positive or negative views towards a given object. In terms of food choice it is assumed that people either like or dislike certain foods and that this value-laden attitude predicts food intake. Recent studies, however, have also explored the role of ambivalence in predicting behavior (Thompson, Zanna, and Griffin, 1995) and this has been applied to food choice (Sparks et al., 2001). Ambivalence has been defined in a variety of different ways. For example, Breckler (1994) defined it as "a conflict aroused by competing evaluative predispositions," and Emmons (1996) defined it as "an approach–avoidance conflict – wanting but at the same time not wanting the same goal object." Central to all definitions of ambivalence is the simultaneous presence of both positive and negative values which seems particularly pertinent to food choice, as individuals may hold contradictory attitudes towards foods in terms such as "tasty," "healthy," "fattening," and "a treat." Sparks et al. (2001) incorporated the concept of ambivalence into the Theory of Planned

Behavior and assessed whether it predicted meat or chocolate consumption. Participants were 325 volunteers who completed a questionnaire, including a measure of ambivalence assessed in terms of the mean of both positive and negative evaluations (e.g "How positive is chocolate?" and "How negative is chocolate?") and then subtracting this mean from the absolute difference between the two evaluations (i.e. "total positive minus total negative"). This computation provides a score which reflects the balance between positive and negative feelings. In line with previous TPB studies, the results showed that attitudes per se were the best predictor of the intention to consume both meat and chocolate. The results also showed that the relationship between attitude and intention was weaker in those participants with higher ambivalence. This implies that holding both positive and negative attitudes to a food makes it less likely that the overall attitude will be translated into an intention to eat it.

A cognitive approach to food choice, however, has been criticized for its focus on individual-level variables only and for the assumption that the same set of cognitions are relevant to all individuals. For example, Resnicow et al. (1997) carried out a large-scale study involving 1,398 schoolchildren as a means to predict their fruit and vegetable intake. The study measured social cognitive variables including self-efficacy and social norms, and added additional cognitive variables including preferences and outcome expectations. The results showed that only preferences and outcome expectations predicted actual food choice but that 90 percent of the variance in food choice remained unaccounted for. The authors concluded from this study that "SCT (social cognition theory) may not be a robust framework for explaining dietary behaviour in children" (p. 275), and suggested that a broader model which included factors such as self-esteem, parental and family dietary habits, and the availability of fruit and vegetables may be more effective.

Problems with a cognitive model

A cognitive model of food choice highlights the role of cognitions and makes explicit the cognitions which remain only implicit within a developmental perspective. It provides a useful framework for studying these cognitions, and highlights their impact upon behavior. However, there are some problems with this approach, as follows:

- Most research carried out within a cognitive perspective uses quantitative methods and devises questionnaires based on existing models. This approach means that the cognitions being examined are chosen by the researcher rather than offered by the person being researched. It is possible that many important cognitions are missed which are central to understanding food choice.

- Although focusing on cognitions, those incorporated by the models are limited and ignore the wealth of meanings associated with food and body size.

- Research from a cognitive perspective assumes that behavior is a consequence of rational thought and ignores the role of affect. Emotions such as fear (of weight gain, of illness), pleasure (over a success which deserves a treat), and guilt (about overeating) might contribute towards food choice.

- Some cognitive models incorporate the views of others in the form of the construct "subjective norm." This does not adequately address the central role that others play in a behavior as social as eating.

- At times the cognitive models appear tautological, in that the independent variables do not seem conceptually separate from the dependent variables they are being used to predict. For example, is the cognition "I am confident I can eat fruit and vegetables" really distinct from the cognition "I intend to eat fruit and vegetables"?

- Although the cognitive models have been applied extensively to behavior, their ability to predict actual behavior remains poor, leaving a large amount of variance to be explained by undefined factors.

In summary, from a social cognitive perspective food choice can be understood and predicted by measuring an individual's cognitions about food. The research in this area points to a consistently important role for attitudes towards food (e.g. "I think eating a healthy meal is enjoyable") and a role for an individual's beliefs about behavioral control (e.g. "How confident are you that you could eat a healthy diet?"). There is also some evidence that ambivalence may moderate the association between attitude and intention. However, there is no evidence for either social norms or other hypothesized variables. Such an approach ignores the role of a range of other cognitions, particularly those relating to the meaning of food and the meaning of size, and at times the associations between variables is weak, leaving much of the variance in food choice unexplained.

Psychophysiological Models of Food Choice

The third theoretical approach to understanding food choice draws upon a psychophysiological perspective and focuses on hunger and satiety. Hunger is generally regarded as a state which follows food deprivation and reflects a motivation or drive to eat. It also describes a more conscious state reflecting a feeling or desire to eat (Blundell, Hill, and Lawton, 1989). Satiety is considered the polar opposite to hunger: the motivation to stop eating and the conscious feeling that enough food has been consumed. The study of hunger and satiety is central to understanding food choice and implicitly relates to both the developmental and social cognitive approaches to eating described above. Hunger and satiety have been explicitly studied, mainly with a focus on the psychophysiology of food intake. This approach explores the interplay between cognitions, behavior, and an individual's physiology, and will be considered in terms of the effect of the senses on food selection, the impact of psychopharmacological drugs and neurochemicals on hunger and satiety, the effect of food on cognitions and behavior, and the relationship between stress and eating.

The role of chemical senses

Food may reduce hunger, but it also has several sensory properties which influence food choice. First, food has an appearance, and research shows that the degree of illumination used to display foods, and a poor appearance, particularly with a large amount of fat on view, can change food choice (MacDougall, 1987). Second, food has an odor which can influence food selection, and third, food has a taste. Research indicates that taste and odor play a central role in food choice, and has specifically examined the impact of sweet, fatty, and salty tastes. For example, some studies indicate that a preference for sweet foods as shown by hedonic measures is related to the consumption of such foods (Mattes, 1985; Mattes and Mela, 1986). Similarly, a preference for bitter tastes has been shown to relate to the percentage of energy derived from bitter-tasting foods (Mattes, 1985), and a preference for creamy foods relates to the consumption of high-fat milk (Pangborn, Bos, and Stern, 1985). However, there are inconsistencies in this literature. For example, Pangborn and Giovanni (1984) found no relationship between hedonic rating for sweetness and sugar intake, and Mattes (1985) found no relationship between preference for sweet and bitter foods and intake. In terms of salt intake, the literature is also contradictory. Some research shows no association between preference for salty tastes and salt intake (Pangborn and Pecore, 1982; Mattes, Keumanyika, and Halpern, 1983), while others have illustrated a relationship (Shepherd, Farleigh, and Land, 1984; Shepherd and Farleigh, 1986a and b). Shepherd and Farleigh (1989) reviewed this research and suggested that the conflicting results may be due to the use of different measures of both sensory attributes and intake. Further, they argued that although preference is a useful proxy measure for the sensory response to a food, it is probably related to many other factors which are neither being held constant nor being directly measured.

Psychopharmacological drugs and neurochemicals

The study of the impact of drugs on food choice provides a means to understand the neurochemical basis for hunger and satiety (Blundell, Hill, and Lawton, 1989). Most of this research has been carried out on animals in the laboratory; only some has been carried out on humans. The effects of drugs on hunger can be considered according to their clinical classification: recreational, anti-psychotics, antidepressants, analgesics, and appetite suppressants.

Recreational

Nicotine has been shown to decrease food intake in animals, and studies suggest that this effect is greater with highly palatable foods (Munster and Battig, 1975; Grunberg, Bowen, and Morse, 1984). For humans, there is research showing that smokers generally weigh about 7 lbs less than nonsmokers (US Department of Health and Human Services, 1990), that dieters use smoking as a weight loss strategy (Ogden and Fox, 1994), and that smoking cessation results in an increased consumption of calories, particularly from sweet foods (Ogden, 1994). Amphetamines are also closely linked with food intake. In particular, they have been shown to have a dramatic suppressant impact on both subjective hunger and food intake (Silverstone and Stunkard, 1968; Silverstone and Kyriakides, 1982), and have been offered both legally and illegally to dieters for many decades. Other recreational drugs include marijuana and alcohol, both of which influence food intake. Marijuana has been shown to increase both hunger and food intake (Hollister, 1971). Studies on the relationship between alcohol and food intake are contradictory with some studies indicating that it has a weak inhibitory effect while others show that it might "perk up" hunger (e.g. Hollister, 1971).

Anti-psychotics

Anti-psychotic drugs are given to those suffering from some form of psychosis, mainly schizophrenia or manic depression. Studies on these drugs show that both lithium and chlorpromazine cause weight gain (Robinson, McHigh, and Folstein, 1975; Vendsborg, Bech, and Rafaelson, 1976).

Antidepressants

Until the past decade the drug treatment of depression involved the use of tricyclic antidepressants, and studies have shown that amitryptiline has a small effect on hunger and is associated with a craving for sweet food and weight gain (Paykel, Mueller, and De La Vergne, 1973; Stein, Stein and Linn, 1985). More recently, doctors have started to prescribe a new type of drug for their depressed patients called SSRIs. These antidepressants do not appear to induce either weight gain or an increased desire for sweet foods, and may even promote weight loss (Blundell, Hill, and Lawton, 1989).

Analgesics

These are drugs which are used for pain relief and have been shown to influence hunger and satiety. For example, naloxone can decrease food intake (Trenchard and Silverstone, 1983), and morphine has a weak depressant effect on hunger (Beecher, 1959).

Appetite suppressants

Some drugs are marketed specifically for their ability to reduce appetite. For example, fenfluoramine and dexfenfluoramine have been shown to have a consistent depressant effect on hunger and to reduce food intake (Hill and Blundell, 1986; Blundell and Hill, 1988) but have now been removed from the market. Likewise, tryptophan and sibutramine can also reduce eating behavior (Blundell and Hill, 1987; Kopelman, 1999b). In addition, hormones of the small intestine such as cholecystokinin (CCK) have been shown to inhibit food intake (Kissileff et al., 1981), although this does not exist as a prescribed drug.

These drug effects are relevant to understanding the psychophysiology of hunger and satiety, as they provide a window into the chemical and metabolic processes involved and have been described as "pharmacological scalpels which may be used to dissect the structure of eating behaviour" (Blundell, Hill, and Lawton, p. 85).

The psychophysiology of food intake highlights the role of three main neurotransmitters which influence appetite and are situated in either the

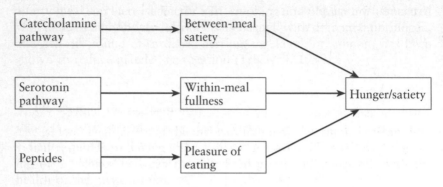

Figure 3.5   Neurochemicals and food choice

central or the peripheral nervous system. These are the catecholamines, serotonin, and peptides. Many of the drugs described above have their impact on the individual's experience of hunger and satiety by influencing these pathways. In particular, amphetamines, amitryptiline, and other tricyclics influence the catecholamine pathway, the SSRIs, fenfluoramine, and tryptophan influence the serotonin pathway, and naloxone and morphine, as well as the hormone CCK, are peptides. Some of the drugs have nonspecific effects, including chlorpromazine and lithium which influence both the catecholamine and serotonin pathways, and nicotine and marijuana which have generalized effects. Blundell et al. (1989) suggested that these three neurotransmitters influence appetite in different ways, which are illustrated in figure 3.5. It is argued that the serotonin pathway influences the feelings of fullness within a meal, thus causing the meal to end, that catecholamines influence satiety between meals, thereby triggering hunger and determining the spaces between eating, and that peptides in general influence the reward and hedonic properties of food. Therefore the drugs which have been shown to influence hunger and weight gain provide insights into the physiology of hunger and satiety and illustrate the extent to which the neurotransmitters affected by these drugs influence the end of eating, the start of eating, and the pleasure of food intake. Further details about the physiology of food intake can be found in Mela and Rogers (1997).

The effect of food on cognitions and behavior

Much psychological research has explored the impact of cognitions on food choice (see earlier). Some research has also examined the reverse relationship, namely the influence of what we eat on our mood and cognitive state. This section reviews the effects of caffeine, carbohydrates, and chocolate.

Caffeine

Over the past few decades there has been much research into the effects of caffeine, which is mostly consumed through coffee (about 60 mg per cup of instant coffee) or tea (about 40 mg per cup), although some is also consumed through cola drink (34 mg per 12 oz cup). The early literature produced highly conflicting results, with some studies showing that caffeine increased alertness and decreased calmness (e.g. Clubley et al., 1979; Leathwood and Pollet, 1983), and some showing no effect (e.g. Svensson, Persson, and Sjoberg, 1980). Other studies showed that caffeine improved performance on cognitive tasks (Regina et al., 1974; Lieberman et al., 1987), while some reported no such improvement (Loke and Meliska, 1984). Such variation has been attributed to methodological differences including the choice of mood measurement, the performance task used, and the dose of caffeine give (Lieberman, 1989). More recent work has addressed these concerns, and it is now generally accepted that caffeine has a positive effect on mood by increasing vigor and alertness and decreasing anxiety and depression, particularly when low doses are used (Lieberman et al., 1990). In addition, it has been shown that caffeine also improves performance in terms of reaction times and vigilance (Lieberman et al., 1987).

Carbohydrates

There is some evidence that carbohydrate meals can impair performance on experimental cognitive tasks and induce sleepiness (Lieberman, Spring, and Garfield, 1986). The research indicates, however, that this is not consistent for all individuals and that the effect it is often small and hard to detect. Research does show, however, that those individuals who generally consume a carbohydrate-rich meal and derive most of their calories from carbohydrates are more likely to show mood and performance changes following carbohydrate consumption. For example, Lieberman, Wurtman, and Chew (1986) gave obese participants who were classified as either high or low carbohydrate eaters a non-sweet, high-carbohydrate, protein-free lunch, and completed measures of their mood states before and after this intervention. The results showed that the high-carbohydrate eaters reported a decrease in depression, and that the low-carbohydrate eaters showed increases in depression, fatigue, sleepiness, and anxiety, and decreases in alertness. Carbohydrates may influence mood but this effect is dependent on the individual's normal eating patterns.

Chocolate

The term "chocoholism" was coined at the beginning of the 1990s (Hetherington and Macdiarmid, 1993) to describe the common craving for chocolate, and the experience of needing chocolate and feeling better when chocolate has been eaten. Those who define themselves in this way have been shown to consume about 12 bars of chocolate per week, to crave chocolate about 6 times per week, and to show higher levels of other forms of eating-related problems. Studies also showed that "chocoholics" reported an increase in arousal, greater craving, and lowered mood when exposed to chocolate-related cues. Actually eating chocolate, however, increased feelings of guilt but had no effect on depression (Hetherington and Macdiarmid, 1993; Macdiarmid and Hetherington, 1995; Tuomisto et al., 1999). Therefore, although it is often believed that chocolate can make people feel better, there is no evidence to support this, and any positive consequences of eating chocolate may be quickly accompanied by feelings of guilt.

Stress and eating

One psychophysiological approach to food choice has focused on the relationship between stress and eating behavior. The stress–eating link, however, is complex and the research is often contradictory. Some research has indicated that stress causes a reduction in food intake. For example, animal studies using high levels of stress reported a reduction in eating (Rowland and Antelman, 1976; Robbins and Fray, 1980), laboratory studies on humans reported that subjects ate less when stressed (Willenbring, Levine, and Morley, 1986), and a similar decrease in eating has been reported in Marines during combat situations (Popper et al., 1989). One longitudinal study collected daily records of stress and eating for 84 days from 158 subjects, and reported that eating less was the predominant response to stress (Stone and Brownell, 1994). In contrast, studies have also shown the reverse relationship. For example, animal studies using interventions such as tail pinching, handling, and social disruption to elicit stress have reported an increase in food intake

(Morley, Levine, and Rowland, 1983; Meisel et al., 1990), and a similar increase has been reported in obese people (Pine, 1985). Further, in a study of students' perceptions of the relationship between stress and snacking, 73 percent of respondents reported that stress increased their snacking while decreasing their consumption of "meal type" foods (Oliver and Wardle, 1999). In addition, a naturalistic study of work stress concluded that high workload periods were associated with greater intakes of energy, saturated fats, and sugar (Wardle et al., 2000). Likewise, stress is considered to elicit eating as a coping response (Spillman, 1990), to be a possible trigger for binge eating (Herman and Polivy, 1975), and to be a precipitant of weight gain in both adults and children (Bradley, 1985; Mellbin and Vuille, 1989).

At times, therefore, stress decreases food intake while at others it causes an increase. This contradictory relationship between stress and eating has been called the "stress eating paradox" by Stone and Brownell (1994). Greeno and Wing (1994) proposed two hypotheses to explain this paradox: first, the general effect model, which predicts that stress changes food intake generally, and second, the individual difference model, which predicts that stress only causes changes in eating in vulnerable groups of individuals. More recent research has focused on the individual difference model, and has examined whether the variability in the response to stress relates to aspects of the individual. Some research has focused on the role of gender. For example, Michaud et al. (1990) reported that exam stress was related to an increase in eating in girls but not boys, and similar results were reported by Rosenfield and Stevenson (1988). In contrast, Stone and Brownell (1994) concluded from their longitudinal study that even though men were more likely to eat less than more when they were under stress, women were even more likely to show a reduction in their food intake particularly when stress levels were at their highest.

Research has also addressed the role of dietary restraint (see chapter 7). For example, Cools, Schotte, and McNally (1992) reported that stress was related to increased eating in dieters only, and similar results have been reported following a naturalistic study of work stress (Wardle et al., 2000). Therefore, gender and levels of dieting seem to be important predictors of a link between stress and eating. The research, however, is not always consistent with this suggestion. For example, Conner, Fitter, and Fletcher (1999) examined the link between daily hassles and snacking in 60 students who completed diaries for seven consecutive days. The results showed a direct association between increased daily hassles and increased snacking, but showed no differences according to either gender or dieting. Similarly, Oliver, Wardle, and Gibson (2000) reported no impact of dietary restraint on stress-induced eating but indicated a role for emotional eating, with emotional eaters eating more following experimentally induced stress.

As a further means to explain the impact of stress on food intake, some studies have addressed a possible physiological pathway. For example, one experimental study examined the impact of stress-induced arousal (blood pressure and heart rate), and reported that arousal predicted food consumption but only in non-dieters (Rutledge and Linden, 1998). Impaired physiological recovery rates were also only associated with food intake in the dieting group. In a similar vein, Epel et al. (2001) measured cortisol levels following experimentally induced stress, and concluded that high cortisol reactivity following stress was related to an increased consumption of calories. Epel et al. (2000) also reported an association between a high waist-to-hip ratio and cortisol reactivity following stress. These studies suggest that stress may relate to food intake via a physiological pathway by increasing arousal and/or cortisol.

In summary, stress is associated with food choice. However, this association is often contradictory, and it has been hypothesized that individual factors may explain this paradox. In particular, research has highlighted a role for gender, dieting, and physiological changes. These factors may individually influence food intake or may work in association with each other. The research is still in its early stages.

Problems with a psychophysiological model

A psychophysiological approach to food choice focuses on the biological aspects of eating and emphasizes the importance of hunger and satiety. It acknowledges the role of both learning and cognitions and illustrates in part how these factors might impact upon physiology. However, there are several problems with this perspective, as follows:

- Much psychophysiological research has taken place in laboratories and some has used animals as models for human food choice. The extent to which research derived from these conditions can be transferred to understanding human behavior remains unclear.
- Food choice may relate to neurochemicals and brain pathways. However, eating is an inherently social behavior as it usually takes place in the context of others, with food acquiring and representing a range of social meanings. A psychophysiological approach to food choice does not explicitly incorporate either social learning or social meanings.

- A psychophysiological model emphasizes eating as a result of hunger and satiety. However, as food is a social behavior such biological drives are consistently moderated and modified by social drives.
- This approach assumes that an individual will respond to hunger by eating and to satiety by ceasing to eat. However, many individuals override the physiological drive to eat due to factors such as a desire to be thin, a dislike of food, and a fear of losing control. They can also override the drive to stop eating due to a desire for a treat, social cues to continue eating, or the availability of more food.

In summary, a psychophysiological model of food choice examines the effect of the senses on food selection, the impact of psychopharmacological drugs and neurochemicals on hunger and satiety, the effect of food on cognitions and behavior, and the relationship between stress and eating. This perspective emphasizes the biological basis to eating and minimizes the social context surrounding food intake.

Conclusion

There are many different approaches to understanding food choice. This chapter has focused on three overarching theories. First it has described a developmental perspective which emphasizes the impact of learning though exposure, social learning, and associative learning. This approach highlights the role of important others, cues, and associations in the development of food preferences, and draws on the central tenets of learning theory. Secondly it has described a cognitive approach to food choice which emphasizes food choice as the end-product of a series of interacting cognitions. Finally it has described a psychophysiological model with an emphasis on chemical senses, the impact of psychopharmacological drugs, and neurochemicals on hunger and satiety, the effect of food on cognitions and behavior, and the relationship between stress and eating.

Towards an integrated model of diet

Theories of food choice have been developed as a means to understand why people eat what they eat and how they can be encouraged to eat more healthily. A developmental perspective, a focus on cognitions, and a psychophysiological approach are central to understanding the complexity of food choice. However, these theoretical frameworks, with their focus on the individual, minimize the complex meanings surrounding food and body shape and size. Food choice takes place within a set of social meanings concerning individual foods, meals as a social and cultural experience, the importance of thinness, and the stigma attached to being overweight. Developmental models address these issues implicitly though the role of learning, as these meanings are learned via observation and association. But their place within such models remains marginal. Similarly, cognitive models address these factors through cognitions such as social and moral norms. But the complexity of such meanings is ignored. Finally, psychophysiological perspectives predominantly focus on the individual's physiological makeup. The next two chapters explicitly address the complex meanings associated with food and body size.

chapter four

The Meaning of Food

Psychological theories of food choice examine the individual factors which influence eating behavior, with an emphasis on learning, beliefs, attitudes, and the individual's psychophysiological makeup. Such work is based on the premise that food choice is a product of more than the nutritional content of the food concerned. Food choice is also more complicated than the psychological makeup of the individual doing the choosing. Food choice takes place within a network of social meanings. Some of these meanings relate to the food itself and, as described by Douglas, should also be the focus for analysis: "Nutritionists know that the palate is trained, that taste and smell are subject to cultural control . . . [yet research] seeks to screen out cultural effects as so much interference. Whereas . . . the cultural controls on perception are precisely what needs to be analysed" (Douglas, 1975, p. 59). This chapter explores the complex social and cultural meanings of food. In particular it describes food classification systems which are offered as a means to understand food and its consumption. It examines the ways in which food represents aspects of self-identity in terms of gender, sexuality, conflicts, and self-control, and the ways in which it is central to social interaction as a communication of love and power. Finally it explores food as a symbol of cultural identity in terms of religion, social power, and a delineation between culture and nature.

This chapter covers:

- Food classification systems
- Food as a statement of the self
- Food as social interaction
- Food as cultural identity

Food has a complex array of meanings; as described by Todhunter (1973):

> food is prestige, status and wealth . . . It is a means of communication and
> interpersonal relations, such as an "apple for the teacher" or an expres-
> sion of hospitality, friendship, affection, neighbourliness, comfort and sym-
> pathy in time of sadness or danger. It symbolises strength, athleticism,
> health and success. It is a means of pleasure and self gratification and a
> relief from stress. It is feasts, ceremonies, rituals, special days and nostal-
> gia for home, family and the "good old days". It is an expression of
> individuality and sophistication, a means of self expression and a way
> of revolt. Most of all it is tradition, custom and security . . . There are
> Sunday foods and weekday foods, family foods and guest foods; foods
> with magical properties and health and disease foods. (p. 301)

This chapter draws mostly upon sociological and anthropological literatures on the meaning of food which are influenced by the theoretical
work of Lévi-Strauss (e.g. 1965), Douglas (1966, 1975) and Mennell
(1987). It also draws on the experiences and writings of psychotherapists such as Orbach (1978, 1986) and Lawrence (1984).

Food Classification Systems

Lévi-Strauss (e.g. 1965) and Douglas (1966) argued that food can be
understood in terms of a deep underlying structure which is common
across different cultures. Drawing on this perspective, Helman (1984)
outlined five types of food classification systems:

- **Food versus non food** delineates things which are edible and those
  which are not. For example, wheat is food, grass is not food; frogs
  can be food, worms rarely are.
- **Sacred versus profane foods** differentiates between those foods
  which are validated by religious beliefs and those which are not.
  For example, cloven-hoofed animals which chew the cud are
  sacred for Muslims and Jews (as long as they are Kosher), pig
  products are profane for Jews and Muslims, and beef is profane
  for Sikhs and Hindus.
- **Parallel food classifications** indicates how foodstuffs can be
  described as "hot" (e.g. wheat, potato, garlic) or "cold" (e.g. rice,
  peas, beans). Within this framework health is equated as a balance
  between hot and cold foods. "Cold" illnesses such as arthritis are
  treated with hot foods and sometimes blamed on eating too many
  cold foods, and hot illnesses are treated with cold foods. Whether

a food is considered "hot" or "cold" does not depend upon its temperature but upon the symbolic value attached to each foodstuff, and may vary from culture to culture.

- **Food as medicine, medicine as food** describes the separation and overlap between food and medicine. For example, certain foods are used or avoided during states such as pregnancy, lactation, or menstruation, and are given to remedy problems such as diarrhea, dyspepsia, and general ill health.
- **Social foods** describes the social function of food. Food can be understood in terms of affirming and developing relationships, symbolizing status by offering rare, expensive, or delicious dishes, and creating group identity through traditional food patterns such as breakfast, lunch, and dinner, or through traditional food types such as "the national dish" or "the family meal."

Work from this perspective argues that all foods can be understood using this framework, which provides insights into the function and role of food within any given culture. Some writers have criticized the search for a deep underlying structure to food and have suggested that this approach neglects the capacity of food meanings to vary across cultures and time. The alternative analysis is that food should be regarded as the medium through which a range of meanings are communicated. For example, in the same way that different jeans can be "read" by adolescents but not by their parents, and interior design can be understood by adults but not by children, food is embedded with meanings within a specific time and space. Some studies have focused on the meanings of individual foods. For example, Wilson (1973) argued that tomatoes were thought to be dangerous and were largely avoided in England until the later eighteenth century, Mintz (1985) pointed to how sugar was originally seen as a medicine rather than a food, and Barthes (1961) illustrated how sweet foods, particularly chocolate, and bitter foods, symbolize the difference between the working and upper classes. Most research, however, has emphasized eating as a communicative act and explored the meanings that food can communicate. In particular, food communicates a sense of self, it acts as a medium of communication between individuals, and it is central to the establishment of a cultural identity. These meanings are illustrated in figure 4.1.

Food as a Statement of the Self

Food provides information about individual identity and acts an a communication of internal needs, internal conflicts, and a sense of self.

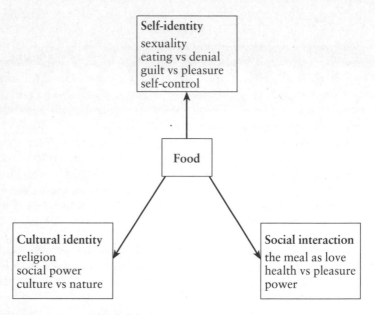

Figure 4.1   The meaning of food

Day-to-day-cooking, shopping for food, home economics at school have all traditionally been female activities, as shown by cross-cultural surveys, magazines, cookbooks, advertising, and studies of newly married couples (Murdock and Provost, 1973; Murcott, 1983; Mansfield and Collard, 1988). The individualized meanings of food are therefore closely linked to issues of gender identity and the notion of being female. In particular, food represents sexuality, conflicts between guilt and pleasure, eating and denial, and an expression of self-control.

Food and sexuality

Some foods are linked with sex and sexuality (see figure 4.2). Advertisements for ice cream offer their product as the path to sexual fulfillment; chocolate is often consumed in an erotic fashion; and the best-selling book *The Joy of Sex* by Alex Comfort (1974) was named after the *The Joy of Cooking* and was subtitled "A gourmet guide to love making."

This interrelationship between food and sex permeates many cultures and many times. Rite-of-passage ceremonies marking the onset of sexuality involve practices such as washing with the blood of a goat (Jacobs, 1958) and killing the first animal (Marshall, 1976). Similarly, eating

Figure 4.2   Food and sex (*Source*: Advertising Archives)

meat is considered to arouse sexual drives. For example, Cecil (1929) described how a captain of a slave ship stopped eating meat to keep himself from lusting after female slaves. Similarly, low-meat diets were recommended in the nineteenth and twentieth centuries to discourage masturbation in young males (Punch, 1977). Further, sexual language describing women or sex is often derived from animals or foods such, as "beaver", "bird," "bitch," "chick," "lamb," "meat market," "beef," and "beefy" (Fiddes, 1990). At a more prosaic level, "going out for dinner," "a dinner for two," and "a candlelit dinner" are frequent precursors to sex. Explanations for the association between eating and sex tend to highlight the biological similarity between the two in terms of both being "a basic drive for survival" (Fieldhouse, 1986), and "that both perpetuate life, that both may be pleasurable and that both imply vulnerability by breaching normal bodily boundaries" (Fiddes, 1990, p. 144). But such explanations are essentially biologically reductionist, and neglect the power of society to construct its own social meanings. Food embodies statements about sex and symbolizes the individual as a sexual being.

Eating versus denial

Food is also a forum for many intrapersonal conflicts. One such conflict is between eating and denial. Charles and Kerr (1986, 1987) studied 200 young mothers in an urban area of northern England and concluded that whereas women have to provide healthy and nutritious foods for their families, they are expected to deny themselves food in order to remain thin and sexually attractive. This conclusion is reflected in the work of Murcott (1983), who argued that while food planning and providing takes up a large part of a woman's day, a woman is also aware that she must remain thin and desirable. There is further evidence for this conflict from a content analysis of 48 issues of magazines for men and magazines for women (Silverstein et al., 1986). The results showed that there were 1,179 food ads in the women's magazines and only ten in the men's, 359 ads for sweets and snacks in the women's magazines and only 10 in the men's, and 63 ads for diet foods in the women's magazines and only one in the men's. The message to women was: think about food all the time but stay slim (Silverstein et al., 1986). Lawrence (1984) also described this conflict in her analysis of her patients and observed that "eating is a source of pleasure, but not often for the people who have the primary responsibility for providing it. Women take control of food, while simultaneously denying themselves the pleasure of it" (p. 31). Further, as Orbach states, "women have occupied this dual role of feeding others while needing to deny themselves" and "women must hold back their desires for the cakes they bake for others and satisfy themselves with a brine canned tuna salad with dietetic trimmings" (1986, p. 60). Food therefore communicates and embodies a conflict, particularly for women, between eating and denial.

Guilt versus pleasure

Some foods such as chocolate and cakes are also associated with a conflict between pleasure and guilt. For example, the advertising slogans "forbidden fruit" and "naughty but nice" describe the paradox of having eaten and regretting having done so, and the concept of "sins of the flesh" indicates that both eating and sex are at once pleasurable and guilt-ridden activities (see figure 4.3). Research has explored the feelings and experiences of individuals who consider themselves to be addicted to chocolate and indicates that those describing themselves as "chocoholics" reported eating chocolate in secret (Hetherington and Macdiarmid, 1993) and craving chocolate but feeling guilty afterwards (Macdiarmid and Hetherington, 1995). In line with this Chernin (1992) described her own feelings towards food and how she experienced both the need for food and the subsequent self-loathing. She wrote that she could not "make it as far as lunch without eating a pound of candy" and described how "I ran from bakery to bakery, from street stall to street stall . . . I bought a pound of chocolate and ate it as I ran." Unable to wait her turn any longer in line for a hot dog behind a man who has just ordered his, she writes, "I suddenly dart forward, grab the plate and begin to run . . . I run with a sudden sense of release" (p. 58). Similarly, Levine (1997) described in her book *I Wish I Were Thin I Wish I Were Fat* how "I still feel as if I am sneaking food when I eat something I love. And I still feel guilty when I let it get the better of me" (p. 19). These sweet foods represent pleasure and fulfill a need. Their consumption is then followed by guilt and feelings of "shame," of feeling "self-conscious," "frantic," and "perverse." Food is therefore a forum for conflicts between guilt and pleasure.

Food and self-control

Food also represents self-control or the loss of control (see figure 4.4). Fasting and food refusal have been received with a sense of wonder; the nineteenth century even saw the development of "hunger artists" who, as

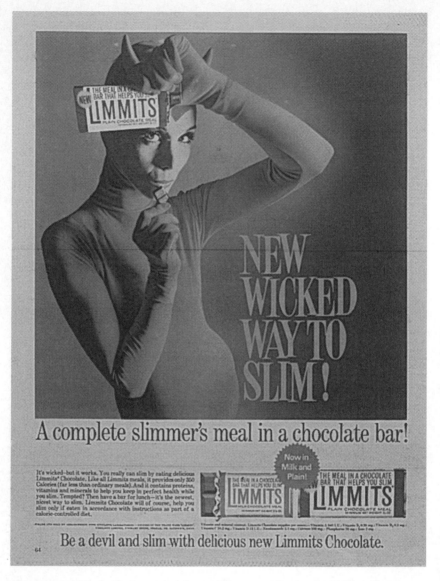

Figure 4.3   Food: Guilt versus pleasure (*Source*: Advertising Archives)

Gordon (2000) noted, "had no moral or religious agenda . . . their food refusal was a sheer act of will and self-control for its own sake" (p. 195). Similarly, Crisp (1984) compared the anorexic to the ascetic in terms of her "discipline, frugality, abstinence and stifling of the passions" (p. 210),

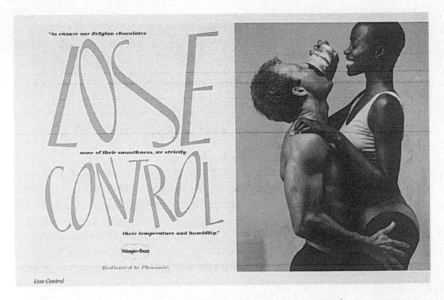

Figure 4.4   Food as self-control (*Source*: Advertising Archives)

and Bruch described the anorexic as having an "aura of special power and super human discipline" (1974). Ogden (1997, 2002) argued that over the past few decades diet has become the perfect vehicle for self-control. Following an examination of psychological and sociological texts over the twentieth century, Ogden (1997, 2002) suggested a shift in their model of the individual from a passive responder, to an interactive individual, to a late twentieth-century self who was reflexive and intra-active. Such an individual is characterized by self-control; it is argued that this focus on self-control is epitomized by the interest in eating behavior as diet becomes the vehicle for this control and the anorexic reflects the ultimate self-controlling intra-active individual.

In summary, food communicates aspects of the self in terms of sexuality, conflicts between guilt and pleasure, eating and denial, and is a statement of self-control.

Food as Social Interaction

The meaning of food has also been explored within the context of its consumption and of its central place in social interaction. In particular, food is a common tool for communication within the family. The dinner table is often the only place where the family gets together, and the family meal can become the forum for sharing experiences of the day. In addition, the types of foods eaten and the way in which they are cooked can create a sense of group identity, as in "The birthday party" and "The Sunday lunch." Some studies have therefore examined the meaning of the meal as a social interaction.

The meal as love

Charles and Kerr (1987) explored the meaning of the meal and suggested that sweet foods are often used to pacify children and to maintain family harmony. They also concluded that healthy and tasty foods are signs of family love and the determination to please and satisfy the different family members (see figure 4.5). In line with this, Lawrence argued that "Food is the medium through which women demonstrate our love and concern for our children, lovers, husbands and friends" and that "taking care over the preparation of food is an act of love" (1984, p. 29).

Health versus pleasure

Food as social interaction can also be a forum for conflict. At times this is a conflict between health and pleasure. For example, Van Otterloo and Van Ogtrop (1989) explored families' eating behavior in the Netherlands and concluded that a desire to feed their children and husbands healthy foods can create conflict in women, as unhealthy foods are often preferred. Similarly, Murcott (1982) concluded from her study of 40 young women and mothers in Wales that on the one hand women are responsible for the health of their family while on the other they wish to please them and show them love by providing foods to their taste. Further, as Lawrence (1984) argued, "good nourishing food is what every mother knows her children need. She also knows that it is usually the last thing they want. Give them junk food and they will love you. But you will also have to live with the guilt about their teeth, their weight, their vitamins" (p. 30) (see figure 4.6).

Power relations

Food can also reflect power relations within a family. Delphy (1979) reported that in nineteenth-century rural France, men regularly received

Figure 4.5   Food and the family (*Source:* Advertising Archives)

larger amounts of food than women, children, or the infirm elderly, and that if poultry or meat was available it was reserved for the men. Millett (1969) also described how "In nearly every patriarchal group it is expected that the dominant male will eat first or eat better and even when

Figure 4.6   Food: Health versus pleasure (*Source*: Advertising Archives)

the sexes feed together the male shall be served by the female" (p. 48). In line with this, Charles and Kerr (1986, 1987) examined the distribution of food within English families and argued that food allocation reflected the power relations and sexual divisions within a family, with larger portions of meat in particular in being given to men. The children and women had subsidiary positions in the family hierarchy. Murcott (1983) similarly concluded from her study that the cooked dinner "symbolises the home, a husband's relation to it, his wife's place in it and their relationship to one another" (p. 179), and that a woman's denial of food both maintained a thinner body and fulfilled a woman's role as the provider for others.

In summary, food is embedded with meaning which is a central form of communication in the interaction of individuals. Within this social context food is a forum for expressions of love and caring and for conflicts between health and pleasure, and is a symbol of power relations within a family.

Food as Cultural Identity

Food is a form of communication about an individual's identity and about this identity in the context of others. Ultimately, however, such communications occur within the broader social context, and food can be read for information regarding a cultural identity. Research has explored the notion of food as culture in terms of food as religious identity, food as social power, and food as a symbolic delineation between culture and nature, with an emphasis on the meaning of meat.

Food as religious identity

Food and family meals play a central role in the establishment of religious identity. For example, Starr Sered (1988) specifically explored cooking behavior among Middle Eastern Jewish women. She argued that many of their foods embody Jewish symbols and that their rituals of food preparation create a sense of holiness in their daily domestic work. Further, she argued that the women see feeding others as representing Jewish identity, tradition, law, and holiness. Eating food, preparing food, and providing food for others, therefore, become a medium through which holiness can be communicated within the family (see figure 4.7).

Figure 4.7   Food and religion (*Source*: Advertising Archives)

Food as social power

Food is also a symbol of social status. Powerful individuals eat well and are fed well by others, and as Wolf (1990) argued, "food is the primal symbol of social worth" (p. 189). Early sociological writers such as Engels and Marx regarded food as an essential component of human subsistence and its absence as an illustration of inequality (see Mennell, Murcott, and Van Otterloo, 1992). Food is a statement of social status and an illustration of social power. In parallel, food avoidance also serves to regain control over the social world. When political prisoners need to make a social statement they refuse to eat and initiate a hunger strike. For example, Bobby Sands was a political prisoner in Northern Ireland in the 1980s and refused food to illustrate his political point. He was voted a Member of Parliament by his local constituency just before he died. Similarly, the suffragettes in the early twentieth century also turned to hunger strikes as a form of political protest over gender inequalities. Lady Constance Lytton (1869–1923) describes how she was imprisoned along with other protesters in Liverpool for 14 days following a suffragette demonstration. In protest, she started to scratch the words "Votes for women" on her body, went on a hunger strike, and was promptly force-fed on eight occasions (Lytton, 1914). She told the wardress "We are sorry if it will give you trouble: we shall give as little as possible: but our fast is against the government and we shall fight them with our lives not hurting anyone else" (p. 260), and argued that the "government had been petitioned in every other way" (p. 262). As Gordon (2000) stated, "Historically the hunger strike has been employed by the socially oppressed as a means of embarrassing or humiliating those in control and ultimately extracting concessions from them" (p. 194). Orbach (1986) has regarded eating disorders as a form of "hunger strike," and Wolf has stated "in the public realm, food is status and honor" (p. 189). The presence of food represents a social power and the denial of food is a powerful tool for regaining control over the political world.

Culture versus nature: The meaning of meat

Food, particularly meat, also signifies the relationship between people and nature. For the majority meat is cornerstone of a meal and for vegetarians it is the food to be avoided. Twigg (1983) stated that "meat is the most highly praised of food. It is the centre around which a meal is arranged. It stands in a sense for the very idea of food itself" (p. 21). Following a study of British family meals, Kerr and Charles wrote "meat was mentioned by the women more frequently than any other food . . . Meat or fish as its substitute was usually viewed as an essential ingredient of the main meal of the day" (p. 140). Similarly, Fiddes (1990) argued that "Meat is, to many, synonymous with 'real' food." He also suggested that even for vegetarians "the range of soya based meat analogues . . . testifies to the centrality of the concept of meat" and that "many people wishing to avoid meat feel that the gap left in their habitual food system needs to be filled with a direct equivalent which mimics the form or the nutritional content of meat itself" (p. 16). He further stated that "Even when the form of meat is entirely foregone, a substitute, such as cheese or eggs, is almost always of animal origin" (p. 17). Meat is therefore a central part of what we eat (or avoid eating). On this basis Fiddes (1990) carried out an extensive anthropological analysis of the meanings of meat and said that "meat is more than just a meal; it also represents a way of life" (p. 45). Fiddes drew upon statistical data concerning eating habits, health risks, and the benefits of meat eating, and then integrated these data with quotes from farmers, butchers, members of the general public, and vegetarian campaigners. Fiddes' central argument contended that meat-eating symbolizes the civilizing of human beings. He argued that by separating ourselves from and gaining power over the natural world people have become civilized. He described how studies on the development of human identity have emphasized the extent to which human beings tame, kill, and eat nature. He described how historians analyze how people have dominated nature and suggested that eating meat represents the essence of being human and is central to the separation between culture and nature. To illustrate and support his analysis he drew upon a range of literatures and behaviors as follows.

Hunting

Fiddes pointed to the literature on hunting, and quoted from a modern writer on deer-hunting who "casually defines the birth of humanity by the beginnings of skilled hunting and progress by the development of more efficient technology" (p. 55). He reviewed the evidence and concluded that "hunting . . . may have been even more significant in the evolution of modern humanity than the later development of agriculture" (p. 56). He also stated that "as civilised humans, we have long characterised ourselves as predators and conquerors" as "it is thus more civilised – more human – to hunt wild animals than to stoop to forage all bloody day for berries" (p. 63). Hunting animals signifies the separation of humans from nature.

Blood

Fiddes also highlighted the symbolism of blood. He argued that "bloodshed is central to meat's value" and that "killing, cooking and eating other animals' flesh provides perhaps the ultimate authentication of human superiority over the rest of nature, with the spilling of blood a vibrant motif" (p. 65). He argued that blood represents a life force and that by eating both animal flesh and animal blood "we drain their lifeblood and so seize their strength" (p. 68). By killing animals and spilling their blood, human beings can claim their control over nature: "It is not only the animal which we so utterly subjugate; consuming its flesh is a statement that we are the unquestioned masters of the world" (p. 68).

Cannibalism

Fiddes also supported his argument with an analysis of the categories of what can and cannot be eaten. He explored the notion of cannibalism and quoted Arens (1979), who stated that "the idea of 'others' as cannibals is the universal phenomenon" and "the significant question is not why people eat human flesh, but why one group invariably assumes that others do." Accordingly, the term "cannibalism" is used to designate others as uncivilized; "the cannibalism label [is] used to denote a different level of humanity" (Fiddes, 1990). Fiddes therefore argued that the taboo of cannibalism emphasizes how human beings have become civilized, as they can eat the meat which comes from the natural world (animals) but not the flesh from the cultural world (humans). He stated that the function of the taboo of cannibalism "has been to demarcate the sanctity of human society" and that "our culture is distinguished as civilised, as a higher form of life that cannot be preyed upon" (p. 128). The preoccupation with not eating human flesh and the mythologizing of those who do creates a boundary between the natural world of animals and the civilized world of humans.

Eating pets

Fiddes also explored which animals can and cannot be eaten. He argued that we care for our pets, give them proper names, allow them into our houses, talk to them, "fret when they are unwell and weep when they die; we may even bury them alongside us." He also suggested that the phrase "I'm so hungry I could eat a horse" not only illustrates a large appetite but an appetite so large as to drive the individual to transcend the normal boundaries of what can be eaten. He concluded that "as honorary humans, pets cannot be consumed" and that as humans are not fit for food, "any beast that falls between human and non human, by coming close in some way, tends to be deemed inedible." In line with his central thesis, eating meat symbolizes the civilizing of human beings. We therefore cannot eat humans because they are not natural, but neither can we eat animals which we have let into our civilized world.

In summary, meat holds a privileged position in the diet of many people, either as the central food to their meals or as the food to be avoided. Fiddes (1990) argued this centrality is due to the symbolic nature of meat which represents the power that human beings have over nature and indicates they are cultured, civilized, and no longer part of the natural world. Food, therefore, is a communicative act concerning culture, and reflects a religious identity, a statement of social power, and a delineation of the cultural world and nature.

Conclusion

Food choice occurs within a complex set of meanings. Some research exploring the meaning of food has described a deep underlying classification system which is relevant across all cultures. Other research has analyzed eating as a communicative act providing a statement of the self, as an expression of social interaction, and as reflecting a cultural identity. In particular, food constructs the self as a sexual being, in terms of conflicts between guilt and pleasure, eating and denial, and as a statement of self-control. At the level of social interaction food can represent love and caring, conflicts regarding health and pleasure, and power relations within the family. Ultimately, however, all such meanings are embedded within their social context, and food also provides information about cultural identities. In particular, food creates a sense of religious identity, symbolizes power within a society, and delineates the cultural world from nature.

Towards an integrated model of diet

Psychological research exploring the predictors of food choice highlights individual variables such as learning, beliefs, and cognitions, and points to a role for psychophysiological factors. Such research aims to understand and promote healthy eating. Food, however, is much more than the necessary substance which can promote health or trigger illness. It holds a central position within each culture and is embedded with a multitude of meanings. Understanding why people eat what they eat requires an understanding of these meanings. It is not only food per se, however, which holds so much meaning. The choice to consume or reject food has the power the change the body's size and shape, which is also subject to much social interpretation. The meaning of body size is addressed in the next chapter.

chapter **five**

The Meaning of Size

Once food is eaten it is digested and incorporated into the body, and either used for immediate energy or stored. Food therefore impacts upon the body's physical state and has the capacity to make changes in the way we look. As a result, food choice takes place within the context of the body and the meanings associated with body size and shape. This chapter explores the meaning of size and examines media representations of the body and the meanings associated with these images, and draws upon both the quantitative and qualitative literatures.

This chapter covers:

- Media representations
- The meaning of sex
- The meaning of size

Media Representations

Women and men are represented in all forms of the media from comic strips to television, but they are not represented in the same way, and much research indicates that sexual differentiation pervades all media images.

Comic strips

One study of comic strips reported that men appear more frequently than women as both central and minor characters and that the most invisible women are ethnic minority women (Etter-Lewis, 1988). Another study of 100 randomly chosen comic strips showed that men appeared with a wide range of occupations such as a travel guide, bartender, salesperson, General, information clerk, court jester, vicar, king, Viking, sergeant, cook, farmer, wizard, and flutist. In contrast, when the women were given a job (only 4 percent of the time) they were either a bank teller or a secretary (Chavez, 1985). Brabant and Mooney carried out two studies in this area. First they explored whether the presentation of women had changed between 1976 and 1986, and reported that women still appeared less frequently than men and when they appeared they were still in more passive roles either at home or as child carers. The only change was that the women were less likely to be wearing aprons than they had been ten years earlier (Brabant and Mooney, 1986). Second, they carried out a study on less traditional comic strips where the woman involved did have a job outside of the home. The results showed that these women were also more likely to be shown in the home or caring for children and were portrayed as critical, worrying a great deal, and having stressful sleepless nights (Mooney and Brabant, 1987).

Newspapers

Women are also much less pictured in newspapers, and when they are the text is more likely to mention their appearance, their clothing, and whether they are married or a mother (Foreit et al., 1980; Archer et al., 1983; Luebke, 1989).

Television

The representation of men and women also differs on television. For example, one study showed that women comprised only 29 percent of all characters and 31 percent of major characters on American TV, that they were likely to be younger than the men, and more likely to be shown in the home (Signorielli, 1989). A further study of children's television found that women were seldom presented in prestigious positions, but if they were, they were both beautiful and brilliant (Fossarelli, 1984).

Magazines

Cantor reviewed studies of fiction in the mass media and concluded that the basic message was that sexual relationships were the most important factors in women's lives, more so than politics, economy, war, or peace, and even more important than the family, children, and their careers (Cantor, 1987). Even the women profiled in magazines targeting working women were portrayed in traditional occupations and were less likely to perceive themselves as having responsibility or influence in their jobs. In addition, women were more likely to be presented nude or partially clad (Soley and Kurzbard, 1986). Research has also explored a phenomenon called "face-ism" to describe the degree of facial prominence in any given image, with a score of "0" representing no face shown and "1" representing that only the face was shown. The converse of this reflects "bodyism" (Archer et al., 1983). The authors used this index to assess 1,750 representations of men and women from at least 12 issues of 5 major American magazines and the results showed that the face-ism index for men was 0.65 whereas for women it was 0.45. This indicates that when women were portrayed greater emphasis was placed on their body, whereas the images of men focused more on the face. This approach has been used for publications in different countries and for paintings from different centuries, and suggests that sex differences in face-ism are widespread, have existed for many centuries, and have increased over time.

Women, therefore, appear less frequently in the media than men and when they do appear they are of a lower status, younger, wearing less, showing less face and more body, and are more likely to be described in terms of how they look. So how do they look?

Images of female body size and shape

Much research has addressed the body size and shape of media images of women. Historical analyses of images of women have reported that the preferred woman's body has become consistently smaller over the past century than it had ever been before this time (Orbach, 1978; Fallon, 1990; Grogan, 1999). For example, from the Middle Ages the rounder "reproductive figure" was considered attractive and plumpness was erotic and fashionable. In line with this, the women painted by Rubens in the 1600s had full rounded hips and breasts, and in the 1800s Courbet painted women who would be considered fat by today's standards. In fact Myers and Copplestone (1985) described how Manet's "Olympia" of 1865, which portrays a female nude of average size, was considered obscene as the woman was deemed too thin to be erotic.

Analyses of more recent changes indicate that the current preference for the thin female body can be traced back to the 1920s and the introduction of the "Flapper" look which required a flat-chested boyish appearance (Orbach, 1986). Women at this time bound their breasts and used starvation diets and exercise in attempts to achieve the ideal body shape (Silverstein et al., 1986). Some respite from this image followed World War II with the popularity of actresses such as Jane Russell in the 1940s and Marilyn Monroe in the 1950s, who were known for their curves and large breasts. The body size deemed attractive in the 1920s, however, returned with a vengeance towards the end of the 1950s with Audrey Hepburn and Grace Kelly and took hold in the 1960s with Twiggy setting a new standard of thinness (Grogan, 1999) (see figure 5.1).

These recent changes in desired body size have been explored empirically. For example, Garner et al. (1980) examined the dimensions of *Playboy* centerfolds and reported that they became steadily thinner after 1960. Similarly, Silverstein et al. (1986) explored the shapes of models in women's magazines and reported that they have become less curvaceous since 1950, and Morris, Cooper, and Cooper (1989) examined the physical features of models recruited for a London-based agency which supplied models for magazines such as *Vogue, Cosmopolitan*, and *Woman's Own*, and concluded that they have become more tubular. In addition, data indicate that overweight women have virtually disappeared as models in women's magazines over the past 35 years (Snow and Harris, 1986). It is not, however, only images of women which have become thinner. Studies indicate that Miss America Pageants have become thinner since 1960 (Garner et al., 1980), contestants for Miss Sweden have dropped in weight from 68 kg to 53 kg (Rossner, 1984), movie actresses have become thinner since 1950 (Silverstein, Peterson, and Perdue, 1986) and female actors, advertisers, models, and newsreaders are overwhelmingly young, attractive, and thin (Kilbourne, 1994). In fact even Barbie has become thinner since she was introduced in 1959 (Freedman, 1986). If the average young woman were to look like Barbie she would have to be 24 inches taller, make her chest 5 inches bigger, her neck 3.2 inches longer, and decrease her waist by 6 inches (Brownell and Napolitano, 1995).

Images of male body size and shape

Most of the literature exploring representations of the body has addressed the female body. Changes can also be seen in ways in which the media have presented the male body. Grogan (1999) provided a useful analysis of these changes, beginning with the idealization in Roman and Greek art of the male nude, who was presented as a slim muscular male warrior. From the 1800s the male body as the object of idealization was replaced by the female body until about the 1980s, when images of naked and semi-clothed men re-emerged in the mainstream media. This

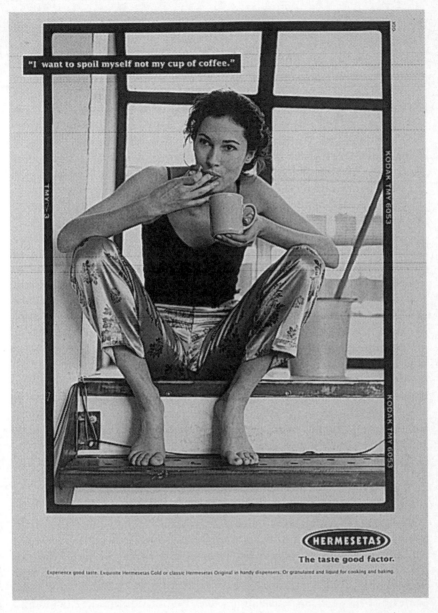

Figure 5.1   Contemporary ideals of beauty (*Source*: Advertising Archives)

re-emergence has been credited to the influence of gay culture (O'Kelly, 1994), and a change from a muscular physique to one that is "slimmed down – the male waif" can be seen. Further, male models have become increasingly hairless, well toned, and narrow-hipped. Men, therefore, have also become the focus of the media, and the male body is increasingly used in films and advertising as an erotic encouragement to purchase whatever product is being offered. In line with their analysis of Barbie, researchers have also examined the body dimensions of Ken. They showed that in order to look like Ken, the average healthy male would have to be 20 inches taller, make his chest 11 inches larger, and his neck 7.9 inches thicker (Brownell and Napolitano, 1995).

Associations with physical characteristics

If men and women are being presented differently by the media, then this may influence the ways in which men and women are thought about. Further, if women are being presented as increasingly thin and men as increasingly muscular, this too may impact upon our conceptualization of what it means to be female or male. Central to this process is the development of stereotypes, which play an important role in the ways in which individuals make sense of their world. They are essential to the efficient assimilation of large amounts of new information and are fundamental to interpersonal perception and communication. Stereotypes involve a network of associations between physical traits which can be easily observed, and personality traits, social roles, and behaviors, which can only be inferred. Two physical characteristics which have been shown to generate powerful associations are sex and body size.

The Meaning of Sex

Stereotypes based on sex involve the assumption that individuals from the same sex have more in common than those from different sexes. The classic studies of sex-role stereotypes were carried in the 1960s and 1970s and involved questionnaires consisting of pairs of adjectives such as "passive/active" and "submissive/dominant." Participants were asked to rate a range of hypothetical people for these characteristics, including a "normal man" and a "normal female," and then to rate a range of people with differing ethnic and religious backgrounds. The results showed clear consistency for the hypothetical man and woman, indicating the existence of stereotypical beliefs. Specifically, the woman was consistently associated with affective traits such as "warm," "expressive," and "sensitive," and the man was associated with "active," "objective," "independent," "aggressive," and "direct" (Broverman et al., 1972). The results also showed that there were more traits associated with the man than the female, that the male traits were considered more socially desirable, and that the female traits were more childlike. This series of studies was criticized on the grounds that they explored only personality, not behavioral traits, that the categories "man" and "woman" were too broad and could not differentiate according to ethnicity, class, or age, and that the chosen methodology forced the participants to make unnatural choices. The studies that followed addressed these methodological issues. For example, Deaux and Lewis (1984) asked participants to list characteristics that they thought were common to males and females. The results showed that a wide range of attributes was chosen, including role behaviors (e.g. financial provider, meal preparer), physical characteristics (e.g. sturdy, graceful), and occupations (e.g. construction worker, telephone operator) as well as the personality traits identified by the Broverman studies. However, although a wider range of attributes emerged, the results still showed consistent differentiation between "the man" and "the woman," with the women being seen as warm, emotional, small, and taking care of children. Deaux, Kite, and Lewis (1985) also explored subgroups of men and women such as "mother," "father," "business woman," "macho man," and "housewife." The results showed two things. First, they indicated that the stereotypes of the subgroups were as strong as they were for the more global terms "man" and "woman." Second, the data indicated that men and women are considered in terms of opposites even when the participants in the study were given a free choice of attributes. Deaux and Lewis (1984) also examined which characteristics were most powerful at triggering stereotypes, and concluded that physical characteristics produced more instant and consistent stereotypes than personality traits, roles, or behaviors.

In summary, being male or female is a physical characteristic which is central to the formation of consistent stereotypes involving the inferred association between sex and a range of personality traits, roles, occupations, and behaviors.

The Meaning of Size

It is not only sex that generates powerful stereotypes. Much literature has also highlighted the stereotypes associated with body size. If the

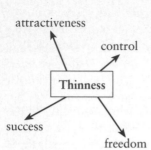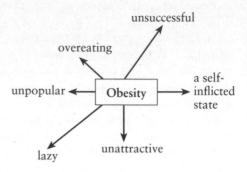

Figure 5.2   The meaning of size

media images of women are becoming thinner, then a larger size reflects unattractiveness and thinness is essentially associated with attractiveness. Body size also generates a range of other associations (see figure 5.2). This has been explored using both quantitative and qualitative methods.

Quantitative research

Quantitative research suggests that people of all ages and sexes and from a number of different cultures stigmatize and consequently discriminate against obese people (Larkin and Pines, 1979; Allon, 1982; Harris, Harris, and Bochner, 1982). In particular, the obese have been rated as more unattractive (Dejong, 1980), lacking in self-discipline (Tiggemann and Rothblum, 1988), lazy (Weiss, 1980), unpopular (Staffieri, 1967), and less active, intelligent, hardworking, successful, athletic or popular (Harris, Harris, and Bochner, 1982) than their thinner counterparts. Studies also indicate that fat women are judged more negatively than fat men and that these stereotypes are independent of the body size of the person doing the rating (Tiggemann and Rothblum, 1988). Research also shows that such negative stereotypes may result in discrimination, as in one study carried out among college students, overweight men and women were less likely to be recommended for employment after being watched performing tasks in an identical fashion to their thinner counterparts (Larkin and Pines, 1979). Such negative views have been reported among a range of populations including business persons (Klesges et al., 1990), rehabilitation counselors (Kaplan, 1984), doctors (Blaxter, 1978), and medical students (Weise et al., 1992). For example, in one early study Maddox and Liederman (1969) asked a group of physicians and medical students to rate their overweight patients for a set of personal characteristics. They found that 97 percent judged them stupid, 90 percent unsuccessful, 90 percent weak, 86 percent lazy, 69 percent not nice, 65 percent unhappy, 60 percent weak-willed, 54 percent ugly, and 55 percent awkward. Therefore, in the same way that gender is associated with a range of personality and behavioral traits, the physical characteristic of size similarly triggers a stereotype.

Research has also evaluated how young we are when we acquire these beliefs. In 1969, Lerner and Gellert showed drawings of different-sized adults to groups of five- and ten-year-old children. The adults were either thin, medium, or overweight. The children were then asked to describe what kind of person the adult would be. The children associated the medium-sized adults with all the positive qualities and the thin and fat adults with all the negative qualities. In a further experiment, the researchers presented the children with five drawings of children: a handicapped child, a child with facial disfigurement, a child with crutches and a leg brace, a child with an amputated left forearm, and an obese child. The children were then asked to "Tell me which boy (girl) you like the best." All the children rated the obese child as the one they liked least. Wadden and Stunkard (1985) also studied children's beliefs about obesity and reported that obese children are regarded as lazy, dirty, stupid, ugly, cheats, and liars by their peers. It has been argued that children develop negative stereotypes of the obese as early as six years of age (Staffieri, 1967) and that such attributions remain relatively constant through to adulthood regardless of level of education (Wooley, Wooley, and Dyrenforth, 1979).

Qualitative literature

The meaning of size is also illustrated in the more qualitative research and in the psychoanalytic writings about eating disorders. Orbach has written extensively about the meaning of thinness in the context both of dieting and of eating disorders (1978, 1986), arguing that thinness and body weight represent a range of meanings and that "how women see and experience their bodies refers to the cultural factors outside themselves" (1986, p. 70). Bordo (1990) in her essay "Reading the slender body," argued that representations of the body can be read to understand the meanings behind them and suggested that current images of thinness reproduce contemporary concerns and anxieties in society. From these perspectives weight, overweight, and thinness have a range of meanings.

Figure 5.3   The meaning of size: Control (*Source:* Advertising Archives)

Control

The central meaning of size is control, in terms of both the ability to control the self and the inclination towards loss of control (see figure 5.3).

For example, Bordo argued that "fat," "bulges," and "flab" reflect factors such as "uncontained desire, unrestrained hunger, uncontrolled impulse" (1990, p. 89), which must be "busted," "destroyed," or "burned," with thinness representing the body's capacity for "self containment and the control of impulse and desire" (p. 90). The thin body therefore means that the thin person has self-control over their inner state; it means that they are psychologically stable and the thinness is a "marker of personal internal order" (Bordo, 1990, p. 94). Lawrence (1984) also argued that "the ability to limit food intake and to lose weight bring with them a far reaching moral kudos, with implications of will power and the capacity to resist temptation" (p. 33). Similarly Orbach (1978) argued that "fat is a social disease" and that "non dieting and self acceptance might be keys to weight loss" (p. 12). This suggests that becoming psychologically stable though self-acceptance could result in a thinner body – the thin body again reflecting psychological control. Bordo (1990) also stated that thinness reflects control over the person's inner world within the context of a culture of consumerism, and that "the slender body codes the tantalizing ideal of a well managed self in which all is 'in order' despite the contradictions of the consumer culture" (1990, p. 97). Thinness represents control over the self within a world which encourages the abandonment of this control. Likewise, Brownell (1991) examined the cultural preoccupation with thinness and stated that society equates thinness with moral perfection and assumes that thinness means hard work, ambition, self-control, and purity whereas being overweight is a sign of laziness and stupidity.

Freedom

Thinness has also been deemed to reflect freedom. First there is a freedom from class. For example, Orbach (1986) described the emergence of thin models and actresses in the 1960s and how they "exemplified . . . an individualistic break with constraints of class society" (p. 72). She argued that "It was a break with the past and seemed to offer the possibility of transcendence of class itself" (p. 73). Therefore, being fat represented the trappings of a lower class and thinness indicated an escape from the class structure.

Second, it has been suggested that thinness represents freedom from reproduction. For example, Orbach (1986) stated that "Slimness is opposed to fertility" and noted that Twiggy's pre-pubescent thinness challenged the association between femininity and childbearing (p. 75). Similarly, Bordo (1990) argued that thinness symbolizes "liberation from a domestic, reproductive destiny" (p. 103) and that the more androgynous body "may symbolise freedom . . . from a reproductive destiny and a construction of femininity seen as constraining and suffocating" (p. 105). Therefore thinness represents an escape from the expectation that women will reproduce.

Success

Finally, thinness also represents success (see figure 5.4). Bordo (1990) stated that fat is "indicative of laziness, lack of discipline, unwillingness to conform and absence of all those 'managerial' abilities that, according to the dominant ideology, confer upward mobility" (p. 95). Similarly she stated that "body weight came to be seen as reflecting moral or personal inadequacy or lack of will" (p. 94). This is similar to Brownell's analysis of thinness as moral perfection (1991).

Throughout both the quantitative and qualitative literatures a larger size is associated with a range of negative meanings. In contrast, a thinner size is associated with positive qualities such as control, freedom, and success.

These associations with size are not, however, consistent across all cultures. For example, Mvo, Dick, and Steyn (1999) carried out a qualitative study to explore the perceptions of ten overweight black women from disadvantaged communities in Cape Town, South Africa. They all had underweight infants and were asked about the culturally acceptable body size for women and children. Some of these women expressed a desire to lose weight for practical reasons. The women, however, placed a high value on food, as food was often scarce, and therefore regarded voluntarily regulating food intake as unacceptable. The participants described increased body mass as a token of well-being, and stated that marital harmony was reflected in being larger. In addition they said that overweight children were seen as a sign of health, as it meant that they had access to sufficient food supply and intake. In line with this Cogan et al. (1996) assessed preferred body size in Ghanaian and American students and reported that the Ghanaian students rated larger bodies as closer to ideal and showed lower levels of body dissatisfaction and dieting. Similarly, Rothblum (1990) reported research findings from Latin

Figure 5.4   The meaning of size: Success (*Source*: Advertising Archives)

America, Puerto Rico, China, and the Philippines and argued that increased body weight is linked with wealth and health, and Sobal and Stunkard (1989) have argued that obesity is a sign of high status in poorer countries.

Why are the overweight and obese judged so negatively in the West?

A larger size triggers an association with a range of negative attributes, whereas a thin body generates consistently positive associations. It has been argued that obesity stereotypes are so negative because obesity is seen as a self-inflicted state. In line with this, Lerner and Gellert (1969) concluded from their study of children's preferences that the children liked the overweight child least because obesity was seen as the fault of the child and not something to sympathize with. It is assumed that the obese have brought their size upon themselves through overeating, and some research has explored the assumptions made about how the obese eat. For example, research has shown that the obese are believed to eat to compensate for other problems (Maimon et al., 1979) or are gluttonous (Maddox, Back, and Liederman, 1968), and that they are rated more negatively when they are described as having lost weight compared to an obese person who is described as having a medical condition (Dejong, 1980). Research has also examined whether eating behavior per se results in negative stereotypes. Some writers have argued that women are judged more positively if seen to eat lightly rather than heavily in public, that "eating like a bird" is regarded as feminine and desirable, and that the control of appetite is seen as virtuous in women (Orbach, 1978; Wolf, 1990; Seid, 1994). Similarly, Mori, Chaiken, and Pliner (1987) indicated that women try to eat less in public to project a more feminine image, and Chaiken and Pliner (1987) concluded that eating lightly does make others judge women as more feminine. One experimental study aimed to explore the underlying mechanisms for negative stereotypes about the obese, with a focus on assumed and actual eating behavior (Ogden and Awal, submitted). Participants were randomly allocated to receive a photograph of a woman eating which had been manipulated according to body size (fat vs thin) and observed eating behavior (eating lightly vs eating heavily). They then completed ratings of social desirability (e.g. femininity, attractiveness, laziness) and assumed eating behavior (e.g. dieting, overeating, motivations for eating) for the target stimulus. The results showed that the fat target woman was consistently rated as less socially desirable and had more negative assumptions made about her eating behavior than her thinner counterpart. Further, the woman eating heavily was not only seen to have different assumed eating behavior but also was rated as less socially desirable than the woman eating lightly, indicating that observed overeating also generates negative stereotypes. In addition, the ratings of some aspects of social desirability and assumed eating behavior for the thin woman varied according to whether she was observed to be eating lightly or heavily. In contrast, the observed eating behavior of the fat woman had only minimal impact on ratings of her attributes. It was concluded from this study that obesity stereotypes are all-pervasive because a larger body size has come to epitomize a socially undesirable trait – overeating. Further, observed eating behavior had virtually no impact on attributions made about the obese, as it cannot override the powerful influence of assumed eating behavior.

Therefore, like sex, size is associated with a range of personality and behavioral traits, with a larger size triggering a complex and consistent negative stereotype, and thinness triggering more positive associations. However, in contrast to the characteristics inferred as a result of someone's sex, which is a biological given, size is associated with eating, which renders being overweight a self-inflicted state. Therefore, as being overweight is considered the fault of the individual, the characteristics associated with it reflect the belief that it is something that could be avoided.

Conclusion

The media represent men more often and more positively than women, and when women are portrayed their images are becoming increasingly thin. Thinness is therefore intricately linked with attractiveness. And in the same way that sex generates a wealth of complex associations, so does body size. In particular, being overweight is associated with laziness and lethargy and is considered a self-inflicted state, creating a sense of blame. In contrast, thinness means control, freedom, and success.

Towards an integrated model of diet

Food choice is studied as a means to understand and promote healthy eating. Psychological models of food choice focus on individual predictors of eating behavior but marginalize the social meanings which surround this behavior. The previous chapter outlined the meanings associated with food, but whatever is eaten has the potential to change body size. Therefore food choice also takes place within the context of the meaning of body size and shape. This chapter has explored these meanings and suggested that the physical attribute of size is loaded with behavioral, role, and personality associations. These meanings can generate weight concern, which can both prohibit and promote food choice. The next two chapters explore weight concern, with a focus on body dissatisfaction and dieting.

chapter six

Body Dissatisfaction

Eating or not eating food can cause changes in the body's size and shape. Worry about such changes constitutes weight concern, which has generated a wealth of work and interest over the past few decades. One form of weight concern is body dissatisfaction, and this has been studied in terms of the development of a range of measures, research into the prevalence of the problem, and an analysis of its causes and consequences. This chapter explores body dissatisfaction and draws upon both the descriptive and experimental literatures.

This chapter covers:

- What is body dissatisfaction?
- Who is dissatisfied with their body?
- Causes of body dissatisfaction
- Consequences of body dissatisfaction

What is Body Dissatisfaction?

Body image has been defined as "the picture of our own body which we form in our mind" (Schilder, 1950), but has also been used to describe perceptions of bodily boundaries, a sense of attractiveness, and the perception of bodily sensations. Over the past few decades researchers, journalists, and broadcasters have become interested in one facet of body image, body dissatisfaction. Magazines contain questionnaires on "How happy are you with your body?" and television programs feature women (and some men) describing how they wish they could be thinner/taller/ have larger breasts or be more muscular. Body dissatisfaction comes in many forms. It has been defined in a range of ways and subsequently measured using a range of techniques. Comprehensive overviews of the measurement of body image and body dissatisfaction can be found in

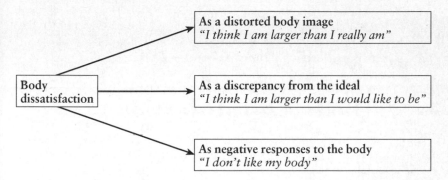

Figure 6.1   Body dissatisfaction

Ben-Tovim and Walker (1991b), Thompson (1990), Cash and Pruzinsky (1990), and Allison (1995).

How is it measured?

The measurement of body dissatisfaction can be considered in terms of three different perspectives, as shown in figure 6.1.

Distorted body size estimation

Some research has conceptualized body dissatisfaction as a distorted body size estimation and a perception that the body is larger than it really is. For example, Slade and Russell (1973) asked anorexics to adjust the distance between two lights on a beam in a darkened room until the lights represented the width of parts of their body such as their hips, waist, and shoulders. The results showed that anorexics consistently over-estimated their size compared to control subjects. Other studies coming from the same perspective have asked subjects either to mark a life-size piece of paper (Gleghorn et al., 1987), to adjust the horizontal dimensions on either a television or video image of themselves (Freeman et al., 1984; Gardner, Martinez, and Sandoval, 1987), or to change the dimensions on a distorting mirror (Brodie, Slade, and Rose, 1989). This research has consistently shown that individuals with clinically defined eating disorders show greater perceptual distortion than nonclinical subjects. The research has also shown that the vast majority of women whether with or without an eating disorder think that they are larger than they actually are.

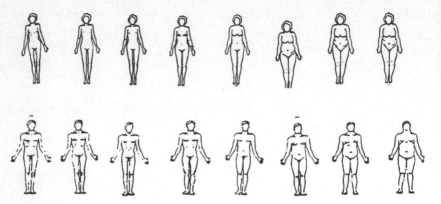

Figure 6.2   Body silhouettes for adults (*Source*: A.J. Stunkard, J.R. Harris, and F. Schulsinger, Use of the Danish adoption register for the study of obesity and thinness, in S. Kety (ed.), *The Genetics of Neurological and Psychiatric Disorders*, New York: Raven Press, 1983)

Discrepancy from the ideal

An alternative approach to body dissatisfaction has emphasized a discrepancy between perceptions of reality versus those of an ideal. In contrast to the approach described above, this perspective does not involve a comparison to the individual's actual size as objectively measured by the researcher. This research has tended to use whole-body silhouette pictures of varying sizes, with the subject asked to state which one is closest to how they look now and which one best illustrates how they would like to look (see figure 6.2).

Stunkard, Sorensen, and Schulsinger (1983) used this approach with normal male and female students, Counts and Adams (1985) used it with bulimics, dieters, and ex-obese females, and Hill, Oliver, and Rogers (1992) used it with pre-adolescent and adolescent children. This approach has consistently shown that most girls and women would like to be thinner than they are and most males would like either to be the same or larger.

Negative responses to the body

The third and most frequent way in which body dissatisfaction is understood is simply in terms of negative feelings and cognitions about the body. This has been assessed using a multitude of questionnaires such as the Body Shape Questionnaire (Cooper et al., 1987), the Body Areas Satisfaction Scale (Brown, Cash, and Mikulka, 1990), the Body Attitudes

Questionnaire (Ben-Tovim and Walker, 1991a), the Body Esteem Scale (Franzoi and Shields, 1984), and the Body Dissatisfaction subscale of the Eating Disorders Inventory (Garner, Olmsted, and Polivy, 1981). These questionnaires ask questions such as "Do you worry about parts of your body being too big?", "Do you worry about your thighs spreading out when you sit down?", and "Does being with thin women make you feel conscious of your weight?" Research has also explored dissatisfaction and criticism of body parts using scales such as the Body Cathexis Scale (Secord and Jourard, 1953) and the Body Satisfaction Scale (Slade et al., 1990). This research has shown that although those individuals with eating disorders show greater body dissatisfaction than those without, dieters show greater body dissatisfaction than non-dieters and women in general show greater body dissatisfaction than men.

In summary, body dissatisfaction can be conceptualized either as a discrepancy between the individual's perception of their body size and their real body size, as a discrepancy between their perception of their actual size as compared to their ideal size, or simply as feelings of discontent with the body's size and shape. Whichever conceptualization is used and whichever measurement tool is chosen to operationalize body dissatisfaction, it seems clear that it is a common phenomenon and certainly not one which is limited to those few individuals with clinically defined eating disorders. So who shows dissatisfaction with their body?

Who is Dissatisfied with their Body?

The occurrence of body dissatisfaction will be explored in terms of gender, age, sexuality, social class, and ethnicity.

Women

Concerns about weight and shape are conventionally associated with women. Fallon and Rozin (1985) asked 227 female students in the US to rate their current figure and ideal figure using body silhouettes, and showed that in general women wanted to be thinner than they thought they were. Similarly, Tiggemann and Pennington (1990) asked 52 students in Australia to repeat this study and found that they also showed body dissatisfaction. Using the same silhouettes, normal-weight women in Britain have also been shown to rate their preferred size as thinner than their perceived actual size (Wardle et al., 1993). Overall, research indicates that many women show a discrepancy between their real and ideal weight, have actively dieted during the past six months, participate in organized weight loss programs, prefer to be thinner, and many engage in both safe and dangerous food-restriction strategies (Klesges, Mizes, and Klesges, 1987; Rozin and Fallon, 1988; Brodie, Slade, and Riley, 1991; Jeffrey, Adlis, and Forster, 1991). This research also shows that women are more likely to show these aspects of body dissatisfaction than men.

Research has also explored which parts of their body women are dissatisfied with. For example, Furnham and Greaves (1994) asked 55 British women to rate a range of body parts and reported that women were most dissatisfied with their thighs, buttocks, and hips. Lee et al. (1996) carried out a similar study and reported that women were most unhappy with the appearance of their stomach, waist, hips, and thighs. A US-based survey of readers of *Psychology Today* magazine showed that 55 percent of women were dissatisfied with their weight, 57 percent were dissatisfied with their mid torso, 50 percent with lower torso, 45 percent with muscle tone, and 32 percent with upper torso (Cash, Winstead, and Janda, 1986). Ogden and Taylor (2000) also examined women's dissatisfaction with body parts using computer-manipulated photographs from magazines and concluded that women would prefer their chests to be larger and their legs, stomachs, bottoms, and overall body shape to be smaller. The majority of women seem to show body dissatisfaction, particularly with their stomach, hips, thighs, and bottoms. They show greater dissatisfaction than men; and such gender differences are apparent in children aged 12 to 13 years (Wardle and Beales, 1986) and even as young as 9 years (Hill, Draper, and Stack, 1994).

Men

When compared to women, men's body satisfaction appears to be high, but men also show body dissatisfaction. For example, Mishkind et al. (1986) asked men to rate a series of body silhouettes ranging from thin to fat and found that 75 percent reported a discrepancy between their ideal and their actual size, with about half wanting to be bigger and half wanting to be thinner. Likewise, Cash, Winstead, and Janda (1986) concluded from their survey that 34 percent of men were dissatisfied with the way they looked and that 41 percent were dissatisfied with their weight. Similarly, Mishkind concluded that 95 percent of American male college students showed body dissatisfaction. Overall, research indicates that some men do diet, are aware of cultural norms of male attractiveness, are concerned with physical attractiveness, upper body strength, and physical condition, and report a preferred size which is different to their perceived shape (Franzoi and Shields, 1984, Klesges, Mizes, and Klesges, 1987; Rozin and Fallon, 1988; Brodie, Slade and Riley, 1991; Jeffrey, Adlis, and Forster, 1991).

Research has also explored which body parts generate body dissatisfaction in men. Furnham and Greaves (1994) asked 47 British men to rate a series of body parts and concluded that the men were most dissatisfied with their biceps, width of shoulders, and chest. Ogden and Taylor (2000) used real photographs and reported that in general men would prefer their arms, chests, and shoulders to be larger and their stomachs and overall body to be smaller. Therefore, some men do show body dissatisfaction, particularly with their arms, shoulders, chests, and stomachs.

Age

Most research exploring body dissatisfaction has focused on young student populations. However, some studies have examined body dissatisfaction in children. For example, Tiggemann and Pennington (1990) asked girls aged 9 to rate age-appropriate silhouettes and concluded that many rated their ideal as thinner than their perceptions of how they actually looked. Similarly, Hill, Oliver, and Rogers (1992) and Grogan and Wainwright (1996) reported body dissatisfaction in girls aged 9 and 8 respectively. Some research has also explored body dissatisfaction in young boys and has shown that although young boys are more satisfied with the way they look than girls, 13-year-old boys show the beginnings of concerns about their bodies (Conner et al., 1996). Across the age spectrum, Pliner, Chaiken, and Flett (1990) asked women ranging in age from 10 to 79 to rate their "appearance self esteem." The results showed no age effects and the authors concluded that women over 60 were just as concerned as young adults and adolescents. Similarly, Lamb et al. (1993) asked men and women across the lifespan to rate their body dissatisfaction and reported that older and younger women and older men would prefer to be thinner. Only the younger men were relatively satisfied with their body size. They also concluded that although both the older women and men wanted to be thinner they preferred larger body sizes than their younger counterparts. This may reflect a more realistic ideal body or it could be illustrative of a cohort effect, with these individuals having been exposed to larger role models in their youth. It would therefore seem that body dissatisfaction is not just a characteristic of young women; it is also present in males and females across the lifespan.

Sexuality

Most research examining body dissatisfaction has ignored the sexuality of the participants being studied. There is some evidence indicating that lesbians and gay men may differ from heterosexuals in their body dissatisfaction. For example, Siever (1994) compared lesbian and heterosexual women's value on appearance and concluded that lesbians were more satisfied with their bodies and placed less importance on their appearance. Similarly, Gettelman and Thompson (1993) reported that lesbian women had lower concerns with appearance, weight, and dieting than heterosexual women. In contrast, Brand, Rothblum, and Soloman (1992) and Striegel-Moore, Tucker, and Hsu (1990) found no differences in their sample between lesbian and heterosexual women and concluded that gender was a better predictor than sexuality. Grogan (1999) suggested that these contradictory findings may illustrate a place for gender role orientation. To explore this possibility, Ludwig and Brownell (1999) asked 188 lesbian and bisexual women to complete measures of their body image and whether they considered themselves to be feminine, masculine, or androgynous in appearance. The results showed that both lesbian and bisexual women who considered themselves to be feminine were more dissatisfied with their bodies, and that this dissatisfaction was greater in women whose friends did not share their sexual orientation.

In terms of gay men, research tends to show that they report higher levels of body dissatisfaction than heterosexual men. For example, Mishkind et al. (1986) reported that gay men were more dissatisfied with their body shape, waist, arms, biceps, and stomachs than heterosexual men, and this has been supported by the findings of Beren et al. (1996), Gettelman and Thompson (1993), and Siever (1994). Furthermore, it has been argued that body dissatisfaction in gay men is higher in those who show the highest affinity with the gay community (Beren et al., 1996). Epel et al. (1996) evaluated the content of personal advertisements in seven different US publications. The results showed that gay men described their body shape more often than both lesbian women and heterosexual men, indicating that body satisfaction is a major concern for this group.

Therefore sexuality may relate to body dissatisfaction. However, whereas homosexuality is associated with lower body dissatisfaction in women, it seems to predict higher body dissatisfaction in men.

Ethnicity

Body dissatisfaction has predominantly been seen as a problem for white women, and this is in part supported by the literature. For example, higher rates of a range of behaviors associated with body dissatisfaction have been found in white women when compared to black and Asian women, including bulimic behaviors (Gray, Ford, and Kelly, 1987), generalized disordered eating (Abrams, Allen, and Gray, 1992; Akan and Grilo, 1995), body dissatisfaction, and eating concerns (Rucker and Cash, 1992; Powell and Khan, 1995). The literature examining the relationship between body dissatisfaction and ethnic group, however, is contradictory, as other studies report the reverse relationship between ethnicity and weight concern. For example, Mumford, Whitehouse, and Platts (1991) reported results from a school in the north of England which indicated that the prevalence of bulimia nervosa was higher among Asian schoolgirls than their white counterparts. In parallel, Striegel-Moore et al. (1995) reported higher levels of a drive for thinness in black girls, and Hill and Bhatti (1995) reported higher levels of dietary restraint in nine-year-old Asian girls when both these samples were compared to white girls. Furthermore, additional studies have suggested that equally high levels of weight concern can be found in women and girls regardless of their ethnicity (Dolan, Lacey, and Evans, 1990; Ahmed, Waller, and Verduyn, 1994; Le Grange, Stone, and Brownell, 1998). Some research therefore indicates that whites are more body-dissatisfied than Asians and blacks, other research shows that whites are less dissatisfied, and some research shows that there is no difference in body dissatisfaction between ethnic groups.

Social class

Body dissatisfaction is generally believed to be a problem for the higher social classes, but the literature on class is also contradictory. Several studies indicate that a range of factors relating to body dissatisfaction are more prevalent in higher class individuals. For example, Dornbusch et al. (1984) examined social class and the desire to be thin in a representative sample of 7,000 American adolescents and concluded that higher class females wanted to be thinner when compared to their lower class counterparts. In parallel, Drenowski, Kurt, and Krahn (1994) reported that the higher class subjects in their sample showed increased prevalence of dieting, bingeing, and vigorous exercise for weight loss, and Wardle and Marsland (1990) reported that although the higher class schoolchildren were thinner, they showed greater levels of weight concern. Similar results have also been reported for the prevalence of anorexia nervosa (Crisp, Palmer, and Kalucy, 1976). In direct contrast to the above studies, Story et al. (1995) concluded from their study of 36,320 American students that higher social class was related to greater weight satisfaction and lower rates of pathological weight-control behaviors such as vomiting. Similar results were reported by Eisler and Szmukler (1985), who examined abnormal eating attitudes. Other studies have found no relationship between social class and factors such as body dissatisfaction, the desire for thinness, the desire for weight loss, and symptoms indicative of eating disorders (Cole and Edlemann, 1988; Whitaker et al., 1989). Therefore, although higher social class is believed to relate to body dissatisfaction, the results remain unclear.

In summary, body dissatisfaction can be conceptualized either as body size distortion involving a comparison with an objective measure of size, as a discrepancy between ideal and perceptions of actual body size, or simply as negative feelings and thoughts about the body. When research into body dissatisfaction was in its early days it was generally believed that it was a problem only shown by those with eating disorders. However, much research shows that although women are more body dissatisfied than men, men also have concerns about their bodies and that such concerns occur across the age range and are apparent in groups which vary in sexuality, ethnicity, and social class. What causes this common problem?

Causes of Body Dissatisfaction

Research has highlighted a role for both social and psychological factors in causing body dissatisfaction.

Social factors and body dissatisfaction

Research exploring the impact of social factors in causing body dissatisfaction has particularly indicated a role for the media, culture, and the family.

The media

The most commonly held belief in both the lay and academic communities is that body dissatisfaction is a response to representations of thin women in the media. Magazines, newspapers, television, films and even novels predominantly use images of thin women. These women may be advertising body-size related items such as food and clothes or neutral items such as vacuum cleaners and wallpaper, but they are always thin. Alternatively, they may be characters in a story or simply passersby to illustrate the real world, but this real world is always represented by thinness. Whatever their role and wherever their existence, women used by the media are generally thin, and we are therefore led to believe that thinness is not only the desired norm but also the actual norm. When, on those rare occasions, a fatter woman appears, she is usually there making a statement about being fat (fat comedians make jokes about chocolate cake and fat actresses are either evil or unhappy), not simply as a normal woman (see chapter 5). Do these representations then make women dissatisfied with their bodies? Some research suggests that this is the case. For example, Heinberg and Thompson (1995) asked white women to rate their body dissatisfaction before and after watching television commercials containing appearance-related material. The results showed that those who already showed body-image disturbance reported more body dissatisfaction after viewing the commercials. In a similar vein, Ogden and Mundray (1996) asked both men and women to rate their body dissatisfaction before and after studying pictures of either fat or thin men or women (the pictures were matched in gender to the participant). The results showed that all participants, regardless of gender, felt more body satisfied after studying the fatter pictures and more body dissatisfied after studying the thinner pictures. The results also showed that this response was greater in the women than the men. Similar results have also been found for other normal-weight women and men, anorexics, bulimics, and pregnant women (Waller, Hamilton, and Shaw, 1992; Hamilton and Waller, 1993; Sumner et al., 1993; Grogan, Williams, and Conner, 1996). If such changes in body dissatisfaction can occur after only acute exposure to these images, then it is possible that exposure in the longer term might be more serious. However, is the effect of the media the only explanation of body dissatisfaction? Are women (and sometimes men) simply passive victims of the whims of the media? Body dissatisfaction also comes from a range of additional sources.

Culture

Research has also examined the impact of an individual's culture on body dissatisfaction, with a particular focus on their ethnicity and their social class. It has been suggested that being from a higher class, white, Asian, or black may relate to developing body dissatisfaction. However, as described above, this research is contradictory, with some research indicating that body dissatisfaction relates to one ethnic group or one class and other research showing either the reverse or no relationship. It has also been argued that moving from one culture to another may also be predictive. For example, Mumford, Whitehouse, and Platts (1991) described a role for acculturation, and argued that body dissatisfaction may emerge as one group attempts to acculturate to its new environment (see chapter 10 for a discussion of acculturation and eating disorders). To date, research exploring the role of culture is limited and conclusions are only tentative.

The family

Research has also focused on the impact of the family in predicting body dissatisfaction. In particular, it has highlighted a role for the mother and suggested that mothers who are dissatisfied with their own bodies communicate this to their daughters, resulting in the daughter's own body dissatisfaction. For example, Hall and Brown (1982) reported that mothers of girls with anorexia show greater body dissatisfaction than mothers of non-disordered girls. Likewise, Steiger et al. (1994) found a direct correspondence between mothers' and daughters' levels of weight concern, and Hill, Weaver, and Blundell (1990) reported a link between mothers' and daughters' degree of dietary restraint. However, research examining concordance between mothers and daughters has not always produced consistent results. For example, Attie and Brooks-Gunn (1989) reported that mothers' levels of compulsive eating and body image could not predict these factors in their daughters. Likewise, Ogden and Elder (1998) reported discordance between mothers' and daughters' weight concern in both Asian and white families.

Research exploring the role of social factors has therefore highlighted a role for the media, culture, and the mother's own body dissatisfaction. However, there are some problems with the literature. First, some of the evidence is contradictory and therefore straightforward conclusions are problematic. Second, even if there were a relationship between social factors and body dissatisfaction, focusing on external sources such as the media or looking for group differences (i.e. white vs. Asian, lower class vs. higher class, mother vs. daughter) doesn't explain how these social influences result in weight concern. Research has also looked for psychological explanations.

Psychological factors and body dissatisfaction

The research suggests that body dissatisfaction may be related to the media. But are women and men just passively influenced by such external sources of information? How does exposure to the media bring about feelings of body dissatisfaction? The results also suggests a role for class, ethnicity, and the family environment, but these relationships are not consistent. Perhaps looking for group differences hides the effect of other psychological causes. From this perspective, ethnicity may relate to body dissatisfaction, but only when ethnicity is accompanied by a particular set of beliefs. Similarly, it may not be class per se which is important, but whether class reflects the way an individual thinks. Further, a mother's body dissatisfaction may only be important if it occurs within a particular kind of relationship. Research has explored the role of beliefs, the mother–daughter relationship, and the central role of control as a means to explain how social influences are translated into body dissatisfaction.

Beliefs

Some research has examined the beliefs held by the individuals themselves and their family members. For example, when attempting to understand ethnicity, studies have highlighted a role for beliefs about competitiveness, the value of achievement, material success, and a parental belief that the child is their future (Ogden and Chanana, 1998). Both Mumford, Whitehouse, and Platts (1991) and Hill and Bhatti (1995) highlighted a role for beliefs about a traditional role for women in explaining weight concern in Asian girls. In a similar vein, when attempting to explain the impact of social class research has highlighted a role for beliefs about achievement, and it has been suggested that eating disorders may be a response to such pressures (Bruch, 1974; Kalucy, Crisp, and Harding, 1977; Selvini, 1988). Lower class individuals may aspire more in terms of family life and having children, which may be protective against weight concern. Cole and Edelmann (1988) empirically tested this possibility and assessed the relationship between the need to achieve and eating behavior, but although the need to achieve was associated with class, it was not predictive of weight concern. It has also been suggested that class may be associated with the value of physical appearance and attitudes towards obesity (Wardle, Volz, and Golding, 1995), and Dornbusch et al. (1984) commented that those from the higher classes placed more emphasis on thinness. In addition, Striegel-Moore,

Silberstein, and Rodin (1986) argued that higher class women are more likely to emulate trendsetters of beauty and fashion, predisposing them to feelings of dissatisfaction with their appearance. The literature, therefore, highlights a range of beliefs which may mediate the impact of ethnicity and social class on body dissatisfaction. These include beliefs about competitiveness, achievement, material success, the role of women, stereotypes of beauty, and the child–parent relationship. Ogden and Chanana (1998) explored the role of these beliefs in Asian and white teenage girls, and Ogden and Thomas (1999) focused on lower and higher class individuals. It was concluded that although social factors such as class and ethnicity may be related to body dissatisfaction, it is likely that their influence is mediated through the role of beliefs held both by the individual who is dissatisfied with their body and by their family members.

Mother—daughter relationship

Some research has also explored the nature of the mother–daughter relationship. For example, Crisp et al. (1980) argued that undefined boundaries within the family and the existence of an enmeshed relationship between mother and daughter may be important factors. Smith, Mullis, and Hill (1995) suggested that a close relationship between mother and daughter may result in an enmeshed relationship and problems with separation in adolescence. Minuchin, Rosman, and Baker (1978) also argued that although optimum autonomy does not mean breaking all bonds between mother and daughter, mother–daughter relationships which permit poor autonomy for both parties may be predictive of future psychopathology. Similarly, Bruch (1974) stated that anorexia may be a result of a child's struggle to develop her own self-identity within a mother–daughter dynamic which limits the daughter's autonomy. Some authors have also examined the relationship between autonomy, enmeshment, and intimacy. For example, Smith, Mullis, and Hill (1995) argued that an increased recognition of autonomy within the mother–daughter relationship corresponds with a decrease in enmeshment and a resulting increase in intimacy. It has also been suggested that such intimacy may be reflected in a reduction in conflict and subsequent psychological problems (Smith, Mullis, and Hill, 1995). The literature therefore highlights many aspects of the mother–daughter relationship which may promote body dissatisfaction. Ogden and Steward (2000) directly explored whether the mother–daughter relationship was important in terms of a "modeling hypothesis" (i.e., the mother is body dissatisfied and therefore the daughter is too) or an "interactive hypothesis" (i.e., it is the relationship between mother and daughter that is important). The study examined both the mothers' and the daughters' own levels of body dissatisfaction and the nature of the relationship between mother and daughter. The results showed no support for the modeling hypothesis, but suggested that a relationship in which mothers did not believe in either their own or their daughter's autonomy and showed a tendency to project their own expectations onto their daughters was more likely to result in daughters who were dissatisfied with their bodies. In a similar vein, Baker, Whisman, and Brownell (2000) examined associations between parent and child's weight-related attitudes and behaviors. The results showed little support for the modeling hypothesis, but the authors highlighted a role for perceived direct criticism from the mother as predictive of weight-loss behaviors in the daughters. These two studies indicate that mother–daughter relationships influence body dissatisfaction via the nature of the relationship and not through the provision of a role model. However, whereas Baker, Whisman, and Brownell (2000) pointed to the daughter's perception of this relationship, Ogden and Steward (2000) highlighted the importance of the mother's own perceptions.

In summary, it would seem that body dissatisfaction may come from the media. Further it may be related to ethnicity, social class, and the mother's own body dissatisfaction. In addition, it is possible that the impact of such social influences is mediated through psychological factors such as beliefs and the nature of relationships.

Consequences of Body Dissatisfaction

If so many women and men show dissatisfaction with their body size and shape, what are the consequences of these feelings?

Women

For women the most common consequence of body dissatisfaction is dieting, with up 70 percent of women dieting in their lives and about 40 percent dieting at any time. Dieting is discussed in detail in chapter 7. Some women also smoke as a means to lose weight, and this has been actively encouraged by the tobacco industry (see figure 6.3). Women also engage in exercise as a means to change their body dissatisfaction, and some undergo cosmetic surgery.

Figure 6.3   Smoking as a response to body dissatisfaction (*Source*: Advertising Archives)

Exercise

Women, particularly those aged between 13 and 18, exercise less frequently than men, but there is some evidence that women exercise more now than they used to do (Cox, Huppert, and Whichelow, 1993). Women who do exercise mainly participate in keep-fit, yoga, dancing, and swimming. Health researchers attempt to encourage exercise by promoting its health benefits. Studies suggest, however, that the main predictors of exercise are not concern about health but ease of access to facilities, low body fat/weight, positive self-image, childhood exercise, high self-motivation, and beliefs that exercise is enjoyable and provides social support (Riddle, 1980; Dishman, 1982; Dishman, Sallis, and Orenstein, 1985; Paxton, Browning, and O'Connell, 1997). In addition, women cite weight control, changing body shape, and attractiveness as the main motivators for exercise (Furnham and Greaves, 1994). Grogan (1999) reported the results from interviews concerning women's body dissatisfaction and concluded that "the primary motivator to exercise for all the women interviewed was to improve muscle tone and lose weight rather than for health" (p. 45), and cited one woman who said that she exercised "entirely for weight. To try to firm up and try to use some calories and I'm always thinking I'm not doing enough. Afterwards . . . I actually feel slimmer" (p. 45).

Cosmetic surgery

A minority of women who are dissatisfied with the way they look resort to cosmetic surgery; however, this minority has been getting larger over recent years in what Wolf (1990) has labelled the "surgical age." The most common forms of cosmetic surgery are rhinoplasty (nose jobs), breast enlargements, and liposuction (Viner, 1997). Whether cosmetic surgery reflects women's right to take control of the way they look and is the result of a free choice (Davis, 1995) or an expression of female oppression and conformity (Morgan, 1991) is currently debated within the feminist literatures. But it is on the increase, and studies have yet to assess whether it removes the problem of body dissatisfaction or simply exacerbates it by making the female body seem even more open to change.

Men

Men are less likely to diet than women and more likely to engage in sports such as football and rugby and solo activities such as jogging and cycling (Fallon and Rozin, 1985; Cox, Huppert, and Whichelow, 1993). The main motivator among men for exercise is a combination of social contact and enjoyment (Dishman, 1982), but many men also exercise to change their body shape. For example, Baker (1994) reported that 500,000 men in the UK use weights to change their body shape and muscle tone, and Grogan (1999) indicated that 65 percent of the men interviewed engaged in sport specifically to improve their body shape. Most men want to develop muscle mass and attain the mesomorphic male ideal. Some become bodybuilders and develop mass to the extreme.

Conclusion

Body dissatisfaction can be conceptualized either as a distorted body image compared to an objective measure of reality, a difference between perceived actual and ideal body size, or simply as negative feelings about the body. At first it was believed that body dissatisfaction was a problem for those with eating disorders. It is now recognized to be a common phenomenon which is apparent in many different groups within society. Women are generally dissatisfied with their bodies as a whole, and particularly dissatisfied with their bottoms, stomachs, hips, and thighs. This seems to be less apparent in lesbians than heterosexual women, but occurs in women from childhood through to old age. Men are generally less dissatisfied with their bodies than women, but many also wish that parts of their body could be changed, and focus on their stomachs, chests, and arms. This is more apparent in homosexual men and less apparent in younger than older men. In terms of the causes of body dissatisfaction, this chapter has described a role for social factors such as the media, ethnicity, social class, and the family, and has indicated that these external influences impact upon body dissatisfaction through beliefs and the nature of relationships. In terms of the consequences of body dissatisfaction, most women diet, some exercise, and a minority resort to cosmetic surgery, whereas men opt for exercise as the solution to their problem.

Towards an integrated model of diet

Many people may be motivated to eat healthily. But food choice is influenced by many factors other than a concern for health. It relates to an individual's learning, cognitions, and physiology. Furthermore it takes place within the context of the wealth of meanings associated with food and body size. A consequence of these meanings is a concern about body weight and body shape. This often takes the form of body dissatisfaction, which involves criticism about the whole body and body parts. Body dissatisfaction can result in dieting, which has direct implications for food choice as dieters attempt to eat less than they would like to as a means to lose weight. Dieting is the focus of the next chapter.

chapter seven

Dieting

Dieting is the most common consequence of body dissatisfaction for women. Some men also diet as a means to change their body size and shape. But dieting is not a simple behavior, and although dieters aim to eat less, research indicates that this aim is rarely achieved. This chapter focuses on dieting behavior, and by placing it within its historical and social context evaluates why body dissatisfaction results in dieting for many people. The chapter then explores what dieting is and examines the consequences of this behavior. In particular, it examines restraint theory, with its emphasis on dieting as a cause of overeating. It then assesses the problems with this perspective.

This chapter covers:

- Putting dieting in context
- The dieting industry
- What is dieting?
- Dieting and overeating
- The consequences of dieting
- Problems with restraint theory

Putting Dieting in Context

Many women and some men diet. For the majority this is the result of body dissatisfaction and a determination to change both body size and shape. People with a desire to change aspects of their bodies, however, have not always dieted; some have bound their bodies, some have worn specially designed clothes, and others have opted for more drastic surgical solutions. To understand why body dissatisfaction translates into dieting it is necessary to explore the history of dieting and the impact of the dieting industry and then to assess the central role for control.

For as long as records have been kept and history has been written, the female body has been seen as something to control and master. Whether it was in the form of foot-binding, female circumcision, or the wearing of corsets or bustles, women's bodies have been viewed with an eye to changing them. Feet, breasts, waists, thighs, and bottoms have either been too large or too small according to the fashion of the day. Padding was used to add size or binding used to reduce. No aspect of the female body has ever been accepted simply as it is. Dieting is the modern-day equivalent (Ogden, 1992). To understand the current preoccupation with dieting it is necessary to understand the history behind the need to change the female form. Although men and women may vary over the years, fashions change, and economic climates alter, men are generally larger than women. They are taller, wider, have larger feet, and broader waists. Changing the female body has often meant emphasizing these differences. This has taken the form of practices such as foot-binding, corset-wearing, and breast-binding.

Chinese foot-binding

An old Chinese saying stated, "If you care for a son, you don't go easy on his studies; If you care for a daughter, you don't go easy on her foot-binding. (Ts'ai-fei lu)" (cited in Daly, 1978, p. 133). Women tend to have smaller feet than men, and the Chinese tradition of foot-binding emphasized this difference. As a central part of Chinese life for about a thousand years, it only began to die out at the beginning of the twentieth century when the Kuomintang encouraged the "letting out of feet." Young girls had their feet bound at about the age of seven. The mutilation process was carried out by the girl's mother and other close female relatives, who would bind each foot so that the large toe pointed upwards and the other toes were tightly bound under the foot. The young girl would then be made to walk and put her weight onto the newly bound foot; the bones would break and the structure of the foot would be rearranged to conform to the "lotus hook" shape (Daly, 1978). This was an excruciatingly painful process and the young girl would be left with three-inch long "hooks" or stumps which meant that she could not run, had to hobble when she walked, or even had to be carried. A foot-bound woman, however, was marriageable material. "Lotus hooks" were regarded as objects of desire for men, one of whom has been quoted saying

the lotus has special seductive characteristics and is an instrument for arousing desire. Who cannot resist the fascination and bewilderment of playing with and holding in his palms a soft and jade-like hook? (cited in Daly, 1978, p. 138)

The lotus hooks also symbolized obedience and ensured that the wife would be incapable of running away. The stumps prevented women from leading any independent life of their own and represented total helplessness and reliance on men. One of the most interesting elements of foot-binding is that it was a tradition for women, executed by women. However, even though women were the mutilators, the goal of male acceptability was an essential element of economic security and social status. The women were prepared to suffer and to pass this suffering on through their family as a sign that they understood and respected male ideas of beauty, and out of fear of being unmarriageable. One man described his sister's ordeal as a child: "Auntie dragged her hobbling along, to keep the blood circulating. Sister wept throughout but mother and auntie didn't pity her in the slightest saying that if one loved a daughter one could not love her feet" (cited in Daly, 1978, p. 137).

Corsets

The corset has played a major role in the world of female fashions. Although an apparently familiar and harmless article, it has possibly been responsible for more fainting fits, more crushed ribs, and more wasting muscles than any other form of bodily control. The "need" for corsets was derived from the idea that women were insufficiently strong to support their own weight. It was believed that the female waist and spine were too weak to support the breasts and stomach. Of course the corset had many other uses, as it created an upright, "regal" appearance, and emphasized the feminine smaller waist. As fashions changed, the corset provided a basis to enlarge or flatten the stomach and to round or flatten the bottom. Women wearing corsets were incapable of bending and so needed to be waited on; constantly breathless, they required a male arm to steady them. In fact, the corset played a central part in creating the very weakness for which it was designed to compensate. As described by Greer (1970) "Nineteenth-century belles even went to the extremity of having their lowest ribs removed so that they could lace their corsets tighter" (p. 35). Molding the body to create the ideal form suggested an acceptance of women's role in society and an understanding of the necessary means to become desirable. It indicated a recognition of the objectification of women and the central role that physical attractiveness played in determining their identity. Of course, men also may use equivalent beauty aids, but men in corsets, built-up shoes, or toupees are laughed at. As Brownmiller (1984) said in her book *Femininity*, such men "have been grist for the jokester's mill, under the masculine theory that real men do not trick themselves out to be pleasing. (They have better ways to prove their worth.) A woman on the other hand is expected to depend on tricks and suffering to prove her feminine nature" (p. 19). The corset represented women's need to be a desirable object to the men who could provide the necessary social acceptability.

Breast-binding

Breasts have always been another problem area. Whether they should be large, small, droopy, or firm has been left to the ever-changing whims of the fashion world and the male appreciators. It is unlikely that any other part of the body has received so much attention, so much criticism, and so much obsessive fixation as the female breast (Greer, 1970). The symbolism of the breast is obvious. It denotes sexuality, fertility, and motherhood. It is also a constant reminder that women are animals and possess "udders" in the same way as cows and all other mammals. Yet the association between breasts and their biological function is constantly denied. Large breasts are hoisted up, pointed out, or flattened down, while flat-chested women pad their breasts out. But women fear the biological destiny of their breasts. As Brownmiller (1984) said, "we have seen too many pictures in *National Geographic* of wizened old females with sagging, shrivelled teats or with udder-like breasts that hang forlornly to the waist. No not sexy. Not pretty and attractive. Entirely too remindful of the she-animal function" (p. 28). Similarly Greer (1970) argued that "breasts are only to be admired for as long as they show no signs of their function: once darkened, stretched or withered they are signs of revulsion" (p. 34).

Women have detached their breasts from their biological function and hoisted them into the realms of a fashion accessory, and fashion dictates their acceptability. For example, in the 1920s women bound their breasts tightly to create the flat-chested, boyish flapper look, but in the 1950s Marilyn Monroe and Jane Russell rendered the flat-chested look unattractive and women wore padded, underwired, push-up bras to make the most of what they had. In contrast, the 1970s meant that bras were out, but only small breasts could survive the lack of support, and the 1980s brought larger breasts back in fashion again with the invention of the "Wonderbra."

Western women have bound their waists and breasts in the same way that Chinese girls had their feet bound. They conform to contemporary ideas of femininity to increase their marriageability and gain economic and social stability. There are physical differences between men and women, and women are taught a variety of tricks, mutilations, and tortures to emphasize these differences and thus emphasize their femininity. If femaleness is defined as the opposite to maleness, then the more different from men, the more female.

The onset of the dieting age

In the late 1960s women traded in wired and laced corsets for the rubber variety which in turn were traded in for freedom. Boadicea-like bras were exchanged for the softer, lighter versions which were in turn exchanged for the luxury of going bra-less. Women were allowed and even expected to release their bodies and to resort to the natural support of flesh and muscles. And then there came the bikini and along with it Twiggy was launched enthusiastically onto the fashion scene. Suddenly at the beginning of an era of natural control and natural support, women were told that they should not have any flesh to control or support. Bikinis gave no protection and represented a freedom that was only available to those without any excess bodily fat. Twiggy did not need to wear a bra or corset; she had no need to squash her body in only for it to reappear elsewhere. But this absence of need did not come from a desire to free the female body, but from the very fact that she had nothing to free. Women could go bra-less as long their breasts revealed only a restrained life of their own, and corsets were out, as long as what was left behind did not need a corset.

For centuries, whalebones, latex, nylon, and cotton had been used to reshape and rearrange any aspect of the body which did not conform. Even in the 1920s with the thin "flapper" days, bras and corsets were an acceptable way to control the female form. But from the 1960s women were free from these artificial devices but were left with only their flesh to control. The messages were the same. Breasts, bottoms, thighs, stomachs should be rounded or flat as determined by the whims of the fashion world, and "in each case the woman is tailoring herself to appeal to a buyer's market" (Greer, 1970, p. 35). But to comply women had to change their actual bodies and this is where dieting raised its head. *Weight Watchers* started in America in 1963 and in Britain in 1967, and the first copy of *Slimming* magazine was issued in Britain in 1969. The sixties represented the onset of the dieting boom, and central to this boom was the dieting industry.

The Dieting Industry

Books, magazines, dieting clubs, newspaper articles, television programs, dieting aids, and exercise videos all make up the dieting industry. Does this industry respond to or create a need?

Responding to a need

Slimmer magazine in the UK sold 142,000 copies between January and June in 1990; "Weight Watchers UK" has an average of 140,000 members, and "Slimmer clubs" have an average of 40,000 members. Wolf (1990) described the $33 billion a year diet industry in the US, Eyton's *The F Plan Diet* (1982) sold 810,000 copies in three weeks, and *Rosemary Conley's Complete Hip and Thigh Diet* (1988, 1989) has sold over two million copies. There seems to be a need for these services, as people respond to their availability. Who are these people whose need is being fulfilled? Dieting clubs and dieting magazines offer their services to a wide audience. According to health guidelines, weight loss should be offered to the obese, as these individuals are at risk of a range of physical and psychological problems (described in chapter 8). Some members of the dieting clubs and buyers of the magazines fall into this category. The dieting industry therefore provides a useful service. It responds to the needs of its audience by offering nutritional information, reinforcement, and social support to those overweight individuals who want to lose weight (described in chapter 9).

The average member of "Weight Watchers" in the UK is 40 lbs overweight, but this number is high due to the few obese members who push up the average. Most members have much less to lose. Likewise, "Slimmer" clubs accept people with only a few pounds to lose. Meal replacements and very low-calorie diets are recommended for the severely overweight only under supervision (Wadden, Van Itallie, and Blackburn, 1990) but are available to anyone who wants to lose weight. Further, while 20 percent of the population is obese, the majority of women diet. Most individuals engaging with the dieting industry are not obese and some are not even overweight. Their desire to lose weight is not driven by health needs but aesthetic ones, and the dieting industry creates this need.

Creating a need

The dieting industry creates the need for its own existence in three ways. First, it perpetuates the stereotypes associated with size described in chapter 5, secondly, it promotes the belief that body size can be changed through dieting, and thirdly, it changes the boundaries of the need for a dieting industry (Ogden, 1992).

Perpetuating the stereotypes of size

The dieting industry creates the need for itself by being part of the media which perpetuate the stereotypes associated with body size. First it promotes the belief that thinness is the most desirable state. Mazel, in her *Beverly Hills Diet* (1981) suggested that if someone should comment "You're getting too thin" you should reply "Thank you." Dieting magazines use slim models to model the latest clothes, and dieting aids such as meal replacements and diet foods are all advertised using very thin women (Ogden, 1992). Magazines publish success stories of women who have lost weight which illustrate how much happier these women feel, and how their lives have changed. As Twigg (1997) says of his "Kensington diet," it can "achieve a huge amount for you, including making you look and feel healthier, happier, younger and more zestful" (p. 20). The industry perpetuates and creates the belief that thinness is attractive and is associated with a wealth of positive attributes.

Second, the industry supports the belief that thinness is associated with being in control. Conley, who developed the "Hip and Thigh Diet" (1989) and others such as the *"Complete Flat Stomach Plan"* (1996) and *Metabolism Booster Diet* (1991), wrote in 1989 that overweight people must have eaten "too many fatty and sugary foods which are positively loaded with calories – bread spread with lashings of butter, an abundance of fried foods, cream cakes, biscuits, chocolates crisps and so on. The types of foods overweight people love" (p. 65). Similarly, in *The Beverly Hills Diet* (1981), Mazel wrote "It is imperative that you exercise control when you eat combinations. Don't let your heart take over. Eat like a human being, not a fat person." Thinness means being in control.

The industry also perpetuates the belief that thinness is a sign of being psychologically stable. For example, Levine (1997), in her book *I Wish I Were Thin I Wish I Were Fat* argued that women unconsciously want to be fat and that this is why they overeat; if they can come to terms with these unconscious desires they can "finally fulfill our conscious wish to be thin" (p. 13). Conley (1996) described one woman who lost weight using her diet, but regained it, and stated that "Vivien has had a few personal problems and has regained some of her weight. However she has resolved to try and lose it again as she was so delighted with her previous success" (p. 30). Being overweight relates to psychological problems and thinness remains the most desirable way to be.

The belief that dieting can change body size

The industry also perpetuates the belief that dieting works and can change a body's size and shape. Diet books all present their product as an inevitable pathway to success (see figure 7.1). For example, Coleman (1990) opened his book *Eat Green – Lose Weight* with the statement "You

Figure 7.1 "Diets work" (*Source:* Advertising Archives)

should buy this book if you would like to get slim – and stay slim – and you are fed up with short term diets which either fail or become boring," and later on claimed "within months you will feel healthier, fitter, stronger and happier" (p. 7). Likewise, De Vries (1989) indicated that his reader should "Make up your mind that this time you will succeed. No more yo-yoing up and down. You're going to lose weight and you are going to lose it permanently" (p. 20), and Twigg (1997), after describing the success of his clients said, "And if it works for them then I promise you – we're going to make it work for you, too!" (p. 17). Even those diets designed not to reduce fat are described as leading to successful weight loss. For example, Lazarides (1999) described fluid as the root of many people's problems, and said that "to be able to sit on the loo and urinate away up to 20 lbs of excess body weight in a few days probably sounds like something out of our wildest dreams" but if you stick to her diet "you will literally be able to urinate much of your excess body weight, sometimes within just a few days" (p. 6). The dieting industry offers its vast range of products as being able to change body weight. It emphasizes the success of its products and by doing so reinforces the belief that body size and shape can be modified and changed by the individual.

Changing the boundaries

If the dieting industry was only aimed at those who needed to diet for health reasons then their audience would be very small. However, by involving all those women who want to be just a few pounds lighter, their audience grows enormously. To this end, not only do diet magazines run articles on losing large amounts of weight, they also run ones which offer "How to lose those extra pounds for summer," and "Clothes feeling tight? lose excess weight quickly and now." The *Bikini Diet* (Earle, 1995) says "the aim of the bikini diet is for you to lose a stone this summer" (p. 7); "Weight Watchers" reported that their members have been getting increasingly lighter over the last few years. The general population is getting gradually heavier (see chapter 8) and yet the population which attends dieting clubs is getting lighter. The dieting industry creates a need for itself by expanding its potential market from people who are fat to those who perceive themselves as fat. It then treats this perception as fact. When dieters say "I feel fat" it is translated into "I am fat," and the industry offers to solve this problem. For example, in the opening to his book *The BBC Diet* (1988) Lynch said, "If you feel fat your body is trying to tell you something: lose weight" (p. 1). Further, in his chapter "A Nation of Fatties," Lynch wrote, "A third of the population are regular users of one or more slimming products. It seems that it's the norm in this country to be overweight" (1988, p. 5). The book translates feeling fat into being fat and assumes that dieters are actually overweight. Conley's *Complete Hip and Thigh Diet* (1989) also illustrates this expansion of the dieting market. She recorded numerous readers' success stories, many from women who say "Although I have never exactly been overweight . . ." (p. 35), "As I was not really over-weight or fat to start with . . ." (p. 31), and "I could hardly be described as overweight" (p. 29). These women were not fat, nor did they see themselves as being fat, but they still dieted. This process expands the dieting market and offers dieting not just to women who are objectively overweight, or even perceive themselves as fat, but to those women who don't even feel fat. Dieting is marketed at everyone regardless of either their health need or their actual size.

The dieting industry responds to a need by providing overweight women (and some men) with information, reinforcement, and social support. The industry also creates this need, first by being part of the media world which both creates and perpetuates the idealization of thinness, secondly by promoting the belief that dieting works, and finally by expanding the boundaries of the need for a dieting industry and treating a perceived problem of body size as an actual problem. It is the perfect industry. It ensures that women will continue to feel fat and to believe that dieting is the solution, and by offering a product which only rarely works it ensures its market never deteriorates (Ogden, 1992).

A backlash

Although the dieting industry in all its permutations continues to thrive, there has been a backlash. In 1982, Katahn subtitled his book "How to stop dieting forever" and his opening statement read "I am writing this book because, frankly I am sick and tired of the nonsense being written that offers dieting as a means for permanent weight control" (p. 9). Likewise, the books *Dieting Makes You Fat* by Cannon and Einzig, and *Breaking the Diet Habit* by Polivy and Herman were published in 1983. But it was not until the 1990s that the backlash gained momentum, and organizations such as "Diet Breakers" were set up, books praising the joys of being overweight were written, and magazines published articles about "alternatives to dieting." For example, Smith (1993) offered her book *Fibrenetics* as a way to "finally kick the whole concept of dieting out of the window" (p. 12), and programs to encourage "undieting" were established by researchers and educationalists such as Polivy,

Herman, and Cileska (e.g. Polivy and Herman, 1992). Particularly in the US and UK, people became skeptical about the value of dieting, and "to be on a diet" became tainted with a sense of conformity. However, this did not stop women dieting. Euphemisms such as "healthy eating," a "healthy lifestyle," and "a good diet" took over, and books were published which while offering themselves as an alternative to dieting still marketed weight loss as their goal. Women (and some men) still tried to eat less and differently as a means to lose weight and change their body shape. But for some this took on a different name. The dieting industry still plays a central role in causing body dissatisfaction and then offers dieting as the solution.

In summary, body dissatisfaction leads to a desire to change the body's size and shape. But rather than using the tricks of the past such as corsets and breast-binding, since the 1960s those dissatisfied individuals have turned to dieting to change the body itself. The dieting industry facilitates the translation of body dissatisfaction into dieting first by perpetuating the belief that thinness is the desirable shape and then by promoting the belief that body size can be changed. The industry also promotes and expands the need for the dieting industry by offering its product not only to those who are overweight, but to all those who just think they are overweight. This transition from body dissatisfaction to dieting illustrates a central role for control.

The central role for control

The previous chapter examined the development of body dissatisfaction and highlighted a role for a range of beliefs. Specifically, it outlined beliefs relating to materialism, competitiveness, achievement, autonomy, the role of women, and a projected relationship between mother and daughter as influencing the development of body dissatisfaction. These beliefs have one thing in common. They are based on the assumption that the object of these beliefs (i.e. the daughter) has control over her destiny (see figure 7.2). It is assumed that she can achieve, she can compete, and she can fulfill the desires of others if only she tries; anything can be achieved if the effort is right. This is a lot of pressure to place on a woman who may well feel that the world is still designed for men. It is even more pressure to place upon a young woman who may feel that the world is designed for adults. Such expectations may result in feelings of being out of control: "How can I achieve all these things?", "What do I have to do?", "I can never fulfill everyone's demands", "My world is

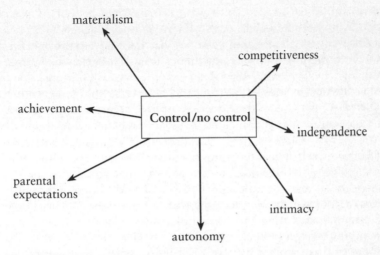

Figure 7.2   The central role for control

simply not that open to change", "Things are not that controllable."
The one factor, however, that women believe can be changed is their
bodies. And this belief is exacerbated by the dieting industry, which
presents body shape as a changeable object and offers dieting as the
means through which such change can be brought about. Feelings
of being out of control may be expressed in the development of body
dissatisfaction, which is then translated into dieting behavior as a means
to regain some control (Orbach, 1978; Brownell, 1991; Ogden, 1992).

What is Dieting?

Dieting is the main consequence of body dissatisfaction. Most dieters are
women and research suggests that a large majority of the female population attempts to restrain their food intake at some time in their life. For
example, Horm and Anderson (1993) reported that 40 percent of their
sample were dieting at any time, and Furnham and Greaves (1994) indicated that 87 percent of their sample had dieted at some time. Dieting is
also found in adolescents and girls as young as nine (Wardle and Beales,
1986; Hill, Oliver, and Rogers, 1992; Hill, Draper and Stack, 1994).
Dieting therefore plays a central role in the lives of many women. In the
late 1970s, a new theory of eating behavior known as "Restraint Theory"
emerged, which emphasized the importance of dieting and suggested

that restrained eating (attempting to eat less) might be a better predictor of food intake than weight per se (Herman and Mack, 1975; Hibscher and Herman, 1977). Restrained eating has become increasingly synonymous with dieting, and restraint theory was developed as a framework to explore this behavior. Restrained eating is measured using scales such as the "Restraint Scale" (Herman and Polivy, 1980; Heatherton et al., 1988), the restrained eating section of the "Dutch Eating Behaviour Questionnaire" (Van Strien et al., 1986) and the dietary restraint section of the "Three Factor Eating Questionnaire" (Stunkard and Messick, 1985). These self-report measures ask questions such as "How often are you dieting?", "How conscious are you of what you are eating?", "Do you try to eat less at mealtimes than you would like to eat?", and "Do you take your weight into account with what you eat?" Other research has categorized dieting into current dieting, a history of dieting, and weight suppression (French and Jeffrey, 1997).

Some studies inspired by restraint theory suggest that dieters eat less than unrestrained eaters (e.g. Kirkley, Burge, and Ammerman, 1988; Thompson, Palmer, and Petersen, 1988; Laessle et al., 1989; see later). Most studies following a restraint theory perspective have argued that although imposing cognitive restraint on food intake may result in dieters eating less or the same as non-dieters, restraint can also lead to episodes of overeating. Research which supports restraint theory is considered first, followed by a discussion of the problems with this perspective.

Restrained eating and overeating

Restraint theory argues that restrained eating results in both under- and overeating, and the first study illustrating overeating in dieters used a preload/taste-test paradigm (Herman and Mack, 1975). This experimental method was a development of the taste-test method originally used by Schachter in the 1960s, and involves giving subjects either a high-calorie preload (e.g. a high-calorie milkshake, a chocolate bar) or a low-calorie preload (e.g. water, a cracker). After eating/drinking the preload, subjects are asked to take part in a taste test. Subjects are asked to rate a series of different foods (e.g. cookies, snacks, ice cream) for a variety of different qualities such as saltiness, preference, and sweetness. The subjects are left alone for a set amount of time to rate the foods and then the amount they have eaten is weighed (the subjects do not know that this will happen). The aim of the preload/taste-test method is to measure food intake in a controlled environment (the laboratory) and to examine

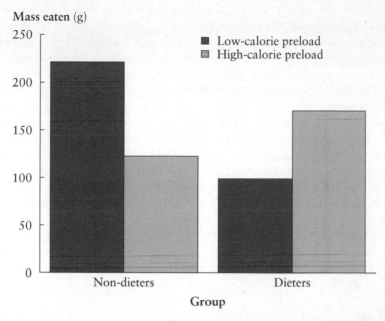

Figure 7.3   Dieting and overeating (*Source*: P. Herman and D. Mack, Restrained and unrestrained eating, *Journal of Personality*, 43 (1975), pp. 646–60)

the effect of preloading on eating behavior. The results from this first study are illustrated in figure 7.3. They indicated that whereas the non-dieters showed compensatory regulatory behavior, and ate less after the high-calorie preload, the dieters consumed more in the taste test if they had had the high-calorie preload than the low-calorie preload. It is equivalent to eating more at lunchtime after eating breakfast than if breakfast has been missed.

This study indicated that although dieters may at times eat less, re-strained eating is also associated with eating more, and restraint theory has described overeating as characteristic of restrained eaters (Herman and Mack, 1975; Spencer and Fremouw, 1979; Herman, Polivy, and Esses, 1987). The Herman and Mack (1975) study illustrated overeating in response to a high-calorie preload. Research suggests that overeating may also be triggered by lowered mood, preloads believed to be high in calorie, a need to escape from self-awareness, smoking abstinence, and food cues (e.g. Herman and Mack, 1975; Spencer and Fremouw, 1979; Heatherton and Baumeister, 1991; Ogden, 1994; Fedoroff, Polivy, and Herman, 1997). Further research has also shown that restrained eaters often eat more per se. For example, Ruderman and Wilson (1979) used

a preload/taste-test procedure and reported that restrained eaters consumed significantly more food than the unrestrained eaters, irrespective
of preload size. Similarly, Klesges, Isbell, and Klesges (1992) examined
the eating behavior of 141 men and 146 women and indicated that
although restrained eaters ingested significantly fewer calories overall
than unrestrained eaters, they were consuming a higher amount of fat.
Several terms have been used to describe the overeating found in restrained eaters. "Counterregulation" refers to the relative overeating
shown following a high-calorie preload compared to a low-calorie one.
The term "disinhibition" has been defined as "eating more as a result of
the loosening of restraints in response to emotional distress, intoxication
or preloading" (Polivy and Herman, 1989, p. 342), and "The What the
Hell effect" (Herman and Polivy, 1984) has been used to characterize
overeating following a period of attempted undereating. The recognition
of overeating in dieters and the development of restraint theory paved
the way for a wealth of research examining when and why dieters sometimes overeat, and the role of restraint in this behavior.

Dieting and Overeating

Research has explored possible mechanisms for the overeating shown by
restrained eaters. These are described below and include the causal model
of overeating, the boundary model of overeating, cognitive shifts, mood
modification, denial, escape theory, overeating as relapse, and the central
role for control.

The causal analysis of overeating

The causal analysis of eating behavior was first described by Herman
and Polivy (Herman and Mack, 1975; Herman and Polivy, 1980, 1988;
Polivy and Herman, 1985). They suggested that dieting and bingeing
were causally linked, and that "restraint not only precedes overeating
but contributes to it causally" (Herman and Polivy, 1988, p. 33). This
suggests that attempting not to eat, paradoxically, increases the probability of overeating, the specific behavior dieters are attempting to avoid.
The causal analysis of restraint represented a new approach to eating
behavior, and the prediction that restraint actually caused overeating
was an interesting reappraisal of the situation. Wardle further developed
this analysis (Wardle, 1980), and Wardle and Beales (1988) experimentally tested the causal analysis of overeating. They randomly assigned 27

obese women to either a diet group, an exercise group, or a no-treatment control group for 7 weeks. At weeks 4 and 6 all subjects took part in a laboratory session designed to assess their food intake. The results showed that subjects in the diet condition ate more than both the exercise and the control group, supporting a causal link between dieting and overeating. From this analysis, the overeating shown by dieters is actually caused by attempts at dieting.

The boundary model of overeating

In attempt to explain how dieting causes overeating, Herman and Polivy (1984) developed the "boundary model," which represented an integration of physiological and cognitive perspectives on food intake. The boundary model is illustrated in figure 7.4.

The boundary model suggests that the food intake of restrained eaters is regulated by a cognitively determined "diet boundary." It indicates that dieters attempt to replace physiological control with cognitive control which represents "the dieter's selected imposed quota for consumption

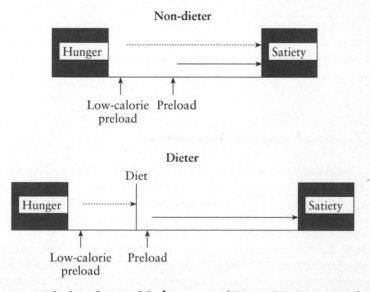

Figure 7.4   The boundary model of overeating (*Source*: C.P. Herman and J.A. Polivy, A boundary model for the regulation of eating, in A.J. Stunkard and E. Stellar (eds), *Eating and its Disorders*, New York: Raven Press, 1984, pp. 141–56)

on a given occasion" (Herman and Polivy, 1984, p. 149). Herman and Polivy (1984) described how after a low-calorie preload the dieter can maintain her diet goal for the immediate future since food intake remains within the limits set by the diet boundary. However, after the dieter has crossed the diet boundary (i.e. eaten something "not allowed"), they will consume food *ad libitum* until the pressures of the satiety boundary are activated. The boundary model proposes a form of dual regulation, with food intake limited either by the diet boundary or the satiety boundary. The boundary model has also been used to examine differences between dieters, binge eaters, anorexics; and normal eaters. This comparison is shown in figure 7.5. A binge eater may not be aware of satiety and so eats to capacity, and the anorexic may not be aware of hunger, or may choose to ignore it and so eats according to cognitive rather than biological drives.

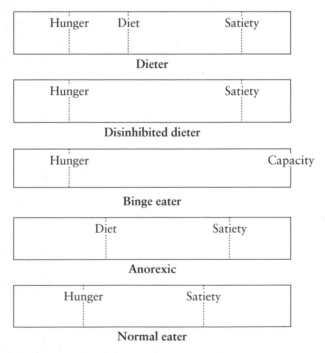

Figure 7.5   A comparison of the boundaries for different types of eating (*Source*: C.P. Herman and J.A. Polivy, A boundary model for the regulation of eating, in A.J. Stunkard and E. Stellar (eds), *Eating and its Disorders*, New York: Raven Press, 1984, pp. 141–56)

Cognitive shifts

The overeating found in dieters has also been understood in terms of shifts in the individual's cognitive set. Primarily this has been described in terms of a breakdown in the dieter's self-control reflecting a "motivational collapse" and a state of giving in to the overpowering drives to eat (Herman and Polivy, 1975, 1980). Ogden and Wardle (1991) analyzed the cognitive set of the disinhibited dieter and suggested that such a collapse in self-control reflected a passive model of overeating, and that the "What the Hell effect" as described by Herman and Polivy (1984) contained elements of passivity in terms of factors such as "giving in," "resignation," and "passivity." In particular, interviews with restrained and unrestrained eaters revealed that many restrained eaters reported passive cognitions after a high-calorie preload, including thoughts such as "I'm going to give into any urges I've got" and "I can't be bothered, it's too much effort to stop eating" (Ogden and Wardle, 1991). In line with this model of overeating, Glynn and Ruderman (1986) developed the Eating Self-Efficacy questionnaire as a measure of the tendency to overeat. This also emphasized motivational collapse and suggested that overeating was a consequence of the failure of this self-control.

An alternative model of overeating contended that overeating reflected an active decision to overeat, and Ogden and Wardle (1991) argued that implicit in the "What the Hell effect" was an active reaction against the diet. This hypothesis was tested using a preload/taste-test paradigm and cognitions were assessed using rating scales, interviews, and the Stroop task, which is a cognitive test of selective attention. The results from two studies indicated that dieters responded to high-calorie foods with an increase in an active state of mind characterized by cognitions such as "rebellious," "challenging," and "defiant," and thoughts such as "I don't care now in a rebellious way, I'm just going to stuff my face" (Ogden and Wardle, 1991; Ogden and Greville, 1993). It was argued that rather than simply passively giving in to an overwhelming desire to eat as suggested by other models, the overeater may actively decide to overeat as a form of rebellion against self-imposed food restrictions. This rebellious state of mind has also been described by obese binge eaters who report bingeing as "a way to unleash resentment" (Loro and Orleans, 1981). Eating as an active decision may at times also indicate a rebellion against the deprivation of other substances such as cigarettes (Ogden, 1994), and against the deprivation of emotional support (Bruch, 1974).

Mood modification

Dieters overeat in response to lowered mood, and researchers have argued that disinhibitory behavior enables the individual to mask their negative mood with the temporary heightened mood caused by eating. This has been called the "masking hypothesis," and has been tested by empirical studies. For example, Polivy and Herman (1999a) told female subjects that they had either passed or failed a cognitive task and then gave them food either *ad libitum* or in small controlled amounts. The results in part supported the masking hypothesis as the dieters who ate *ad libitum* attributed more of their distress to their eating behavior than to the task failure. The authors argued that dieters may overeat as a way of shifting responsibility for their negative mood from uncontrollable aspects of their lives to their eating behavior. This mood modification theory of overeating has been further supported by research indicating that dieters eat more than non-dieters when anxious, regardless of the palatability of the food (Polivy, Herman, and McFarlane, 1994). Overeating is therefore functional for dieters as it masks dysphoria, and this function is not influenced by the sensory aspects of eating.

The role of denial

Cognitive research illustrates that thought suppression and thought control can have the paradoxical effect of making the thoughts that the individual is trying to suppress more salient (Wenzlaff and Wegner, 2000). This has been called the "theory of ironic processes of mental control" (Wegner, 1994). For example, in an early study participants were asked to try not to think of a white bear but to ring a bell if they did (Wegner et al., 1987). The results showed that those who were trying not to think about the bear thought about the bear more frequently than those who were told to think about it. Similar results have been found for thinking about sex (Wegner et al., 1999), thinking about mood (Wegner, Erber, and Zanakos, 1993) and thinking about a stigma (Smart and Wegner, 1999). A decision not to eat specific foods or to eat less is central to the dieter's cognitive set. This results in a similar state of denial and attempted thought suppression, and dieters have been shown to see food in terms of "forbiddenness" (e.g. King, Herman, and Polivy, 1987) and to show a preoccupation with the food that they are trying to deny themselves (Grilo, Shiffman, and Wing, 1989; Ogden, 1995). To date no research has directly applied the theory of ironic processes of thought control to dieting. It is possible, however, that the decision to diet and to not eat undermines any attempts at weight loss. As soon as food is denied it becomes forbidden and therefore desired.

Escape theory

Researchers have also used escape theory to explain overeating (Heatherton and Baumeister, 1991; Heatherton, Herman, and Polivy, 1991; Heatherton et al., 1993). This perspective has been applied to both the overeating characteristic of dieters and the more extreme form of binge eating found in bulimics, and describes overeating as a consequence of "a motivated shift to low levels of self awareness" (Heatherton and Baumeister, 1991). It is argued that individuals prone to overeating show "high standards and demanding ideals" (p. 89) and that this results in low self-esteem, self-dislike, and lowered mood. It is also argued that inhibitions exist at high levels of awareness when the individual is aware of the meanings associated with certain behaviors. In terms of the overeater, a state of high self-awareness can become unpleasant, as it results in self-criticism and low mood. However, such a state is accompanied by the existence of inhibitions. The individual is therefore motivated to escape from self-awareness to avoid the accompanying unpleasantness, but although such a shift in self-awareness may provide relief from self-criticism it results in a reduction in inhibitions, thereby causing overeating. Within this analysis, disinhibitory overeating is indicative of a shift from high to low self-awareness and a subsequent reduction in inhibitions.

Overeating as a relapse

Parallels exist between the under- and overeating of the restrained eater and the behavior of the relapsing smoker or alcoholic. The traditional biomedical perspective on addictive behaviors viewed addictions as being irreversible and out of the individual's control. It has been argued that this perspective encourages the belief that the behavior is either "all or nothing," and that this belief is responsible for the high relapse rate shown by both alcoholics and smokers (Marlatt and Gordon, 1985). Thus, the abstaining alcoholic believes in either total abstention or relapse, which itself may promote the progression from lapse to full-blown relapse. In the case of the restrained eater, it is possible that they too believe in the "all or nothing" theory of excess which promotes the shift from a high-calorie lapse to the "what the hell" relapse characterized by

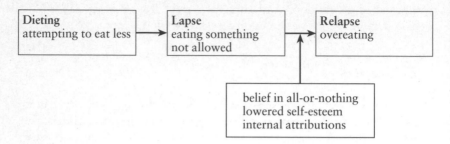

Figure 7.6   Overeating as relapse

disinhibition. This transition from lapse to relapse and the associated changes in cognitions are illustrated in figure 7.6.

These parallels have been supported by research suggesting that both excessive eating and alcohol use can be triggered by high-risk situations and low mood (Brownell, Marlatt, et al., 1986; Grilo, Shiffman, and Wing, 1989). In addition, the transition from lapse to relapse in both alcohol consumption and eating behavior has been found to be related to the internal attributions (e.g. "I am to blame") for the original lapse (e.g. Ogden and Wardle, 1990). In particular, researchers exploring relapses in addictive behaviors describe the "abstinence violation effect" which describes the transition from a lapse (one drink) to a relapse (becoming drunk) as involving cognitive dissonance (e.g. "I am trying not to drink but I have just had a drink"), internal attributions (e.g. "It is my fault") and guilt (e.g. "I am a useless person") (Marlatt and Gordon, 1985). These factors find reflection in the overeating shown by dieters (Ogden and Wardle, 1990).

The role of control

The interview data from a study of 25 women who were attempting to lose weight provide further insights into the mechanisms behind overeating (Ogden, 1992). The results from this study indicated that the women described their dieting behavior in terms of the impact on their family life, a preoccupation with food and weight, and changes in mood. However, the concept of self-control pervades these themes. For example, when describing how she had prepared a meal for her family, one woman said "I did not want to give in, but I felt that after preparing a three course meal for everyone else, the least I could do was enjoy my efforts." The sense of not giving in suggests an attempt to impose control over her

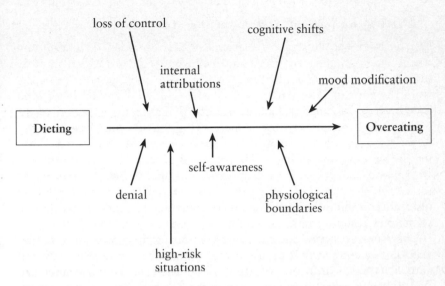

Figure 7.7 From dieting to overeating

eating. In terms of the preoccupation with food, one woman said "Why should I deprive myself of nice food?" and another said "Now that I've eaten that I might as well give in to all the drives to eat." Such statements again illustrate a sense of the importance of self-control and a feeling that eating reflects a breakdown in this control. In terms of mood, one woman said that she was "depressed that something as simple as eating cannot be controlled." Likewise this role of self-control was also apparent in the women's negative descriptions of themselves, with one woman saying "I'm just totally hopeless and weak, and though I hate being fat I just don't have the willpower to do anything about it."

In summary, restraint theory indicates that dieting is linked with overeating, and research inspired by this perspective has explored the processes involved in triggering this behavior. Studies have used experimental and descriptive designs and suggest a role for physiological boundaries, cognitive shifts, mood modification, denial, a shift in self-awareness, and control. These are illustrated in figure 7.7.

The Consequences of Dieting

Dieting sometimes leads to overeating. Research has also explored the consequences of dieting in terms of mood and cognitive state, and weight.

Dieting and mood and cognitive state

The first work to illustrate a relationship between food restriction and mood and cognitive state was a study by Keys et al. in 1950. The study involved 36 healthy non-dieting men who were conscientious objectors from the Korean War. They received a carefully controlled daily food intake of approximately half their normal intake for a period of 12 weeks, and consequently lost 25 percent of their original body weight. Keys stated that they developed a preoccupation with food often resulting in hoarding or stealing it. They showed an inability to concentrate, with mood changes such as depression and apathy being common. At the end of the period of dieting the men were allowed to eat freely and often ate continuously, reporting loss of control over their eating behavior sometimes resulting in binge eating. The authors concluded that these effects were probably due to the restriction of their diet. In a similar vein, Polivy et al. (1994) explored the eating behavior of World War II combat veterans and former prisoners of war. The authors concluded that post-war binge eating was rare in the combat veterans but significantly more common in the prisoners who had suffered massive weight loss in camps during the war.

To examine the effects of dieting without extreme weight loss, Warren and Cooper (1988) investigated the effects of a short period of dieting on both mood and self-control over eating. They placed 14 men and women on a calorie-restricted diet (1,200 kcal per day for women and 1,500 kcal per day for men) for two weeks and monitored daily changes in psychological state using visual analogue scales. Like Keys et al. (1950), they found significant increases in feelings of loss of control of eating and increases in preoccupation with food, but there was no effect on any of the mood ratings, possibly due to the short duration of the study. The interpretation of the results of these studies is limited by the absence of non-restricting control groups, since changes of the kind identified could have resulted from participation in research on eating. However both studies suggest that changes in cognitions and self-control can be identified, which might well exacerbate eating problems. In addition, a feature common to the studies by Keys et al. (1950), Warren and Cooper (1988), and Polivy et al. (1994) is that the food restriction was externally imposed, which is different from the self-imposed food restriction characteristic of dieters. The restriction of food intake was part of the experiment and therefore not entirely a product of the subject's motivation for weight loss. It is possible that the impact of a self-imposed restrictive regimen would be different. To explore this possibility, Ogden (1995) monitored the effects of self-imposed dieting over a six-week period in 23 dieters who completed rating scales of mood and cognitive and motivational states three times a week, and profile questionnaires at the beginning and end of the six-week period of caloric restriction. A control group of 18 non-dieters was also assessed for a comparative period. The results showed some differential changes over the period of the diet, with the dieters showing increases in both depression and loss of control, a decrease in hunger, and a temporary increase in the preoccupation with food compared to the non-dieters. These results suggest that dieting can have several negative consequences which may then trigger subsequent overeating.

The extensive research into obesity treatment is also relevant to the association between dieting and mood. One perspective has been that obese people are depressed as a direct result of being overweight, and that weight loss decreases the overall experience of depression. This has been supported by several studies using a range of methods (e.g. Shipman and Plesset, 1963; Crisp et al., 1980; Wing et al., 1984). In contrast, it has been suggested that obesity and overeating are a defense against depression, and that reducing food intake should result in a lowering of mood (Kornhaber, 1970). Wadden, Stunkard, and Smoller (1986) evaluated the emotional consequences of dieting in a group of obese patients undergoing behavior therapy. The results showed that the subjects reported an increase in negative mood as a response to the treatment regimen. However, as with studies assessing caloric restriction in the non-obese, evaluating the results from the behavioral treatment of the obese is also limited by the absence of a non-dieting control group.

Not all research, however, indicates that dieting results in lowered mood. Polivy and Herman (1999b) questioned why dieters continue to diet when their diets fail, when they show no weight loss, and when dieting has so many negative consequences, and argued that dieters show the "false hope syndrome." They suggested that making a commitment to change, regardless of the outcome of this commitment, results in temporary and immediate rewards. To test this suggestion, subjects either made a commitment to change their weight, a commitment to study more, or no commitment to change. The results showed that for the non-dieters making a commitment resulted in improved mood and self-image. For the dieters, however, there was a mixed response. The dieters showed an immediate deterioration in mood which supported the previous research outlined above. However, they also reported being more hopeful of success. The authors concluded that this provided some support for the "false hope syndrome" but suggested that this positive effect on mood varies according to the dietary history of the individual concerned.

Dieting and weight

Dieting leads to changes in eating behavior, with episodes of both under- and overeating. It also results in changes in mood and cognitive state. As a consequence of such changes it would also seem likely that dieting would result in changes in weight. Some research has explored the impact of dieting on weight fluctuation and weight variability. For example, Heatherton, Polivy, and Herman (1991) indicated that higher levels of dietary restraint were related to greater weight fluctuation. This is discussed further in chapter 9, in the context of dieting and obesity treatment. Some research has pointed to dieting as a contributory factor in the etiology of eating disorders, as the overeating found in dieters is considered analogous to the binge eating shown by some anorexics and bulimics (Herman and Polivy, 1988). This is considered in chapter 10. In addition, dieting is intricately linked with obesity, both as an attempt to lose weight but also as a possible cause of weight problems. In particular, dieting behavior at baseline has been shown to predict greater weight gain in women at follow-up (Klesges, Isbell, and Klesges, 1992; French et al., 1994). The causes of obesity are discussed in chapter 8.

Restraint theory, therefore, suggests that:

- Dieters aim to eat less as a means to lose weight and change their body shape. At times this aim is achieved and they successfully manage to restrict their food intake. Dieters therefore sometimes show undereating. Sometimes they eat the same as non-dieters.
- Dieters, however, also show episodes of overeating, particularly in response to triggers such as high-calorie preloads, anxiety, or smoking abstinence.
- This overeating can be understood in terms of a transgression of boundaries, shifts in cognitive set, mood modification, a response to denial, an escape from awareness, a lapse, or changes in self-control.
- Increasing or promoting dieting can result in an increased preoccupation with food, increased depression, and, paradoxically, increased eating behavior.
- The dieter's aim to eat less and consequently to lose weight is rarely achieved, and this failure may be a product of changes which occur as a direct response to imposing a cognitive structure upon eating behavior.
- Dieting is also related to changes in weight in terms of weight variability, the development of eating disorders, and the onset and progression of obesity.

Problems with Restraint Theory

Although restraint theory has generated a wealth of research and provides an insight into overeating behavior, there are several problems with this theory:

- Central to restraint theory is the association between food restriction and overeating. However, although dieters, bulimics, and bingeing anorexics report episodes of overeating, restricting anorexics cannot be accounted for by restraint theory. If attempting not to eat can result in overeating, how do anorexics manage to starve themselves?
- If attempting not to eat something results in eating it, how do vegetarians manage never to eat meat?
- There are some successful dieters who have been obese, dieted to lose weight, and kept this weight off (see chapter 9). Why do they not also show overeating?

Some recent research has highlighted problems with restraint theory. In particular, this has described the times when restraint leads to undereating, and has addressed the measurement of restraint and the complexity of dieting behavior.

Dieting and undereating

Restrained eating aims to reduce food intake, and several studies have found that at times this aim is successful. Some research has used an experimental methodology. For example, Thompson, Palmer, and Petersen (1988) used a preload/taste-test methodology to examine restrained eaters' eating behavior, and reported that the restrained eaters consumed fewer calories than the unrestrained eaters after both the low- and high-calorie preloads. Similarly, Dritschel, Cooper, and Charnock (1993) examined eating behavior in the laboratory following a preload and concluded that their results provided no support for the counter-regulatory behavior described as characteristic of dieters. Similar results have also been reported by Van Strien, Cleven, and Schippers (2000) and Oliver, Wardle, and Gibson (2000). Therefore, some studies using an experimental design indicate that dieters' attempts to eat less can be successful. Other research has used more naturalistic methods. For example, Kirkley, Burge, and Ammerman (1988) assessed the eating style of 50 women using four-day dietary self-monitoring forms, and reported that the restrained eaters consumed fewer calories than the unrestrained eaters. Laessle et al. (1989) also used food diaries and found that the restrained eaters consumed around 400 kcal less than the unrestrained eaters, with the restrained eaters specifically avoiding food items of high carbohydrate and fat content. Furthermore, Stice (1998) used a longitudinal method to explore the relationship between restrained eating and overeating at follow-up. The results showed that once the temporal stability of the measures had been controlled for, restrained eating did not predict overeating. In fact, the reverse relationship was true. Overeating at baseline predicted future levels of restrained eating. Some studies, therefore, show that restrained eating can result in overeating. Other studies using similar methodologies indicate that restrained eaters can eat less and be successful in their attempts to lose weight. It has been argued that such contradictions in the literature highlight problems with restraint theory, as the restrained eaters in these studies did not show the predicted overeating (Charnock, 1989; Cooper and Charnock, 1990). Other researchers have argued that such episodes of undereating are in line with restraint theory if restrained eating is considered to result in both under- and overeating (Polivy and Herman, 1989). This debate has generated an analysis of the measures used to assess dietary restraint and an assessment of the complexity of dieting behavior.

The measurement of restraint

Most research examining dieting behavior uses formal measures of dietary restraint which have been subjected to both psychometric and conceptual analysis. For example, Ogden (1993) examined dietary restraint as assessed by the Restraint Scale (RS: Herman and Polivy, 1980; Heatherton et al., 1988) and the restrained eating section of the DEBQ (DEBQR: Van Strien et al., 1986) and found that high scorers on these measures were characterized by both successful and failed restriction. It was concluded that these measures confound successful and failed dieting and that restrained eating involves both under- and overeating. In a similar vein, Van Strien (1999) examined restrained eating as measured by the Three Factor Eating Questionnaire (TFEQ: Stunkard and Messick, 1985) and the DEBQR (Van Strien et al., 1986). The results from this study indicated that although these two measures similarly confound success and failure, these two aspects of dieting can be easily unconfounded by using a two-factor approach to dieting. From this perspective dieters can be understood as either successful or unsuccessful dieters. Likewise, Stice, Ozer, and Kees (1997) examined the relationship between restrained eating as measured by the Restraint Scale (Herman and Polivy, 1980; Heatherton et al., 1988) and by the DEBQR (Van Strien et al., 1986), and concluded that although higher restraint scores on both these measures were correlated with overeating (in line with restraint theory), this correlation was lowered for the Restraint Scale when items specifically asking about overeating were removed. Further research in this area has also been carried out by Westenhoefer and colleagues (Westenhoefer et al., 1994; Westenhoefer, Stunkard, and Pudel, 1999). These studies have explored restrained eating as measured by the Restraint Scale, the Three Factor Eating Questionnaire, and the DEBQR, and have indicated that dieting is associated with overeating only in those that score high on questions specifically concerned with overeating and disinhibition. In line with these findings Westenhoefer, Stunkard, and Pudel (1999) have argued that dieters should be conceptualized as having either rigid or flexible control and that those with flexible control are the ones that show overeating.

Therefore, as a result of some of the contradictions in the literature exploring the relationship between restraint and overeating, there has been an increasing amount of research exploring what is being measured by the different restraint scales. This has raised a debate about the different psychometric properties of these measures and their conceptual clarity. In general, it would seem that while some measures assess both undereating and overeating (i.e., the Restraint Scale) others focus mainly on food restriction (i.e., DEBQ and Three Factor Eating Questionnaire). From these analyses, some researchers have concluded that restrained eating is seen to lead to overeating only when it has been measured using items such as "Do you eat sensibly with others and splurge alone?", selecting those dieters with a tendency to overeat who then do so in either a laboratory or naturalistic setting (e.g. Charnock, 1989; Westenhoefer, 1991; Van Strien, 1999).

The complex nature of dieting

Dieting seems to a be a more complex behavior than sometimes thought. As noted, Van Strien (1999) has argued that there are two types of dieters, namely successful and unsuccessful dieters. Westenhoefer, Stunkard, and Pudel (1999) have argued that dieters should be categorized as having either flexible or rigid control. Further, Westenhoefer (1991) also argued that dieters should be considered as those with either high or low disinhibition. These analyses focus on between-subject differences and suggest that dieters can be divided into different groups: those that either do or do not succeed. In contrast, other researchers have focused on within-subject differences and have suggested that rather than dichotomizing the individuals (successful vs unsuccessful dieters), it is the behavior that should be dichotomized into successful vs unsuccessful dieting. For example, Ogden (1993) argued that restrained eating is best conceptualized as an attempt which is only rarely realized, with dieters showing both under- and overeating. Similarly, Heatherton et al. (1988) argued that "the restrained eater who is exclusively restrained . . . is not representative of restrained eaters in general, whereas the restrained eater who occasionally splurges is" (p. 20). From this perspective, "to diet" is probably best understood as "attempting to lose weight but only sometimes doing so" and "an attempt to eat less which often results in eating more."

In summary, restraint theory argues that dieting can lead to overeating and impacts upon cognitions, mood, and weight. Much research has supported this perspective, although there are several problems this analysis. In particular, some individuals do successfully restrict their food intake, and research has illustrated this using both experimental and naturalistic methodologies. These contradictions in the literature have resulted in an analysis of what measures of restrained eating are actually assessing; it would seem that restrained eating can be considered to consist of both under- and overeating, with some measures specifically selecting a population of dieters with a tendency to overeat. Researchers have also explored the nature of dieting itself. One perspective has been to categorize individuals into successful or unsuccessful dieters. From this analysis, restraint theory would hold true only for those categorised as unsuccessful, with the successful dieters not showing overeating behavior. Another perspective has been to categorize by behavior into successful and unsuccessful dieting. From this analysis, restraint theory would hold true for all dieters some of the time. To date, which of these perspectives is most accurate remains unclear. It is probable, however, that given the research illustrating the links between restraint and overeating and between restraint and undereating both analyses are valuable. In line with this, there may be some dieters who are successful all of the time and some who are not. But there may also be many who fluctuate between success and failure. Therefore, dieting can be seen as causing overeating in the majority of dieters some of the time, while the minority see their attempts at eating less more consistently fulfilled.

Conclusion

Many men and women are dissatisfied with their body size and shape. Men tend to take up exercise, but for women body dissatisfaction translates into dieting. The translation of body dissatisfaction into dieting is facilitated by the dieting industry, which perpetuates the belief that thinness is the desired state. Further, the dieting industry encourages the belief that body size and shape can be changed, and then offers dieting as the means through which to change it. However, although dieting aims to reduce food intake and cause subsequent weight loss, much research indicates that dieting causes episodes of overeating. This research has been inspired by restraint theory and has highlighted disinhibitory behavior as a consequence of attempts to impose cognitive limits on food intake. Explanations of disinhibition include the boundary model of overeating, which emphasizes the dieters' cognitive limits, changes in both cognition and mood, a paradoxical response to denial, and escape theory, which highlights the role of self-awareness. Research has also drawn parallels between eating behavior and addictive behaviors. Overeating is not the only consequence of dieting; attempted and actual food restriction can also lead to a preoccupation with food, lowered mood, and feelings of being out of control. Dieting has also been implicated in weight changes in terms of weight variability, eating disorders, and obesity. However, there are problems with restraint theory, with researchers questioning the link between dieting and overeating, the validity of restraint measures, and the nature of dieting itself. It would seem that dieting does not always lead to overeating, and that some measures of restraint specifically select those dieters with a tendency to overeat. It is most likely that there are some dieters who are always successful in their attempts to eat less, but that there is also a majority of dieters who fluctuate between episodes of undereating and episodes of disinhibitory behavior.

Towards an integrated model of diet

Many individuals wish to choose a healthy diet. Food choice, however, takes place within the context of meanings associated with food and size, which can result in weight concern. In particular, women feel dissatisfied with their body size and shape and this dissatisfaction often results in dieting. But the goal of dieting is often sabotaged by the psychological consequences of imposing limits upon food intake, and attempts to chose a healthy diet become more problematic. Eating is also associated with other more extreme problems. Obesity is one of these problems and is the focus of the next chapter.

chapter eight

Obesity

One problem related to eating behavior is obesity. This chapter first examines the prevalence and definition of obesity. It then describes the possible physical and psychological consequences of obesity and focuses on theories which have been developed to explain its etiology. In particular it describes physiological theories including the role of genetics, metabolic rate, fat cells, and the impact of genes on appetite. It then explores behavioral theories, with a focus on the role of physical activity and the impact of diet.

This chapter covers:

- What is obesity?
- How common is obesity?
- What are the consequences of obesity?
- What are the causes of obesity?
- Problems with obesity research

What is Obesity?

There are many definitions of obesity which are used by different researchers and clinicians in different countries. The most commonly used definitions include the following.

Population means

Using population means to define obesity involves exploring mean weights within a specific population and deciding whether someone is below average weight, average, or above average in terms of percentage overweight for a given height. This approach is problematic as it depends on which population is being considered – someone could be obese in India but not in the US. It is therefore not used for adults but is still used for children as it enables the child's height and weight to be examined separately.

Body mass index

Obesity is also defined in terms of Body Mass Index (BMI), which is calculated using the equation weight (kg) / height (m^2). This produces a figure which is categorized as normal weight (18.5–24.9), overweight (grade 1: 25–29.9), clinical obesity (grade 2: 30–39.9), or severe obesity (grade 3: 40+). This is the most frequently used definition of obesity. However, it does not allow for differences in weight between muscle and fat – a bodybuilder would be defined as obese. These gradings are illustrated in figure 8.1.

Waist circumference

BMI is the most frequently used measure of obesity but it does not allow for an analysis of the location of fat. This is important since some problems such as diabetes are predicted by abdominal fat rather than lower body fat. Researchers originally used waist–hip ratios to assess obesity, but recently waist circumference on its own has become the preferred approach. Weight reduction is recommended when waist circumference is greater than 102 cm in men and greater than 88 cm in women (Lean, Han, and Morrison, 1995; Lean, Han, and Seidall, 1998). A reduction in waist circumference is associated with a reduction in cardiovascular risk factors, and abdominal obesity is associated with insulin resistance and the development of Type 2 diabetes (Chan et al., 1994; Han et al., 1997). Waist circumference has been suggested as the basis for routine screening in primary care (Despres, Lemieux, and Prud'homme, 2001), although Little and Byrne (2001) have argued that more evidence is needed before such a program should be implemented.

Percentage body fat

As health is mostly associated with fat rather than weight per se, researchers and clinicians have also developed methods of measuring

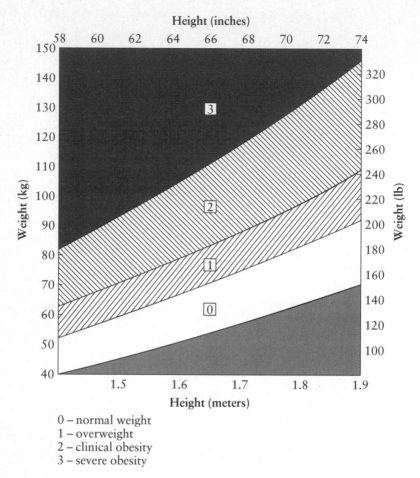

Figure 8.1   Grades of obesity by height and weight

percentage body fat directly. At its most basic this involves assessing skinfold thickness using callipers, normally around the upper arm and the upper and lower back. This is not suitable for those individuals who are severely obese, and it misses abdominal fat. At a more advanced level, body fat can be measured using bio-electrical impedence, which involves passing an electrical current between a person's hand and foot. As water conducts electricity and fat is an insulator, the impedence of the current can be used to calculate the ratio between water and fat and therefore an overall estimate of percentage body fat can be made.

How Common is Obesity?

In the UK, rates of obesity are on the increase. If obesity is defined as a BMI greater than 30, reports show that in 1980, 6 percent of men and 8 percent of women were obese, in 1993, 13 percent of men and 16 percent of women were obese, and in 1996 this had risen further, to 16 percent of men and 18 percent of women (Department of Health, 1995; Prescott-Clarke and Primatesta, 1998). It is predicted that by the year 2005 18 percent of men and 24 percent of women will be obese. For children in England, Chinn and Rona (2001) reported that in 1994, 9 percent of boys and 13.5 percent of girls were overweight, that 1.7 percent of boys and 2.6 percent of girls were obese, and that these figures were more than 50 percent higher than ten years earlier. Estimates for the US suggest that roughly half of American adults are overweight, that a third are obese, that women particularly have grown heavier in recent years, and that the prevalence of overweight children has doubled in the past 20 years (Flegal, Harlan, and Landis, 1988; Kuczmarski et al., 1994; Ogden et al., 1997; National Institutes of Health, 1998). Across the world, the highest rates of obesity are found in Tunisia, the US, Saudi Arabia, and Canada, and the lowest are found in China, Mali, Japan, Sweden, and Brazil; the UK, Australia, and New Zealand are all placed in the middle of the range. Across Europe the highest rates are in Lithuania, Malta, Russia, and Serbia, and the lowest are in Sweden, Ireland, Denmark, and the UK. Overall, people in northern and western Europe are thinner than in eastern and southern Europe, and women are more likely to be obese than men. In general BMI increases with age for both men and women until age 64, when it decreases slightly into old age. The prevalence of obesity is slightly higher in women, particularly working-class women, but lower in vegetarians and smokers regardless of their sex (Fehily, 1999).

What are the Consequences of Obesity?

Obesity is associated with a range of both physical and psychological problems.

Physical problems

Obesity has been associated with cardiovascular disease, diabetes, joint trauma, back pain, cancer, and hypertension and mortality (e.g. Bray,

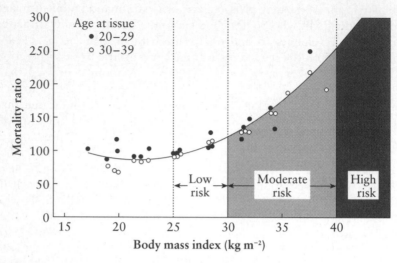

Figure 8.2   The relationship between BMI and mortality

1986; Chan et al., 1994; World Health Organization, 1998). The effects of obesity are related to where the excess weight is carried, with weight stored in the upper body, particularly in the abdomen, being more detrimental to health than weight carried on the lower body. It is interesting to note that although men are more likely than women to store fat on their upper bodies, and are therefore more at risk if obese, women are more concerned about weight than men, and most treatment studies examine women. It has been suggested that most problems seem to be associated with severe obesity and weights in the top 10 percent (Wooley and Wooley, 1984); however a study of 14,077 women indicated a direct linear relationship between BMI and risk factors for heart disease including blood pressure, cholesterol, and blood glucose (Ashton, Nanchahal, and Wood, 2001). Similar studies have also reported a relationship between BMI increases in the lower range of the spectrum and hypertension (National Institutes of Health, 1998), diabetes (Ford, Williamson, and Liu, 1997), and heart attack (Willett et al., 1995). The relationship between BMI and mortality is shown in figure 8.2.

Psychological problems

Research has also examined the relationship between psychological problems and obesity. The contemporary cultural obsession with thinness, the aversion to fat found in both adults and children, and the attribution of blame to the obese may promote low self-esteem and poor self-image in those individuals who do not conform to the stereotypically attractive thin image (see chapters 5 and 6). In line with this, Bull et al. (1983) reported that both obese patients waiting for a gastric bypass operation and normal obese patients rated themselves as more depressed than average-weight subjects, although the levels of depression did not reach clinical proportions. Hopkinson and Bland (1982) also indicated that one-fifth of their sample of obese subjects, also waiting for surgical treatment, reported having at least one period of clinical depression requiring treatment. Likewise, Halmi, Stunkard, and Mason (1980) indicated that just over 28 percent of a group of 80 patients waiting to have a gastric bypass operation were (or had been) clinically depressed. In addition, Rand and McGregor (1991) concluded that individuals who had lost weight following gastric bypass surgery stated that they would rather be deaf, dyslexic, diabetic, have heart disease or acne than return to their former weight. These studies suggest a relationship between body size and depression (see figure 8.3). However, it is possible that depressed obese individuals are more likely to seek treatment for their obesity than the ones who are not depressed and that there may be many obese individuals who are quite happy and therefore do not come into contact with health professionals. Ross (1994) addressed this possibility and interviewed a random sample of more than 2,000 adults by telephone. These were individuals who varied in weight and were not necessarily in the process of seeking help for any weight-related issues. The results from this large-scale study showed that overweight was unrelated to depression. A small subgroup in Ross's study who were both overweight and depressed tended to be the most educated. Ross argued that these individuals were also dieting to lose weight, and that it was the attempt to lose weight rather than the weight per se which was distressing. Therefore, although some obese people may be depressed, there is no consistent support for a simple relationship between body size and psychological problems.

What are the Causes of Obesity?

There are many theories about the causes of obesity and it is generally believed that the variation in body fat relates to a complex interplay of genetic, nutritional, energy expenditure, psychological, and social factors. This chapter explores physiological theories concerned with genetics, metabolic rate, fat cells, and appetite regulation, and behavioral theories, which focus on physical activity and eating behavior.

Figure 8.3   Weight and depression (*Source*: Advertising Archives)

Genetic theories

Size appears to run in families and the probability that a child will be overweight is related to their parents' weight. For example, having one obese parent in a family results in a 40 percent chance of producing an obese child and having two obese parents results in an 80 percent chance. In contrast, the probability that thin parents will produce overweight children is very small, about 7 percent (Garn et al., 1981). This observation has been repeated in studies exploring populations from different countries and living in different environments (Maes, Neale, and Eaves, 1997). Parents and children share both environment and genetic constitution, so this likeness could be due to either factor. To address this problem, research has examined twins and adoptees.

Twin studies

Twin studies examine the weight of identical twins reared apart, who have identical genes but different environments. Studies also examine the weights of non-identical twins reared together, who have different genes but similar environments. The results show that the identical twins reared apart are more similar in weight than non-identical twins reared together. For example, Stunkard et al. (1990) examined the BMI in 93 pairs of identical twins reared apart, 154 pairs of identical twins reared together, 218 pairs of non-identical twins reared apart, and 208 pairs of non-identical twins reared together. The authors concluded that genetic factors accounted for 66–70 percent of the variance in their body weight, suggesting a strong genetic component in determining obesity, and stated that "genetic influences on body-mass index are substantial, whereas the childhood environment has little or no influence." Similarly, Allison et al. (1996) estimated the heritability of obesity in twins from the US, Finland, and Japan. They concluded that 50 percent of the total variance found in BMI resulted from genetic factors. However, the role of genetics appears to be greater in lighter twin pairs than in heavier twin pairs.

Adoptee studies

Research has also examined the role of genetics in obesity using adoptees. Such studies compare the adoptees' weight with both their adoptive parents and their biological parents. Stunkard, Stinnett, and Smoller (1986) gathered information in Denmark about 540 adult adoptees, their adopted parents, and their biological parents. The results showed a strong relationship between the weight class of the adoptee (thin, median weight, overweight, obese) and their biological parents' weight class, but no relationship with their adoptive parents' weight class. This suggests a major role for genetics and was also found across the whole range of body weight. Interestingly, the relationship to the biological mother's weight was greater than the relationship to the biological father's weight.

Research therefore suggests a strong role for genetics in predicting obesity. Research also suggests that the primary distribution of this weight (upper vs lower body) is inherited (Bouchard et al., 1990). Furthermore it is argued that the inheritance of obesity is controlled by both major gene effects and polygenic effects. This means that for some individuals a single gene appears to determine obesity, whereas for others obesity is related to a complex combination of small effects resulting from a range of genes. A good review of the role of genetics in obesity can be found in Kopelman (1999a). How this genetic predisposition expresses itself is unclear. Metabolic rate, the number of fat cells, and appetite regulation may be three factors influenced by genetics.

Metabolic rate theory

The body uses energy to carry out the chemical and biological processes which are essential to being alive (e.g. respiration, heart rate, blood pressure). The rate of this energy use is called the resting metabolic rate, which has been found to be highly heritable (Bouchard et al., 1990). One theory of obesity has argued that the obese may have lower metabolic rates, that they burn up fewer calories when they are resting, and therefore require less food intake to carry on living.

There is some tentative support for this suggestion. For example, research in the US evaluated the relationship between metabolic rate and weight gain. A group in Phoenix assessed the metabolic rates of 126 Pima Indians by monitoring their breathing for a 40-minute period. The study was carried out using Pima Indians because they have an abnormally high rate of obesity – about 80 to 85 percent – and were considered an interesting population. The subjects remained stationary and the levels of oxygen consumed and carbon dioxide produced were measured. The researchers then followed any changes in weight and metabolic rate for a four-year period and found that the people who gained a substantial amount of weight were the ones with the lowest metabolic rates at the beginning of the study. In a further study, 95 subjects spent 24 hours in a respiratory chamber and the amount of energy used was measured. The subjects were followed up two years later and the researchers found that those who had originally shown a low level of energy use were four times more likely to also show a substantial weight increase (Ravussin, Lilioja, and Knowler et al., 1988; Ravussin, 1993).

These results indicate a relationship between metabolic rate and the tendency for weight gain. If this is the case, then some individuals are predisposed to become obese because they require fewer calories to survive than thinner individuals. A genetic tendency to be obese may therefore express itself in lowered metabolic rates. However, most research does not support this theory. In particular, there is no evidence to suggest that obese people generally have lower metabolic rates than thin people. In fact, research suggests that overweight people tend to have slightly higher metabolic rates than thin people of similar height (Garrow, 1987). The obese also expend more energy than thin people for a given activity (Prentice et al., 1989). To explain these apparently contradictory findings it has been suggested that obese people may have lower metabolic rates to start with, which results in weight gain and this weight gain itself results in an increase in metabolic rate (Ravussin and Bogardus, 1989). This view has not gone unchallenged, however, and Garrow and Webster (1985) have argued that this is an unlikely explanation which is unsupported by the evidence. In sum, the "slow metabolism" theory of obesity may be held by many laypeople. But it is no longer considered to be backed by research.

Fat cell theory

A genetic tendency to be obese may also express itself in terms of the number of fat cells. People of average weight usually have about 25 to 35 billion fat cells, which are designed for the storage of fat in periods of energy surplus and the mobilization of fat in periods of energy deficit. Mildly obese individuals usually have the same number of fat cells but they are enlarged in size and weight. Severely obese individuals, however, have more fat cells – up to 100–125 billion (Sjostrom, 1980). It was originally believed that the number of fat cells was determined by genetics and early infancy and remained constant throughout life (Hirsch, 1975). It is now recognized that when the existing number of cells has been used up, new fat cells are formed from preexisting preadipocytes, and that preadipocytes can be turned into adipocytes across the lifespan (Roncari, Kindler, and Hollenberg, 1986). Therefore, it would seem that if an individual is born with more fat cells, then there are more cells immediately available to fill up, making excessive weight gain easier in some people than others. In addition, research suggests that once fat cells have been made they can be emptied but never lost (Sjostrom, 1980). However, even a person born with a lower number of fat cells can create them if they are needed for the storage of fat.

Appetite regulation

A genetic predisposition may also be related to appetite control. Over recent years researchers have attempted to identify the gene or collection of genes responsible for obesity. Some work using small animals has identified a single gene which is associated with profound obesity (Zhang et al., 1994). Other animal work has explored the impact of minor and major genes on food intake and energy expenditure. However, for humans the work is still unclear but tends to fall within three areas of research: leptin production, genetic disorders, and candidate genes.

Leptin

One area of research has focused on the production of a protein called leptin, which is thought to inhibit eating and regulate energy expenditure. Research has shown that leptin levels are positively correlated with BMI and percentage body fat, and are high in the obese and lowered in sufferers of anorexia. Further, leptin levels fall in the obese when weight is lost (Considine et al., 1995; Ferron et al., 1997). It has therefore been argued that obesity may result from leptin resistance, with the high levels of leptin in the obese being ignored by the body's satiety mechanisms. In contrast, leptin deficiency has also been linked to obesity. Two children have been identified with a defect in the "ob gene" which produces leptin and is responsible for telling the brain to stop eating (Montague et al., 1997). To support this, researchers have given these two children daily injections of leptin, which has resulted in a decrease in food intake and weight loss at a rate of 1–2 kg per month (Farooqi et al., 1999). Therefore both too much and too little leptin may result in weight gain and obesity.

Genetic disorders

An alternative train of research has focused on genetic diseases which have obesity as part of their expression. Such diseases include Prader Willi syndrome and Bardet-Biedel syndrome, and research has studied these diseases as a means to map the genes involved in body weight. To date this research is in its infancy.

Candidate genes

A final area of research has explored candidate genes which are a part of the DNA molecule responsible for the production of polypeptide chains central to a particular disease. To date some candidate genes have been identified as linked to obesity, and research in this area will expand given the development of marker libraries following the human genome project.

In summary, there is strong evidence for a genetic basis to obesity. But how this genetic basis expresses itself remains unclear, as the research on lowered metabolic rate and high fat cells has mostly been refuted and the genetics of appetite control remains in its infancy. There are also some problems with genetic studies which need to be considered. For example, the sample size of studies is often small, zygosity needs to be confirmed, and there remains the problem of the environment. Twin studies assume that the environment for twins is constant and that only the genetic makeup of non-identical twins is different. It is possible, however, that identical twins are brought up more similarly because they are identical whereas parents of non-identical twins emphasize their children's differences. In addition, adopted children often go to the homes of parents who are similar to their biological parents. Further, the identification of individual genes responsible for obesity is problematic, as most genes function by interacting either with each other or with the environment or both. There also remains a substantial amount of the variance in body fat which is unexplained by genetics, and the recent increased prevalence of obesity in the West within populations whose gene pool has remained relatively constant points to a role for additional factors. As Prentice (1999) argued, "Obesity can only occur when energy intake remains higher than energy expenditure, for an extended period of time. This is an incontrovertible cornerstone on which all explanations must be based" (p. 38). Research has therefore examined the role of behavior in explaining obesity; behavioral theories of obesity focus on physical activity and eating behavior.

Physical activity

Increases in the prevalence of obesity coincide with decreases in daily energy expenditure due to improvements in transport systems, and a shift from an agricultural society to an industrial and increasingly information-based society. As a simple example, a telephone company in the US has suggested that in the course of one year an extension phone saves an individual approximately one mile of walking, which could be the equivalent of 2–3 lbs of fat or up to 10,500 kcals (Stern, 1984). Furthermore, at present only 20 percent of men and 10 percent of women are employed in active occupations (Allied Dunbar, 1992) and for many people leisure times are dominated by inactivity (Central Statistical Office, 1994). Although data on changes in activity levels are problematic, there exists a useful database on television viewing which shows that whereas the average viewer in the 1960s watched 13 hours of television per week, in England this has doubled to 26 hours per week (General Household Survey, 1994). This is further exacerbated by the increased use of videos and computer games by both children and adults. It has therefore been suggested that obesity may be caused by inactivity. To examine the role of physical activity in obesity, research has asked "Are changes in obesity related to changes in activity?", "Do the obese exercise less?", "What effect does exercise have on food intake?", and "What effect does exercise have on energy expenditure?" These questions will now be examined.

Are changes in obesity related to changes in activity?

This question can be answered first by using epidemiological data on a population, and second by using prospective data on individuals.

In 1995 Prentice and Jebb published a paper entitled "Obesity in Britain: Gluttony or sloth?", in which they presented epidemiological data on changes in physical activity from 1950 to 1990 as measured by car ownership and television viewing and compared these to changes in the prevalence of obesity. The results from this study suggested a strong association between an increase in both car ownership and television viewing and an increase in obesity. These results are shown in figure 8.4. Prentice and Jebb argued that "it seems reasonable to conclude that the low levels of physical activity now prevalent in Britain must play an important, perhaps dominant role in the development of obesity by greatly reducing energy needs" (Prentice and Jebb, 1995). However, their data were only correlational. Therefore it remains unclear whether obesity and physical activity are related (the third-factor problem – some other variable may be determining both obesity and activity) and whether decreases in activity cause increases in obesity, or whether in fact increases in obesity actually cause decreases in activity. In addition, the data are at the population level and therefore could miss important individual differences (i.e. some people who become obese could be active and those who are thin could be inactive).

In an alternative approach to assessing the relationship between activity and obesity, research has used prospective designs to explore the impact of changes in activity levels on changes in body weight. A large Finnish study of 12,000 adults examined the association between levels of physical activity and excess weight gain over a five-year follow-up

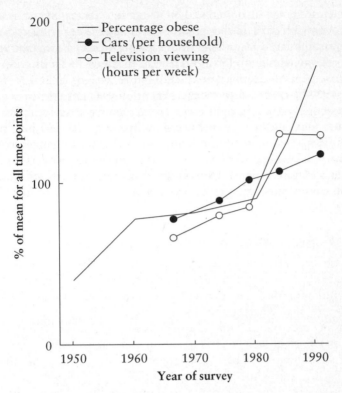

Figure 8.4   Changes in physical activity and obesity (*Source*: A.M. Prentice and S.A. Jebb, Obesity in Britain: Gluttony or sloth?, *British Medical Journal*, 311 (1995), pp. 437–9, reprinted by permission of The British Medical Journal Publishing Group)

(Rissanen et al., 1991). The results showed that lower levels of activity were a greater risk factor for weight gain than any other baseline measures. Similarly, Haapenen et al. (1997) monitored 5,000 working adults in Finland over a ten-year period and examined their leisure time physical activity and subsequent weight gain. The results showed that those who reported no physically active leisure time both at baseline and follow-up, and those who showed reduced activity by follow-up, were twice as likely to have gained more than 5 kg over the ten years than those who reported two sessions of vigorous activity per week. In a similar vein, Williamson et al. (1993) examined the relationship between activity and weight gain in over 9,000 US men and women. The results from this study also showed that low levels of physical activity predicted weight gain at follow-up. A link between sedentary lifestyle and weight gain in children has also been shown, using television viewing as a measure of activity (Gortmaker et al., 1996). Furthermore, research has used the doubly labelled water method to assess energy expenditure. For example, Ravussin et al. (1993) reported that low levels of minor physical movements (fidgeting) predicted future weight gain and Roberts et al. (1988) reported low energy expenditure at baseline in six babies who later became overweight by the time they were one year old. However, although all these studies were prospective it is still possible that a third factor may explain the relationship (i.e. those with lower levels of activity at baseline were women, the women had children and therefore put on more weight). Unless experimental data are collected, conclusions about causality remain problematic.

Do the obese exercise less?

Research has also examined the relationship between activity and obesity using a cross-sectional design to examine differences between the obese and non-obese. In particular, several studies in the 1960s and 1970s examined whether the obese exercised less than the non-obese. Using time-lapse photography, Bullen, Reed, and Mayer (1964) observed obese and normal-weight girls at a summer camp. They reported that during swimming the obese girls spent less time swimming and more time floating, and while playing tennis the obese girls were inactive for 77 percent of the time compared to the normal-weight girls, who were inactive for only 56 percent of the time. This approach indicated that the obese exercise less than the non-obese. Other early studies observed who used the stairs versus the escalators on public transportation, and used movement sensors on chairs. More recently, research has used the doubly labelled water method. Using this method Schulz and Schoeller (1994) reported high correlations between percentage body fat and energy expenditure. Whether reduced exercise is a cause or a consequence of obesity, however, remains unclear. It is possible that the obese exercise less due to factors such as embarrassment and stigma and that exercise plays a part in the maintenance of obesity but not in its cause.

What effect does exercise have on food intake?

The relationship between exercise and food intake is complex, with research suggesting that exercise may increase, decrease, or have no effect on eating behavior. For example, a study of middle-aged male joggers who ran approximately 65 km per week suggested that increased calorie intake was related to increased exercise, with the joggers eating more than the sedentary control group (Blair et al., 1981). In contrast, another study of military cadets reported that decreased food intake was related to increased exercise (Edholm et al., 1955). A review of the literature in 1997 by King, Blundell, and Tremblay concluded that there is no clear evidence for a relationship between energy expenditure and energy intake.

What effect does exercise have on energy expenditure?

Exercise burns up calories. For example, ten minutes of sleeping uses up to 16 kcals, standing for ten minutes uses 19 kcals, running uses 142 kcals, walking downstairs uses 88 kcals, and walking upstairs uses 229 kcals (Brownell, 1989). In addition, the amount of calories used increases with the individual's body weight. Therefore, exercise has long been recommended as a weight loss method (see chapter 9). However, the number of calories exercise burns up is relatively few compared to those in an average meal. In addition, although exercise is recommended as a means to increase metabolic rate, only intense and prolonged exercise appears to have a beneficial effect.

In summary, population data illustrate a correlation between decreased activity and increased obesity. Prospective data support this association and highlight lower levels of activity as an important risk factor. Cross-sectional data also indicate that the obese appear to exercise less than the non-obese. However, whether inactivity is a cause or consequence of obesity remains unresolved. It is also possible that an unidentified third factor may be creating this association. In addition, whether exercise has a role in reducing food intake and promoting energy expenditure is also debatable. Therefore the role of exercise in causing obesity remains unclear. But exercise may benefit the obese in terms of promoting weight loss, maintaining any weight losses, improving their health status, or making them feel better about themselves (see chapter 9).

Eating behavior

In an alternative approach to understanding the causes of obesity, research has examined eating behavior. Research has asked "Are changes in food intake associated with changes in obesity?", "Do the obese eat for different reasons than the non-obese?", "Do the obese eat more than the non obese?", and "How does dieting influence obesity?"

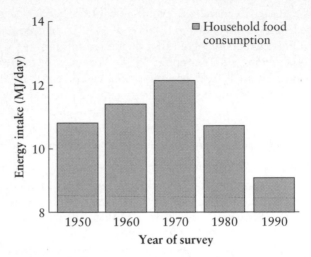

Figure 8.5 Changes in food intake over 40 years (*Source*: A.M. Prentice and S.A. Jebb, Obesity in Britain: Gluttony or sloth?, *British Medical Journal*, 311 (1995), pp. 437–9, reprinted by permission of The British Medical Journal Publishing Group)

Are changes in food intake associated with changes in obesity?

The UK National Food Survey collected data on food intake in the home which could be analyzed to assess changes in food intake over 40 years. The results from this database illustrated that although overall calorie consumption increased between 1950 and 1970, since 1970 there has been a distinct decrease in the amount people eat. This is shown in figure 8.5.

In their paper, "Obesity in Britain: Gluttony or sloth?", Prentice and Jebb (1995) examined the association between changes in food intake in terms of energy intake and fat intake and changes in obesity. Their results indicated no obvious association between the increase in obesity and the changes in food intake. These results are shown in figure 8.6.

Therefore, using population data, there appears to be no relationship between changes in food intake and changes in obesity.

Do the obese eat for different reasons than the non-obese?

Early studies of obesity were based on the assumption that the obese ate for different reasons than people of normal weight (Ferster, Nurnberger, and Levitt, 1962). Schachter's externality theory suggested that although all people were responsive to environmental stimuli such as the sight, taste, and smell of food, and that such stimuli might cause overeating,

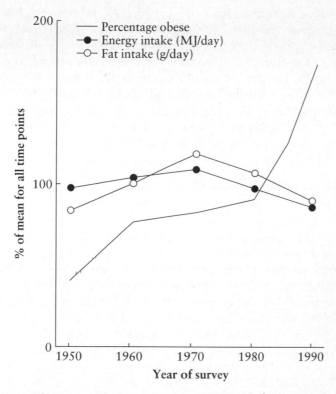

Figure 8.6 Changes in calorie consumption and obesity (*Source:* A.M. Prentice and S.A. Jebb, Obesity in Britain: Gluttony or sloth?, *British Medical Journal*, 311 (1995), pp. 437–9, reprinted by permission of The British Medical Journal Publishing Group)

the obese were highly and sometimes uncontrollably responsive to external cues. It was argued that normal weight individuals mainly ate as a response to internal cues (e.g. hunger, satiety) while obese individuals tended to be underresponsive to their internal cues and overresponsive to external cues. Within this perspective, research examined the eating behavior and eating style of the obese and non-obese in response to external cues such as the time of day, the sight of food, the taste of food, and the number and salience of food cues (e.g. Schachter, 1968; Schachter and Gross, 1968; Schachter and Rodin, 1974). Schachter and colleagues also developed the emotionality theory of obesity. This argued that not only were the obese more responsive to external cues, but that they also ate more than the non-obese in response to emotions such as anxiety, fear, boredom, and depression (e.g. Schachter and Rodin, 1974). This approach was also supported by Bruch (e.g., 1974) in her psychosomatic theory of eating behavior. She argued that some people interpret the sensations of emotions as an emptiness similar to hunger and that food is used as a substitute for other forms of emotional comfort. The results from these studies produced fairly inconsistent support for either the externality or emotionality theories of obesity. But the theories have been subsequently successfully applied to dieting behavior and eating disorders (see chapters 7, 10, and 11). Therefore, research has also examined whether the obese eat more than the non-obese.

Do the obese eat more than the non-obese?

Research exploring the amount eaten by the obese has either focused on the amount consumed per se or on the type of food consumed.

Because it was believed that the obese ate for different reasons than the non-obese it was also believed that they ate more. Research therefore explored the food intake of the obese in the laboratory (Wooley, Wooley, and Dunham, 1972) and in more naturalistic settings such as restaurants and at home, and also examined what food they bought. For example, Coates, Jeffrey, and Wing (1978) suggested that the obese might be overeating at home and went into the homes of 60 middle-class families to examine what was stored in their cupboards. They weighed all members of the families and found no relationship between body size and the mass and type of food they consumed at home. In an attempt to clarify the problem of whether the obese eat more than the non-obese, Spitzer and Rodin (1981) examined the research into eating behavior and suggested that "of twenty-nine studies examining the effects of body weight on amount eaten in laboratory studies . . . only nine reported that overweight subjects ate significantly more than their lean counterparts." Over recent years, however, researchers have questioned this conclusion for the following reasons. First, much of the early research was based on self-report data, which are notoriously unreliable, with most people consistently underreporting how much they eat (Prentice et al., 1986; Heitmann and Lissner, 1995). Second, when the obese and non-obese are either over- or underfed in a controlled environment, these two groups gain or lose weight at the same rate, suggesting that the obese must eat more in order to maintain their higher weight (Jebb et al., 1996). Finally, it has been argued that assessing food intake in terms of gross amount without analyzing the types of food being eaten misses the complex nature of both eating behavior and food metabolism (Prentice, 1995b). Therefore, the answer to the question "Do the obese eat more than the non-obese?" appears to be "Sometimes, but not consistently so."

If, however, overeating is defined as "compared to what the body needs," then the obese do overeat, because they have excess body fat.

More recent research has focused on the eating behavior of the obese not in terms of calories consumed, or in terms of amount eaten, but more specifically in terms of the type of food eaten, with a particular emphasis on the ratio between carbohydrate and fat. Population data indicate that calorie consumption has decreased since the 1970s and that this decrease is unrelated to the increase in obesity (see figures 8.4 and 8.5). However, these data also show that the ratio between carbohydrate consumption and fat consumption has changed; whereas we now eat less carbohydrate, we eat proportionally more fat (Prentice and Jebb, 1995, see figure 8.7). One theory that has been developed is that although the obese may not eat more calories overall than the non-obese, they may eat proportionally more fat. Further, it has been argued that not all calories are equal (Prentice, 1995b), and that calories from fat may lead to greater weight gain than calories from carbohydrates. In support of this theory, one study of 11,500 people in Scotland showed that men consuming the lowest proportion of carbohydrate in their diets were

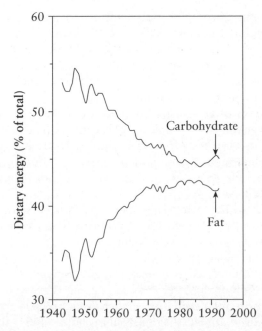

Figure 8.7 Changes in the carbohydrate/fat ratio and obesity (*Source*: A.M. Prentice and S.A. Jebb, Obesity in Britain: Gluttony or sloth?, *British Medical Journal*, 311 (1995), pp. 437–9, reprinted by permission of The British Medical Journal Publishing Group)

four times more likely to be obese than those consuming the highest proportion of carbohydrate. A similar relationship was also found for women, although the difference was only two- to threefold. Therefore, it was concluded that relatively higher carbohydrate consumption is related to lower levels of obesity (Bolton-Smith and Woodward, 1994). A similar study in the UK also provided support for the fat proportion theory of obesity (Blundell and Macdiarmid, 1997). This study reported that high-fat eaters who derived more than 45 percent of their energy from fat were 19 times more likely to be obese than those who derived less than 35 percent of their energy from fat. These studies suggest that the obese may not eat consistently more overall than the non-obese, or more calories, or carbohydrate, or fat per se. But they eat more fat compared to the amount of carbohydrate; the proportion of fat in their diet is higher. So how might a relative increase in fat consumption relate to obesity?

As a possible explanation of these results research has examined the role of fat and carbohydrates in appetite regulation. Three possible mechanisms have been proposed, as follows (Blundell et al., 1996; Blundell and Macdiarmid, 1997):

- **The benefits of complex carbohydrates to energy use:** First, it has been suggested that it takes more energy to burn carbohydrates than fat. Further, while carbohydrate intake is accompanied by an increase of carbohydrate oxidation, increased fat intake is not accompanied by an increase in fat oxidation. Therefore, carbohydrates are burned, fat is stored.
- **The benefits of complex carbohydrates to hunger:** Second, it has been suggested that complex carbohydrates (such as bread, potatoes, pasta, rice) reduce hunger, causing reduced food intake due to their bulk and the amount of fiber in them. In addition, they switch off the desire to eat. Therefore carbohydrates make you feel fuller faster.
- **The costs of fat to hunger:** Third, it has been suggested that fat does not switch off the desire to eat, making it easier to eat more and more fat without feeling full.

How does dieting influence obesity?

Many people who are already obese diet in an attempt to lose weight. The success of these attempts is reviewed in chapter 9. Dieting, however, may not only be a consequence of obesity but also a cause. The research reviewed in chapter 7 indicated that dieting is often characterized by periods of overeating which are precipitated by factors such as lowered mood, cognitive shifts, and shifts in self-awareness. There is also some evidence that dieting is reflected in weight variability. For example, Heatherton, Polivy, and Herman (1991) weighed 24 restrained and unrestrained subjects daily for six weeks and again after six months and concluded that restraint was a better predictor of weight variability than relative body weight. This suggests that the episodes of under- and overeating resulting from dieting are translated into fluctuations in weight. There is also some evidence that overeating is also reflected in weight gain, particularly in women. For example, French et al. (1994) reported the results from a cross-sectional and longitudinal study of 1,639 men and 1,913 women who were involved in a worksite intervention study for smoking cessation and weight control. The cross-sectional analysis showed that a history of dieting, current dieting, and previous involvement in a formal weight-loss program were related to a higher body weight in both men and women. Similarly, the prospective analysis showed that baseline measures of involvement in a formal weight-loss program and dieting predicted increases in body weight at follow-up. However, this was for women only. In particular, women who were dieting or who had been involved in a formal weight-loss program at baseline gained nearly 2 lbs more than those who had not. Klesges, Isbell, and Klesges (1992) reported similar results in their study of 141 men and 146 women who were followed up after one year. The results showed that both the dieting men and women were heavier than their non-dieting counterparts at baseline. Higher baseline weight and higher restraint scores at baseline also predicted greater weight gain at follow-up in women. Dietary restraint is therefore associated with weight fluctuations in dieters of both genders and overall weight gain in women. If dieters perceive themselves to be overweight, but are not necessarily obese, and if dieting causes overeating and subsequent weight gain, then dieting could predictably play a causal role in the development of obesity. It is possible that dieting also results in the relative overconsumption of high-fat foods as these are the foods that dieters try to avoid.

What does all this research mean?

The evidence for the causes of obesity is complex and can be summarized as follows:

- There is good evidence for a genetic basis to obesity. The evidence for how this is expressed is weak.
- The prevalence of obesity has increased at a similar rate to decreases in physical activity.

- Low levels of activity predict weight gain at follow-up.
- There is some evidence that the obese exercise less than the non-obese.
- The prevalence of obesity has increased at a rate unrelated to the overall decrease in calorie consumption.
- There is some evidence that the obese sometimes but not consistently consume more calories than the non-obese.
- The relative increase in fat is parallel to the increase in obesity.
- The obese may eat proportionally more fat than the non-obese.
- Dieting may have a causal role in the development of obesity by triggering overeating and subsequent weight gain in those who feel fat but are not always fat.

Therefore, it would seem that:

- Some individuals have a genetic tendency to be obese.
- Obesity is related to underexercise.
- Obesity is related to consuming relatively more fat and relatively less carbohydrate.
- Dieting may contribute to this relative overconsumption.

Problems with Obesity Research

There are several problems with the literature on obesity which can be considered in terms of the following stages of research.

The problem being studied

Obesity has been described as having a dynamic phase (becoming obese) and a static phase (maintaining a level of obesity) (Garrow, 1974). Research indicates that it may take fewer calories to maintain a level of obesity than it does to become obese in the first place. Therefore, obese individuals may overeat (compared to the non-obese) in the dynamic phase and undereat (compared to the non-obese) in the static phase.

Data collection

Measuring food intake is extremely problematic – laboratory studies, diary studies, and observation studies may actually change what people eat. Observational studies do not involve people in controlled conditions, and self-report studies are open to forgetting and social desirability. Underreporting of food intake is found in most populations but particularly in the obese, who omit snack foods and foods high in fat from food checklists and food diaries (Prentice et al., 1986; Heitmann and Lissner, 1995). In addition, measuring and comparing food intake of groups of individuals ignores the variability in the energy requirements of these individuals due to their body size, composition, and activity levels.

Data analysis

Much of the data is correlational (e.g. associations between changes in obesity and changes in activity/food intake). This does not enable conclusions about causality to be drawn (i.e. does inactivity cause obesity or obesity cause inactivity?). Further, it is possible that a third factor (as yet unknown) is responsible for the associations reported. Much of the data is also cross-sectional (e.g. obese vs non-obese). This also does not allow conclusions about causality to be made (i.e. how someone eats when they are obese may not reflect how they ate to become obese). In addition, some data are measured at the population level – for example, changes in activity levels, calorie intakes and fat intakes are all based on measures of populations. Other data are measured at the level of the individual – for example, differences between the obese and non-obese. Comparing population data and individual data is open to the "ecological fallacy:" population data can hide a multitude of individual differences, for the data at the population level may show one pattern which is completely different to the pattern at the individual level.

Data interpretation

If the obese do eat proportionally more fat than the non-obese, and this causes obesity via loss of appetite control, why do the obese not eat more of everything than the non-obese? (i.e. the fat that they consume doesn't cause them to feel full so they then eat more of all types of food). If relative increases in fat affect appetite control, why are the population increases in relative fat consumption not reflected in overall population increases in food intake? (i.e. the more fat we eat relatively, the more we eat overall). Finally, if relative increases in fat affect appetite control, which causes eating more overall, why isn't eating more overall associated with an increase in obesity? (i.e. as the population eats relatively more fat, it eats more overall, and gets more obese). It has been suggested that this reflects underreporting of calories and accurate reporting of the proportion of fat and carbohydrate, but this remains unsupported.

The values of the researchers

"Overeating" assumes that this behavior is "wrong" because it may lead to weight gain. This judgment is only accepted within a culture where food is freely available and weight gain is regarded as unacceptable. For other cultures, eating to maintain weight could be seen as "undereating."

Conclusion

The prevalence of obesity is on the increase in the West. It is associated with a range of physical problems such as heart disease and diabetes, and it may be linked to psychological problems such as depression and low self-esteem. Much research has explored the causes of obesity and has focused on two main mechanisms. The first emphasizes a physiological process which highlights the role of genetics, metabolism, and fat cells, and also the role of genetics in appetite regulation. The second emphasizes behavior in terms of both physical activity and food intake. Overall, the research suggests that some individuals have a genetic tendency to be obese, that obesity is related to under-exercise and to the consumption of relatively more fat than carbohydrate.

Towards an integrated model of diet

Attempts to eat a healthy diet are complicated by the meanings associated with food and body size which can result in weight concern. For many this weight concern takes the form of body dissatisfaction which is translated into dieting and attempts to eat less. However many dieters end up overeating, and experience lowered mood and a preoccupation with food. In those individuals with a genetic predisposition to becoming obese, these episodes of overeating may result in weight gain which over many years can result in obesity. Researchers and clinicians have developed approaches to treat obesity, which are the focus of the next chapter.

chapter nine

Obesity Treatment

Interventions designed to treat obesity have been developed by nutritionists, psychologists, dieticians, and the medical profession. This chapter examines the usefulness of dietary interventions, which form the basis of the majority of treatment approaches. It then explores the role of restrained eating in obesity treatment and asks whether obesity should be treated at all. The use of exercise, drug therapy, and surgery as complementary and alternative methods is then assessed. The chapter then explores the minority of obese individuals who have succeeded in losing and maintaining weight loss, and finally, examines the recent shift in emphasis towards prevention.

This chapter covers:

- Dietary interventions
- Should obesity be treated at all?
- The treatment alternatives
- The success stories
- Preventing obesity

Dietary Interventions

Dietary interventions range from relatively simple traditional approaches to more recent complex multidimensional packages.

Traditional treatment approaches

The traditional treatment approach to obesity was a corrective one, and encouraged the obese to eat "normally." This consistently involved putting them on a diet. Stuart (1967) and Stuart and Davis (1972) developed a behavioral program for obesity involving monitoring food intake, modifying cues for inappropriate eating, and encouraging self-reward for appropriate behavior, which was widely adopted by hospitals and clinics. The program aimed to encourage eating in response to physiological hunger, and not in response to mood cues such as boredom or depression or external cues such as the sight and smell of food or other people eating. In 1958, Stunkard concluded his review of the past 30 years' attempts to promote weight loss in the obese with the statement "Most obese persons will not stay in treatment for obesity. Of those who stay in treatment, most will not lose weight, and of those who do lose weight, most will regain it" (Stunkard, 1958). More recent evaluations of their effectiveness indicate that although traditional behavioral therapies may lead to initial weight losses of on average 0.5 kg per week (Brownell and Wadden, 1992), "weight losses achieved by behavioural treatments for obesity are not well maintained" (Stunkard and Penick, 1979).

Multidimensional behavioral programs

The failure of traditional treatment packages for obesity resulted in increases in treatment length, an emphasis on follow-up, and the introduction of a multidimensional perspective to obesity treatment. Recent comprehensive, multidimensional cognitive-behavioral packages aim to broaden the perspective for obesity treatment and combine traditional self-monitoring methods with nutritional information, exercise, cognitive restructuring, attitude change, and relapse prevention (e.g. Brownell, 1990, 1999). Brownell and Wadden (1991) emphasized the need for a multidimensional approach and also highlighted the importance of screening patients for entry onto a treatment program, and argued that each patient should be matched to the most appropriate package. This can involve using motivational interviewing, which is derived from the Stages of Change Theory, as a means to assess whether an individual is ready to change their behavior and to evaluate their degree of motivation (Prochaska and DiClemente, 1984; see figure 11.2 below). Further, the concept of a reasonable weight which is negotiated by the patient and the therapist is used, and such approaches focus on long-term lifestyle change rather than short-term "quick fixes" (Brownell and Wadden, 1991; Brownell, 1998, 1999). Some approaches have also attempted to change the carbohydrate/fat ratio in patient's diets rather than simply recommending a reduction in calorie intake (Astrup et al., 2000; Saris et al., 2000). Other dietary interventions have used very low-calorie diets (Wadden, Van Itallie, and Blackburn, 1990). A multidimensional approach to obesity treatment is illustrated in figure 9.1.

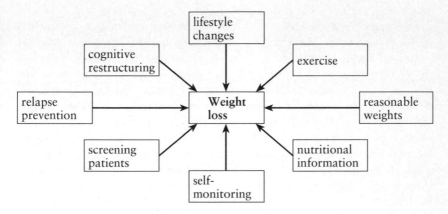

Figure 9.1   Multidimensional packages for obesity

Some individual studies show that multidimensional long-term inter-ventions including components such as relapse prevention, problem-solving therapy, motivation, behavioral skills training, and group support produce good initial weight losses and some degree of weight maintenance (e.g. Sherman et al., 2000; Perri et al., 2001). A broader analysis of the effectiveness of multidimensional treatment approaches suggests that average weight loss during the treatment program is 0.5 kg per week and that approximately 60 to 70 percent of the weight loss is maintained during the first year (Brownell and Wadden, 1992). Low fat/high carbohydrate diets have been shown to been more effective than low-calorie diets for shorter term weight loss, particularly in heavier subjects (Astrup et al., 2000; Saris et al., 2000) and very low-calorie diets have been shown to be of some use in the short term for the severely obese (Wadden, Van Itallie, and Blackburn, 1990). At three- and five-year follow-ups, however, the data tend to show weight gains back to baseline weight (Brownell and Wadden, 1992). In a comprehensive re-view of the treatment interventions for obesity, Wilson (1995) suggested that there has been an improvement in the effectiveness of obesity treat-ment since the 1970s. However, long-term success rates are still poor. In 1993, Wadden also examined both the short- and long-term effective-ness of both moderate and severe caloric restriction on weight loss (Wadden, 1993). He examined all the studies involving randomized con-trolled trials in four behavioral journals and compared his findings to those of Stunkard (1958). Wadden concluded that "Investigators have made significant progress in inducing weight loss in the 35 years since

Stunkard's review." He stated that 80 percent of patients will now stay in treatment for 20 weeks and that 50 percent will achieve a weight loss of 20 lbs or more. Therefore, modern methods of weight loss produce improved results in the short term. Wadden also concluded, however, that "most obese patients treated in research trials still regain their lost weight." This conclusion has been further supported by a systematic review of interventions for the treatment and prevention of obesity, which identified 92 studies which fitted the authors' inclusion criteria (NHS Centre for Reviews and Dissemination, 1997). The review examined the effectiveness of dietary, exercise, behavioral, pharmacological, and surgical interventions for obesity, and concluded that "the majority of the studies included in the present review demonstrate weight regain either during treatment or post intervention." In real terms, between 90 percent and 95 percent of those who lose weight regain it within several years (Garner and Wooley, 1991). Accordingly, the picture for long-term weight loss remains a pessimistic one.

Problems with weighing

Intrinsic to the definition and treatment of both obesity and eating disorders is the process of weighing. An individual is weighed in order to compare their weight with that recommended by the health professionals, and repeated weighing is used in order to provide both negative and positive feedback during a treatment program. Weighing is also used by many normal-weight individuals to facilitate their own weight control. Underlying the use of weighing is the assumption that the individual will benefit from being weighed, as this practice will encourage them to adhere to any treatment recommendations. It also assumes that even if weighing has no actual benefits, it can do no harm. The focus on weighing, however, shifts the desired outcome of any treatment program from improved health and well-being to actual weight loss defined by the number on the scale. In addition, weighing involves a comparison with social norms, which may facilitate any existing self-perceptions of abnormality. In an experimental study to explore the immediate impact of weighing, normal-weight subjects were weighed and sequentially allocated to either the "average weight," the "underweight," or the "overweight" group according to a fictional height/weight chart (Ogden and Evans, 1996). The results indicated that subjects who were told that they were overweight showed a deterioration in mood and self-esteem but no change in body image when compared to both the "underweight" and the "average" weight groups. In a similar study McFarlane, Polivy, and

Herman (1998) concluded that dieters who were told that they weighed 5 lbs more than they actually did also reported lower mood and lower self-esteem than the dieters who were told that they were lighter or were not weighed at all. In addition, these dieters also ate more food in a subsequent taste test. The effect of repeated weighing was also examined in a small-scale exploratory study (Ogden and Whyman, 1997). The results indicated that subjects who weighed themselves every day for two weeks reported increases in both anxiety and depression and decreased self-esteem. Weight stability or gain was related to increased depression and body dissatisfaction, whereas weight loss was related to increased body satisfaction. These studies suggest that even in the short term, weighing may not be the benign intervention it is assumed to be, and has negative consequences for those who do not show the desired outcome of treatment. The potential problems with weighing are illustrated by Judy Mazel, in *The Beverly Hills Diet*. She said that the scales have "more effect on us than an atom bomb" and described:

> When I looked in the mirror my hip bones had vanished . . . I was terrified. The whale that I had once been was looming. I inched onto the scale with dread and horror. With one eye shut, barely breathing, I looked down. Three numbers stared up at me – 102. I had not gained an ounce! . . . I was overcome with joy and relief, and when I looked in the mirror again, my hip bones had reappeared. (Mazel, 1981)

Should Obesity be Treated At All?

The problems with treating obesity raise the question of whether it should be treated at all, and this debate has been argued within both the professional and the lay press. For example, Garrow remains a strong advocate of obesity treatment, and concluded a paper in 1994 with the statement "I have been running a hospital obesity clinic for more than 20 years . . . Obesity is often treated badly. The solution is not to pretend it does not matter but to treat it well" (1994, p. 655). In contrast, Wooley, who is a vocal skeptic about obesity treatment, argued in a paper with Garner in 1994 "We should stop offering ineffective treatments aimed at weight loss . . . Only by admitting that our treatments do not work – and showing that we mean it by refraining from offering them – can we begin to undo a century of recruiting fat people for failure" (Wooley and Garner, 1994, p. 656). They also argued that treatments should be withheld until they can be proved to be effective, in the same way that "the drug industry has to show both safety and efficacy" (p. 655). Brownell, although an advocate of obesity treatment, has also questioned whether obesity should always be treated and has questioned how much weight should be lost (e.g. Brownell, 1991). He has argued that the belief that body size and shape are changeable can result in victim blaming: "When individuals do not meet the implied responsibilities, they are blamed and are assumed to have negative personal characteristics" (p. 308). In order to answer the question "Should obesity be treated?", it is first necessary to examine the costs and benefits of treatment and then to explore the treatment alternatives.

The costs of obesity treatment

With the exception of the surgical interventions now available, all obesity treatment programs involve recommending dieting in one form or another. Traditional treatment programs aimed to correct the obese individual's abnormal behavior, and recent packages suggest that the obese need to readjust their energy balance by eating less than they usually do. But both styles of treatment emphasize imposing cognitive restraint upon eating behavior. They recommend that the obese deny food and set cognitive limits to override physiological limits of satiety. And this brings with it the potential psychological and physical consequences of restrained eating described earlier, in chapter 7.

Psychological problems and obesity treatment

Wadden, Stunkard, and Smoller (1986) reported that dieting resulted in increased depression in a group of obese patients, and McReynolds (1982) reported an association between ongoing obesity treatment and psychological disturbance. In addition, results from a study by Loro and Orleans (1981) indicated that obese dieters reported episodes of bingeing precipitated by "anxiety, frustration, depression and other unpleasant emotions." This suggests that the obese respond to dieting in the same way as the non-obese, with lowered mood and episodes of overeating, both of which are detrimental to attempts at weight loss. The obese are encouraged to impose a cognitive limit on their food intake, which introduces a sense of denial, guilt, and the common response to such limits – overeating. Consequently, any weight loss may be precluded by episodes of overeating which are a response to the many cognitive and emotional changes which occur due to dieting.

Physical problems and obesity treatment

In addition to psychological consequences are the physiological changes which accompany attempts at food restriction. In particular, research suggests that shifts in weight, in addition to weight per se, may be an important predictor of the health of the individual, and that treating obesity with dieting may result in weight variability. For example, research examining men indicates that a single weight cycle of weight gain and weight loss is a risk factor for coronary heart disease, but not for death from all causes (Hamm, Shekelle, and Stamler, 1989). Lissner et al. (1989) reported that weight variability (which is the standard deviation/mean) calculated at three time-points predicted coronary heart disease in men (not women) and all-cause mortality in both men and women. Furthermore, Lissner and colleagues (1991) evaluated data from the Framingham Heart Study and assessed the effects of weight variability in 5,127 men and women over 32 years. The results suggested that weight variability was associated with all-cause mortality, and with mortality and morbidity from coronary heart disease, in both sexes. Likewise, research on rats suggests that repeated attempts at weight loss followed by weight regain result in further weight loss becoming increasingly difficult due to a decreased metabolic rate and an increase in the percentage body fat (Brownell, Greenwood et al., 1986). Lissner and Brownell (1992) reviewed the literature on weight fluctuations and concluded that there was consistent evidence for an association between weight fluctuation and all-cause mortality, particularly coronary mortality. Therefore, as dieting in the non-obese can cause weight fluctuation (Heatherton et al., 1991; see chapter 7 above) yo-yo dieting in the obese may similarly cause weight cycling and be more detrimental to physical health than remaining statically obese. The research into the relationship between weight variability and health, however, remains controversial, as some work has found no association between these factors (Muls et al., 1995). In addition, it has been argued that weight fluctuation may simply be a proxy measure for diseases such as irritable bowel syndrome, tuberculosis, coronary heart disease, or diabetes (Muls et al., 1995). From this perspective weight fluctuations are seen as a marker of other causes of mortality rather than the cause per se. The debate is still in its preliminary stages, but the focus has shifted from weight per se as a predictor of health status to accepting a role for weight variability regardless of baseline weight.

Restraint theory suggests that dieting may have negative consequences (see chapter 7), and yet most obesity treatments recommend dieting as a solution. This paradox can be summarized as follows:

- Obesity treatment aims to reduce food intake, but restrained eating can promote overeating.
- The obese may suffer psychologically from the social pressures to be thin (although evidence of psychological problems in the non-dieting obese is scarce), but failed attempts to diet may leave them depressed, feeling a failure and out of control, which is also detrimental to health.
- Weighing is central to most treatment of obesity but may not be the benign intervention it is considered to be, contributing to lowered mood and self-esteem and changes in food intake.
- Obesity is a physical health risk, but restrained eating may promote weight cycling.

Dieting is therefore offered as a cure for obesity but may bring with it the adverse consequences of dieting. If restraint theory is applied to obesity, the obese should not be encouraged to restrain their food intake, since although obesity may not simply be caused by overeating, overeating may be triggered if restrained eating is offered as a cure. However, there are also many benefits of obesity treatment.

The benefits of treatment

Although failed obesity treatment may be related to a preoccupation with food, negative mood, and lowered self-esteem, actual weight loss has been found to be associated with positive changes such as elation, self-confidence, and increased feelings of well-being (Stunkard, 1984). This suggests that whereas failed dieting attempts are detrimental, successful treatment may bring with it psychological rewards. The physical effects of obesity treatment also show a similar pattern of results. Yo-yo dieting and weight fluctuation may increase chances of coronary heart disease and death, but actual weight loss of only 10 percent may result in improved blood pressure and benefits for Type 2 diabetes (Blackburn and Kanders, 1987; Wing et al., 1987). Likewise, a reduction in waist circumference is associated with a reduction in cardiovascular risk factors (Han et al., 1997). Halmi, Stunkard, and Mason (1980) also reported significant psychological and physical benefits of weight loss in the severely obese. They compared a group of severely obese who underwent surgery with a comparable group who received a behavioral diet program. The results indicated that the surgery group showed higher rates of both weight loss and weight maintenance, and the diet group reported significantly higher changes in psychological characteristics such as preoccupation with food and depression than the surgery group. Thus, permanent weight loss through surgery brought both physical and psychological benefits. Weight loss in the obese can be beneficial if treatment is successful and the results permanent. An argument for treating obesity can be made if a positive outcome can be guaranteed, as failed treatment may be more detrimental than no treatment attempts at all.

The Treatment Alternatives

Dieting offers only small chance of weight loss accompanied by the risk both of negative physical and psychological consequences. The successful treatment of obesity brings with it both psychological and physical benefits. Alternative treatment approaches have therefore been developed, including exercise, drugs, and surgery.

Exercise-based treatments of obesity

Over the past few years exercise has played an increasingly important role in the treatment of obesity, either as an adjunct to dieting or as a stand-alone approach. For example, Brownell (1995, 1998) argued that exercise should be central to any intervention and that "it would be difficult to argue that any factor is more important than exercise" (1995). The impact of exercise on obesity has been explored in terms of its effects on weight loss, weight maintenance, and overall health.

Exercise and weight loss

Exercise can take many forms, including structured sports such as tennis or aerobics, and incidental physical activity such as stair-climbing. As a result of this variability, assessments of the effectiveness of exercise as a treatment for obesity are problematic. Several reviews and meta-analyses, however, have been carried out. Ballor and Poehlman (1994) examined 46 diet-based weight loss programs published between 1964 and 1991 and concluded that adding exercise to diet-based treatments had no impact on changes in body weight or fat mass. Garrow and Summerbell (1995) conducted a meta-analysis and calculated that over 30 weeks, exercise added 3 kg extra weight loss in men and over 12 weeks exercise added 1.4 kg weight loss for women. They also concluded that exercise resulted in greater loss of fat mass and improved preservation of fat-free mass, although Kopelman (1997) has argued that the impact of exercise on fat reduction remains unsupported by a substantial evidence base. Fox (1999) reviewed the literature exploring exercise and weight loss and concluded that "aerobic exercise cannot compete with dietary methods for rapid weight loss" but that it should be "considered as an accompaniment to a moderate dietary regime" (p. 166).

Exercise and weight maintenance

Exercise seems to have a more important role to play in weight mainte-nance. For example, Pavlou, Krey, and Steffee (1989) randomly alloc-ated male participants to receive either dietary intervention or diet plus exercise, which included stretching, moderate to vigorous aerobics, and callisthenics three times per week. The results showed that exercise had no effect on immediate weight loss. By 8 and 18 months, however, only the exercisers were maintaining any weight loss. Svendsen, Hassager, and Christiansen (1994) and Van Dale, Saris, and ten Hoor (1990) reported similar results for women. Although it is possible that the effects of exercise are physiological, research also indicates a role for psychological factors, with exercise improving self-esteem, confidence, body image, and sense of mastery (Brownell, 1995).

Exercise and health

The aim of obesity treatment is to improve health, and it is generally believed that weight loss by whatever means is the correct pathway. Exercise is therefore recommended as a means to lose weight and bring about improvement in health status. There is much evidence, however, that physical activity regardless of weight can create better health for the individual. Physical activity is related to cholesterol levels, blood pres-sure, and blood lipids (Powell et al., 1987), all of which are risk factors for the obese. In addition, physical activity has also been shown to link directly to mortality. Blair has carried out much research in this area and has argued that increases in fitness and physical activity can result in significant reductions in the relative risk of disease and mortality (Blair et al., 1989, 1995, 1996; Blair, 1993). The data from one study are shown in figure 9.2.

This study indicated that overweight men and women who showed low fitness scores had a high risk of all-cause mortality. Those over-weight individuals, however, who showed either medium fitness scores or high fitness scores showed a substantial reduction in this risk. In sum,

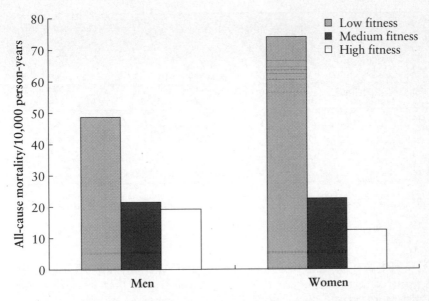

Figure 9.2   Mortality and fitness level in individuals with a BMI > 25.4
(*Source*: S.N. Blair, Evidence for success of exercise in weight loss and control,
Annals of Internal Medicine, 199 (1993), pp. 702–6)

physical activity may not be that effective at promoting weight loss in the short term, but may be more helpful in promoting any maintenance of weight loss. Regardless of any changes in weight, exercise may be very effective at improving health.

Drug treatments of obesity

If both dietary and exercise treatments have failed then an obese individual may turn to drugs; as Hirsch said in 1998, "Who would not rejoice to find a magic bullet that we could fire into obese people to make them permanently slim and healthy?" (p. 1136). Doctors have been offering weight-loss drugs for many years (see figure 9.3), and often used to prescribe amphetamines, but this practice was stopped due to their addictive qualities.

In 1987 it was estimated that in the UK the National Health Service spent £4,000,000 per year on appetite-suppressant drugs. A *Which?* magazine survey in the 1980s suggested that up to half the women who consulted their doctors about their weight were offered drugs. Further, *The Observer* newspaper carried out a study in 1988 involving three

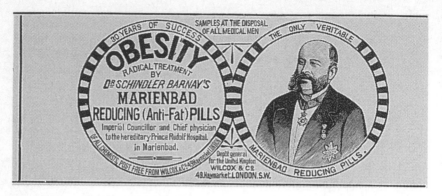

Figure 9.3   Searching for the magic bullet for obesity (*Source:* Advertising Archives)

journalists who went to dieting centers and asked for help to lose weight. None of them was obese, or even overweight, but they were all offered different forms of "diet pills." They were given no counseling, and asked no questions as to why they wanted to be thinner. The drugs varied from placebos to amphetamines, and were presented without any medical advice.

Nowadays, drug therapy is only legally available to patients in the UK with a BMI of 30 or more, and government bodies have become increasingly restrictive on the use of anti-obesity drugs. For example, both fenfluoramine and dexfenfluoramine were recently withdrawn from the market because of their association with heart disease, even though they were both quite effective at bringing about weight loss. There are currently two groups of anti-obesity drugs available which are offered in conjunction with dietary and exercise programs. Those in the first group act on the gastrointestinal system and the more successful of these reduce fat absorption. Orlistat is one of these and has been shown to cause substantial weight loss in obese subjects (James et al., 1997; Sjostrom et al., 1998; Rossner et al., 2000). It can, however, be accompanied by a range of unpleasant side effects, including liquid stools, an urgent need to go to the toilet, and anal leakage, which are particularly apparent following a high-fat meal. Although Orlistat is designed to work by reducing fat absorption it probably also has a deterrent effect, as eating fat causes unpleasant consequences. Drugs in the second group work on the central nervous system and suppress appetite. The most commonly used of these are phentermine, which acts on the catecholamine pathway, and sibutramine, which acts on the noradronergic and serotonergic pathways (see chapter 3). There is some evidence for the effectiveness of these drugs although they can also be accompanied by side-effects such as nausea, dry mouth, and constipation (Lean, 1997). Current recommendations state that drugs should be used only when other approaches have failed, and that they should not be prescribed for longer than three months in the first instance and should be stopped if a 10 percent reduction in weight has not been achieved. Continued drug use beyond this time should be accompanied by review and close monitoring (Kopelman, 1999b).

Surgical treatments of obesity

The final approach to obesity is surgery, which is reserved for the morbidly obese and is offered when all other attempts at weight loss have repeatedly failed. Although there are 21 different surgical procedures for obesity (Kral, 1995), the two most popular are the gastric bypass and the vertical stapled gastroplasty (e.g. Mason, 1987; Kral, 1995) (see figures 9.4 and 9.5). Both these procedures impose dietary control on the patient and therefore remove the need for the patient to restrict their own eating behavior. The gastric bypass involves excluding most of the stomach, the duodenum, and a 40–50 cm segment of the proximal

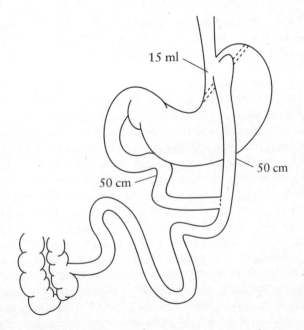

15 ml

50 cm

50 cm

Figure 9.4   Gastric bypass (*Source:* after J.G. Kral, Surgical interventions for obesity, in K.D. Brownell and C.G. Fairburn (eds), *Eating Disorders and Obesity,* New York: Guilford Press, 1995, pp. 510–15)

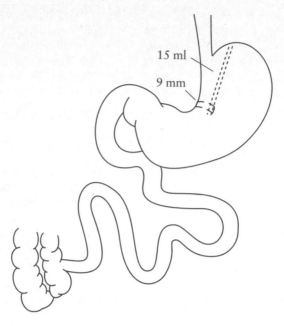

15 ml

9 mm

Figure 9.5   Vertical stapled gastroplasty (*Source*: after J.G. Kral, Surgical interventions for obesity, in K.D. Brownell and C.G. Fairburn (eds), *Eating Disorders and Obesity*, New York: Guilford Press, 1995, pp. 510–15)

jejunum. This promotes weight loss in two ways. First it reduces the amount of food that can be eaten, as large quantities of food cause discomfort, and second it reduces how much food is absorbed once it has been eaten. The vertical stapled gastroplasty involves a line of staples which divides the stomach into a small upper pouch with the capacity of about 15 ml which communicates with the rest of the stomach via a narrow stoma. This procedure promotes weight loss by restricting food intake, as once the pouch is full any further food induces vomiting until the pouch has emptied its contents into the rest of the stomach.

Halmi, Stunkard, and Mason (1980) reported high levels of weight loss and maintenance following surgery, with accompanying changes in satiety, body image, and eating behavior. Likewise, Stunkard, Stinnett, and Smoller (1986) indicated that after one year, weight losses average at 50 percent of excess weight. Stunkard (1984) also stated that "Severe obesity . . . is most effectively treated by surgical measures, particularly ones that reduce the size of the stomach and of its opening into the large gastrointestinal tract" (p. 171). More recently, researchers in Sweden have carried out the large-scale Swedish Obese Subjects (SOS) study, which explored nearly 1,000 matched pairs of patients who received either surgery or conventional treatment for their obesity (Torgerson and Sjostrom, 2001). The results showed an average weight loss of 28 kg in the surgical group after two years, compared to only 0.5 kg in the conventional group. After eight years the weight loss in the surgical group remained high (average of 20 kg), while the control group had gained an average of 0.7 kg. The weight loss in the surgical group was associated with a reduction in diabetes and hypertension at two years and in diabetes at eight years. This study indicates that surgery can be effective for both weight loss and maintenance and brings with it a reduction in the risk factors for cardiovascular disease. However, in parallel to the problems with dieting, individuals who have surgery can show complete weight regain or no initial weight loss. In addition, they are subjected to the dangers of any operation and the accompanying problems with anesthetics (Mason, 1987). The surgical management of obesity has been endorsed by expert committees in the US (Institute of Medicine, 1995) and the UK (Anon., 1997) and is recommended for those with a BMI over 40 who have not lost weight with nonsurgical interventions, as long as they made aware of the possible side-effects.

In summary, to answer the question "Should obesity be treated at all?" it is necessary to consider the following points:

- Obesity is a health risk.
- Obesity is caused by a combination of physiological and behavioral factors.
- Treating obesity with dieting is effective in the short term but many individuals regain any lost weight by follow-up.
- Dieting in the obese can be associated with psychological and physical changes such as lowered mood and self-esteem, overeating, and weight variability.
- Weight variability may be more detrimental to health than stable obese weight.
- Successful treatment does bring with it both psychological and physical benefits.
- Exercise is less effective than dieting in the short term but more effective in the longer term. Exercise also improves health regardless of any weight loss.
- Drug therapy can bring about weight loss but can be accompanied by unpleasant side effects.
- Treating obesity with surgery often results in weight loss and even weight maintenance but may result in medical complications and weight regain.

Embarking upon a treatment intervention for obesity should involve weighing up the potential benefits of any weight loss (e.g. improved self-esteem, reduced risk of mortality and morbidity) against the potential costs of intervention (e.g. lowered self-esteem, guilt, overeating, weight fluctuations). If weight loss and maintenance could be "guaranteed" then the intervention is worthwhile. If not, then failed treatment may be worse than no treatment at all. Many researchers and clinicians persist in treating obesity and attempting to improve treatment outcomes (e.g. Garrow, 1994). In contrast, those more skeptical researchers such as Wooley and Garner (1994) argue that it is time to shift the emphasis from the physical consequences of obesity and address some of the contextual factors such as blame, stigma, and stereotyping which can make being obese an unpleasant experience.

The Success Stories

Randomized control trials examining the effectiveness of interventions indicate that although the majority of individuals may lose weight initially, the large majority eventually return to their baseline weight. Within each trial, however, a small minority not only lose weight initially but successfully maintain this loss. Klem et al. (1998) examined the psychological states of 784 men and women who had both lost weight and maintained their weight loss and concluded that weight suppression was not associated with psychological distress. In contrast, Wooley and Wooley (1984) suggested that the minority of "success stories" are "in fact condemned to a life of weight obsession, semi starvation and all the symptoms produced by chronic hunger . . . and seem precariously close to developing a frank eating disorder" (p. 187).

What factors distinguish between the majority of failures and the minority of long-term successes? To date some studies have specifically examined this minority group. This research, together with data from the trials of obesity treatment, provides some preliminary insights into the factors which predict and/or correlate with successful weight loss and maintenance. In particular, the literature highlights a role for a range of variables which can be conceptualized as profile characteristics, historical factors, help-seeking behaviors, and psychological factors.

Profile characteristics

Research suggests that baseline BMI predicts weight loss and maintenance; however, while some studies indicate that lower baseline weight is predictive of greater success (Stuart and Guire, 1978; Neumark-Sztainer, Kaufmann, and Berry, 1995; Ogden, 2000a), other studies show the reverse effect (Wadden et al., 1992). Research also suggests that employment outside of the home, higher income, and being older are predictive of weight loss and maintenance (Neumark-Sztainer, Kaufmann, and Berry, 1995; Wong et al., 1997; Ogden, 2000a). Some research has also looked at gender, although the data remain contradictory (e.g. Colvin and Olson, 1983).

Historical factors

Some research points to an individual's previous dieting attempts and their weight history as important for successful weight loss and maintenance. In particular, studies indicate that a longer history of dieting and a higher number of dieting attempts predict success (Hoiberg et al., 1994; Ogden, 2000a). In contrast, Kiernan et al. (1998) concluded from their study that success was greater in those who did not have a history of repeated weight loss. Whether the "try, try, and try again" ethos holds for dieting therefore remains unclear. It is also possible that changes in smoking behaviour (e.g. Klesges and Klesges, 1988) and an individual's reproductive history may be contributory factors to success, as weight gain and maintenance often follows smoking cessation and childbirth (e.g. Ohlin and Rossner, 1990; see below).

Help-seeking behaviors

There appear to be several help-seeking factors which are predictive of success. Primarily, research highlights a role for the types and intensity of weight-loss methods used. For example, many studies have emphasized the importance of dietary changes (e.g. Kayman, Bruvold, and Stern, 1990; McGuire et al., 1999) although Ogden (2000a) reported that calorie-controlled diets were associated with weight loss and regain rather than maintenance. Many studies have also highlighted the role of exercise and general increases in physical activity (Haus et al., 1994; Hoiberg et al., 1994; French and Jeffrey, 1997; Klem et al., 1997; Wong et al., 1997). Furthermore, research has highlighted the relative effectiveness of different interventions involving contact with a range of health professionals. These include psychological interventions such as Cognitive Behavioral Therapy (CBT), counseling, self-help groups, and medical interventions involving drug therapy and surgery (see NHS Review, 1997 for a review). The general conclusion from this research is that the more intense the intervention, the longer the follow-up period, and the greater the professional contact, the higher the probability of successful weight loss and maintenance.

Psychological factors

Rodin and colleagues (Rodin et al., 1977) reported the results from a study designed to assess the baseline psychological predictors of successful weight loss. Their results indicated a role for the individual's beliefs about the causes of obesity and their motivations for weight loss. A similar focus on motivations was also reported by Williams et al. (1996), whose results indicated that motivational style was predictive of weight loss and maintenance. Likewise, Kiernan et al. (1998) indicated that individuals who were more dissatisfied with their body shape at baseline were more successful, suggesting that motivations for weight loss guided by a high value placed on attractiveness may also be important. Ogden (2000a) examined differences in psychological factors between weight-loss regainers, stable obese, and weight-loss maintainers, who were classified as those individuals who had been obese (BMI > 29.9), lost sufficient weight to be considered non-obese (BMI < 29.9), and maintained this weight loss for a minimum of three years. The results showed that the weight-loss maintainers were more likely to endorse a psychological model of obesity in terms of its consequences such as depression and low self-esteem, and to have been motivated to lose weight for psychological reasons such as wanting to increase their self-esteem and feel better about themselves. Further, they showed less endorsement of a medical model of causality including genetics and hormone imbalance. These results suggested that it is not only what an individual does which is predictive of success, but also what they believe. Accordingly, for an obese person to lose weight and keep this weight off it would seem that they need both to change their behavior and believe that their own behavior is important. Further, they need to perceive the consequences of their behavior change as valuable.

In summary, a small minority of individuals show successful weight loss and maintenance which relates to their profile characteristics, dieting history, help-seeking behaviors, and beliefs about obesity.

Preventing Obesity

In light of the increased prevalence of obesity and the apparent intractable nature of this problem, there has been an developing interest in its prevention. Preventing obesity involves both public-health and individualistic approaches.

Public-health interventions

A public-health approach to obesity involves targeting populations rather than individuals. Possible public-health approaches include:

- **Advertising:** Ads for high-fat foods could contain health warnings or be restricted or banned in line with cigarette ads.
- **Cost:** High-fat foods could be taxed at a higher rate to deter their consumption. Fruit and vegetables could be subsidized.
- **Retailers:** Shops could be restricted from selling candy and high-fat foods to children, or could place them on high shelves where children cannot reach them.
- **Exercise:** Cycle paths could be built to encourage cycling rather than car use. Footpaths could be made safer and have better lighting to encourage walking. Car access to cities could be restricted or banned to encourage the use of public transportation. The use of elevators could be restricted to the elderly, disabled, and those with children, and stairs could be an available alternative.
- **Schools:** Schools could be subsidized to provide healthier meals and could place a greater emphasis on the benefits of exercise.

Such approaches require financial investment and motivation from governments. To date there is no evidence for either the effective introduction of such approaches or their effectiveness once established.

Individualistic approaches

Individualistic approaches to prevention could involve providing an intervention for all in the form of dietary information or encouragement to exercise. However, whereas studies show that exercise can prevent weight gain in the longer term (Klesges, Isbell, and Klesges, 1992; French et al., 1994), intensive interventions providing dietary and exercise information to large populations have no significant impact on BMI (Taylor et al., 1991; Jeffery et al., 1995). Therefore, some researchers have highlighted the need to target those individuals at risk of obesity including pregnant women and high-risk children.

Pregnancy

Weight gain in pregnancy should be sufficient to meet the growth and development of the fetus and extra maternal tissue. Some research indicates, however, that a substantial number of pregnant women gain much more weight than necessary during pregnancy (Olsen and Mundt, 1986; Parham, Astrom, and King, 1990). Such weight gain has been shown to relate to postpartum weight retention (Greene et al., 1988; Schauberger, Rooney, and Brimer, 1992), and many obese women state that their excessive weight was initiated by pregnancy (Ohlin and Rossner, 1990). Research also indicates that women who have become obese during pregnancy have gained 4 kg more than controls at six weeks postpartum (Hunt et al., 1995). Preventive interventions could therefore target women who are either trying to get pregnant or are in early pregnancy.

At-risk children

As children with obese parents are more likely to become obese (see chapter 8), preventive interventions could target these "at-risk" children. In addition, obese children are at risk of becoming obese adults. In line with this, Epstein et al. (1994) designed a family-based intervention and recruited 6–12-year-old obese children and their parents. All subjects received comparable advice on diet and exercise but were randomly allocated to one of three groups. In one group both parent and child were rewarded for changing their behavior, in the second group only the child was rewarded, and in the third group the family was rewarded for attendance only. The results showed that this intervention had a significant impact on weight at five and ten year follow-ups. Specifically, those families who had received rewards for both parent and child showed a 11.2 percent reduction in the average percentage that people were overweight after five years and a 7.5 percent reduction in overweight after ten years. In contrast those in the control group showed a 7.9 percent increase and a 14.3 percent increase respectively. In sum, targeting both parent and child reduced overweight at follow-up.

Prevention is therefore an important approach to managing the increasing prevalence of obesity. It requires a commitment from funding bodies and governments to consider obesity a serious problem, and involves both population and individual changes. To date there is little evidence of the effectiveness of preventive interventions.

Conclusion

Over the past few decades treatment approaches for obesity have been developed by a range of professionals from a variety of disciplinary perspectives. Most have involved dietary modification, with more recent multidimensional interventions adding elements such as exercise, cognitive restructuring, relapse prevention, and intensive long-term follow-ups. Some have also addressed the fat/carbohydrate ratio and others have used very low-calorie diets. The results from these interventions suggest that short-term weight losses are better than they were in the past. Longer term weight maintenance, however, remains poor, with between 90 and 95 percent returning to their weights at baseline. This has raised the question as to whether obesity should be treated at all. A cost–benefit analysis of obesity treatment shows that dieting in the obese and overweight also brings with it many of physical and psychological problems described by restraint theory, such as lowered mood and self-esteem, overeating, and weight variability. Successful treatment, however, can result in both psychological and physical health benefits. Alternative treatment approaches including exercise, drugs, and surgery are now recommended. Exercise adds nothing for short-term weight loss but aids longer term weight maintenance. Exercise also has a direct influence on health regardless of weight change. Drug therapy can bring about weight loss and even weight maintenance, but is sometimes accompanied by side-effects, and the weight loss can be followed by weight regain. Surgery has recently been shown to be effective for both weight loss and maintenance, particularly for those individuals who have failed using other methods. Those who show long-term weight loss and maintenance, however, still remain in the very small minority. But this minority provides some insights into successful dieting, and the research indicates that it is not only what people do that is important but also what they think, with a psychological model of obesity in terms of both causes and consequences being associated with success. The prevention of obesity in terms of public health and individualistic approaches has also been explored. A prevention perspective is still in its infancy, and although recommendations can be made, the effectiveness of any preventive intervention remains unknown.

Towards an integrated model of diet

Choosing healthy food is complicated due to the complex meanings associated with food and body size. These meanings can result in weight concern, which has implications for eating behavior problems, as dieting can cause overeating and a preoccupation with food. Another problem associated with eating is obesity. Obesity is linked to a strong genetic tendency to gain weight, but it is also associated with activity levels and food intake. Treatment interventions therefore emphasize a need to change an individual's behavior. Eating behavior is also linked to the problems of anorexia and bulimia. These are the focus of the next chapter.

chapter ten

Eating Disorders

Clinical textbooks describe a range of eating-related disorders. This chapter focuses on anorexia nervosa (AN) and bulimia nervosa (BN) and examines their definition and their prevalence. The chapter explores the consequences of these problems in terms of physical complications ranging from constipation through to cardiac problems and death, and psychological complications such as anxiety and depression. Finally it examines the different theoretical approaches to understanding their etiology. In particular it describes a genetic model, a psychoanalytic approach, a cognitive behavioral approach, a family systems analysis, a sociocultural model, and an approach which emphasizes significant events.

This chapter covers:

- Anorexia nervosa
- What are the consequences of anorexia nervosa?
- Bulimia nervosa
- What are the consequences of bulimia nervosa?
- Causes of eating disorders
- Conclusion

Anorexia Nervosa

A disorder involving severe emaciation and amenorrhea (loss of periods) was first described by Lasegue as "L'anorexie hysterique" in 1873 and by Gull in 1874 as "Anorexia nervosa," meaning "nervous loss of appetite." These early descriptions placed food avoidance at the core of the problem. More recent observers of this problem have focused less on the patients' behavior and more on their psychological disturbance. For example, Crisp (1967) described a "weight phobia," and Russell (1970) described a "morbid fear of fatness." Anorexia has also been described in terms of self-control. For example, Garfinkel and Garner (1986) suggested that the achievement of ever-decreasing weight becomes a sign of mastery, control, and virtue. Crisp, in 1984, likewise compared the anorexic to the ascetic in terms of his or her "discipline, frugality, abstinence and stifling of the passions" (p. 210), and analyzed anorexia as resulting from a determination to keep "the impulse to ingest at bay" and as a consequence of a "never ending vigilance and denial." Similarly, Bruch described the anorexic as having an "aura of special power and super human discipline" (1985).

Currently, the definition of anorexia nervosa most frequently used by researchers and clinicians is that described in DSM-IV (1994). This states that anorexia nervosa involves the following factors:

- Refusal to maintain body weight at or above a minimally normal weight for age and height (e.g., weight loss leading to maintenance of body weight less than 85 percent of that expected, or failure to make expected weight gain during period of growth, leading to body weight less than 85 percent of that expected).
- Intense fear of gaining weight or becoming fat even though underweight.
- Disturbance in the way in which body weight or shape is experienced, undue influence of body weight or shape on self-evaluation, or denial of the current low body weight.
- In post-menarcheal females, amenorrhea, i.e., the absence of at least three consecutive menstrual cycles. (A woman is considered to have amenorrhea if her periods occur only following hormone – e.g., estrogen – administration.)

DSM-IV also describes two types of anorexia nervosa. The first is restricting anorexia, which involves food restriction and no episodes of bingeing or purging. The second is binge eating/purging anorexia, which involves both food restriction and episodes of bingeing or purging through self-induced vomiting or the misuse of laxatives, diuretics, or enemas.

This classification system can be used for the diagnosis of anorexia nervosa and is currently central to much clinical work and research. It can be regarded as the medico-clinical approach to the disorder. In contrast, Brumberg (1988) argued for a more sociocultural approach to understanding eating disorders, and suggested that the presentation of anorexia nervosa has and will change according to the social norms of any particular time. She stated that "we should expect to see anorexia nervosa 'present' differently in terms of both predisposing psychological factors and actual physical symptoms," and therefore argued that a

too-rigid classification of anorexia nervosa ignored the potential variation in anorexia nervosa and risked locating it within one particular
time-frame. This need for flexibility is also reflected in cultural differences in the expression of eating disorders. For example, although anorexic patients have been identified in Hong Kong (Lee, Chiu, and Chen,
1989; Hsu and Lee, 1993) such individuals avoid food and show weight
loss but show only a minor or absent fear of fatness. Lee, Chiu, and
Chen (1989) pointed out that the pursuit of thinness is much less in
Hong Kong than in the West, and Hsu and Lee (1993) argued that by
imposing strict classification criteria on anorexia nervosa we may be
committing a "contextual fallacy" by failing "to understand the illness
in the context of its culture." Therefore, from a medico-clinical perspective the definition of anorexia nervosa involves a simple and clear set of
criteria. From a sociocultural perspective such criteria may miss the
potential for the expression of anorexia to vary across time and space.

The prevalence and incidence

Estimating the prevalence of anorexia is problematic, and attempts to do
so have been hindered by several factors. First, it is rare, which means
that large samples are needed; second, its illness course is variable, which
means identifying who has the problem and for how long can be difficult; and third, sufferers are often reluctant to take part in population
studies. However, one study in Sweden managed to overcome many of
these problems and used growth charts recorded by school nurses,
together with interview assessment. They concluded that 0.7 percent of
girls up to the age of 16 fulfilled the criteria for anorexia nervosa. This is
generally considered an accurate estimate of prevalence in a Western
population (Szmuckler and Patton, 1995). In terms of the incidence of
anorexia, estimates face similar problems, with rates ranging from 4 per
100,000 per year to 14 per 100,000 per year depending on the time and
place of survey (Russell, 1995).

Changes in incidence

The popular belief is that the incidence of anorexia nervosa has increased dramatically over the past 30 years. Many studies have addressed
how common anorexia is using different definitions, different measurement tools, and different populations. As a means to control for these
factors, Russell (1995) summarized the data from studies which had
collected data using the same definitions and measurement tools of the

same populations at different periods in time. The surveys he selected were in south Sweden, north-east Scotland, Switzerland, and Monroe County, New York and Rochester, Minnesota in the US (Theander, 1970; Kendell et al., 1973; Jones et al., 1980; Willi and Grossman, 1983; Szmuckler et al., 1986; Willi, Giacometti, and Limacher, 1990; Lucas et al., 1991). These results showed that in Sweden, Scotland, Switzerland, and Monroe County from periods ranging from the 1930s to the 1980s the incidence of anorexia nervosa had changed from less than one in a million per year in the 1930s to around 4 per 100,000 per year in the 1980s. Russell (1995) also considered the data from the Rochester study (Lucas et al., 1991) which involved a painstaking examination of 40 years of records of cases presenting to hospital services with a range of diagnoses with clinical similarities to anorexia nervosa. These results showed no increase in the incidence of anorexia nervosa, and are particularly important as the study covered the period before 1960 when incidence rates were thought to be low, and included patients from a range of services. However, when the data for females aged 15 to 24 were examined in isolation, these results also showed an increased incidence between the periods 1935–9 and 1980–4 which was particularly marked after 1950. Following this analysis Russell (1995) concluded that "there is persuasive evidence in support of a rising incidence of anorexia nervosa from the 1950s until the 1980s" (p. 11). This would seem to be particularly apparent in the 15-to-24 age band.

The increased incidence in anorexia has not gone unchallenged and has been called the "medical myth" by Williams and King (1987). They argued that data illustrating an increase are problematic due to factors such as deficiencies in the psychiatric case registers, changes in the referral rates, differences in case definition, demographic changes within a given population, and a rise in readmission rates. These factors would result in an increase in new cases appearing in hospital units and old cases being recounted as new. This challenge to the purported rise in anorexia nervosa has also been supported by studies based on local and national case registers (Nielsen, 1990; Willi, Giacometti, and Limacher, 1990). Therefore, while much research points to an increase in the occurrence of anorexia, this conclusion should be treated with caution given the potential for many methodological problems.

The incidence of anorexia nervosa can be considered in terms of demographic factors including age, gender, social class, and ethnicity. The stereotype of the anorexic often involves an emaciated woman looking into the mirror. She is always a woman. She is young, usually white, and considered to be from a higher class background (see figure 10.1). Research has explored the extent to which this stereotype holds true.

Figure 10.1   A common portrayal of an anorexic patient

Gender

The vast majority of sufferers of anorexia nervosa are women. This has been the experience of clinicians since anorexics started to be admitted into inpatient units, and is supported by both clinical and community studies, with the male/female ratio currently standing at 1:10 (e.g. Beumont, Beardwood, and Russell, 1972; Rastam, Gillberg, and Garton, 1989; Hsu, 1990; Touyz, Kopec-Schrader, and Beumont, 1993). Some research has indicated that male anorexia may be on the increase, particularly within vulnerable groups such as models, dancers, and jockeys, who are required to have a lower body weight (Buckley, Freyne, and Walsh, 1991). Research has also shown that gay men may be at higher risk than heterosexual men of eating disturbances, with about one-third of men who present with eating disorders being gay (Schneider and Agras, 1987). This has been supported by community-based studies which have shown higher frequencies of disturbed eating attitudes and behaviors among gay participants (Siever, 1994). Several explanations have been put forward for this phenomenon, including the internalization of social homophobia, over-identification with a gay scene which emphasizes youthfulness, slimness, and attractiveness, and an emphasis on healthiness in the context of HIV (Williamson, 1999).

Age

Clinical and register-based studies indicate that the age of onset for anorexia nervosa peaks at mid to late adolescence (Szmukler et al., 1986), with the mean age of onset being 17. There has been some recent evidence, however, that the incidence in younger girls may be increasing, with studies on girls as young as eight and nine showing a concern about weight and shape (Hill, Draper, and Stack, 1994). Clinical records also show that girls this young are increasingly likely to report symptoms of full-scale anorexia (Lask and Bryant-Waugh, 1992). This is reflected in the increase in inpatient units specifically for younger sufferers. However, not all anorexics are young. Anorexia also occurs in those of middle age and the elderly, and is often associated with severe depression or obsessive compulsive disorder (Cosford and Arnold, 1992). For example, Beck, Casper, and Anderson (1996) reviewed all cases of eating disorders who had been admitted to three university hospital programs in the US. They reported that 1 percent of all cases (n = 11) showed first onset of the disorder after the age of 40, with two patients reporting onset at ages 75 and 77.

Social class

It is mainly assumed that anorexics come from the higher classes. However, the research examining the relationship between class and a clinical diagnosis is contradictory. For example, Kendell et al. (1973) reported data from a small-scale clinical register study and concluded that those individuals who fulfilled the criteria for anorexia nervosa were of a higher class than those who did not. However, a larger study found no such relationship (Szmukler et al., 1986). This inconsistency may reflect problems with defining social class, as definitions can include parental occupation, own occupation, educational status, and income which are problematic due to an overreliance on male data and the changing nature of the job market. This inconsistency may also indicate that class per se is only a proxy measure for other factors which relate to eating disorders. Gard and Freeman (1996) reviewed all papers written between 1970 and 1994 which assessed socioeconomic status and eating disorders. They concluded from their analysis that "the relationship between anorexia nervosa and high socioeconomic status remains to be proved" (p. 1), and suggested that clinical impression, referral bias, and methodological bias had contributed to the perpetuation of this stereotype.

Ethnicity

Research has also addressed the extent to which the incidence of ano-rexia is related to ethnicity within Western populations, and many clin-ical reports show that the majority of patients with anorexia are white. However, a number of UK patients are Asian or Arabic (Bryant-Waugh and Lask, 1991; Mumford, Whitehouse, and Platts, 1991) or black (Holden and Robinson, 1988; Lacey and Dolan, 1988), and black patients have also been reported in the US (Hsu, 1987). Only a few studies, however, have examined cases of anorexia using validated inter-view techniques. Research also suggests that eating disorders may be more common in those individuals who have moved away from their background environment to a new society. For example, Fichter et al. (1988) reported that anorexia was more common in Greek girls living in Germany than in two Greek towns. Likewise, Nasser (1986) reported higher levels of disordered eating in Arab female undergraduates living in London than in those living in Cairo. Mumford, Whitehouse, and Platts (1991) have described these results in terms of acculturation, and have argued that eating disorders may emerge as one group attempts to acculturate to its new environment. In a similar vein, DiNicola (1990) has suggested that eating disorders can be considered a "culture change syndrome" which emerge during periods of rapid social change. How-ever, the incidence of cases in these studies was so small that only tent-ative conclusions can be made. Much research has also examined the relationship between ethnicity and measures of dieting, body dissatisfac-tion, and attitudes towards food. These data have been considered in detail in chapter 6.

Research has also examined the prevalence of anorexia in non-Western populations. Such research has included anecdotal clinical evid-ence, cross-sectional community studies, and the use of case registers, and has generally shown that the prevalence of anorexia nervosa is very low. For example, Lee, Chiu, and Chen (1989) reported ten cases out of a population of 500,000 psychiatric patients in China, and Mumford and colleagues reported no cases of anorexia in a sample of 640 Pakistani schoolgirls (Choudry and Mumford, 1992; Mumford, White-house, and Choudry, 1992). The prevalence appears to be higher among Westernized segments of non-Western populations such as in Hong Kong (Lee 1991) and areas of India, Africa, Malaysia, and New Guinea (DiNicola, 1990), and Mumford (1993) argued that higher rates were apparent in countries undergoing rapid Westernization. The prevalence is also particularly high in Japan (Suematsu, Ishikawa, and Inaba, 1986). Research exploring the relationship between ethnicity is made difficult, however, by problems with applying one definition of caseness across a range of cultures and using assessment tools which have been translated into different languages. The problem of language was specifically studied by King and Bhugra (1989), who concluded from their study that mis-interpretations of Western-based questions by non English-speaking par-ticipants are common. For example, while statements such as "Cut my food into small pieces" and "display self-control around food" may reflect disturbed eating in the West, they can be interpreted as desirable behaviors in other cultures. Similarly, while "eat diet foods" and "en-gage in dieting behaviors" are used in Western questionnaires to assess disordered eating, in other cultures they could relate to religious fasting.

In summary, anorexia is stereotypically regarded as a problem for young white women from the higher classes. The evidence for this suggests that the age and gender profile is fairly accurate. Data on social class and ethnicity remain unclear.

What do anorexics do?

All anorexics restrict their food intake. Most are extremely knowledge-able about the nutritional content of food, and count every calorie. When they do eat they tend to eat small meals predominantly made up of fruit and vegetables. They eat very slowly, sometimes cutting the food into small pieces. They avoid all fatty foods and often drink coffee and fizzy drinks, chew gum, or smoke to minimize their hunger (e.g. Reiff, 1992). The diet of anorexics is often repetitive and ritualized and they eat from a very limited repertoire. Many anorexics cook elaborate meals for others and often buy and read magazines and books containing recipes and pictures of food. Some anorexics refuse to swallow their food and chew it and then spit it out. Others will binge on large quantities of food and then purge by using laxatives or diuretics or making themselves sick. Anorexics are also often very physically active and will fidget when sitting, or march backwards and forwards as a means to burn up calories. Some sufferers of anorexia also hoard food. Good descriptions of what anorexics actually do can be found in literature from survivors of anorexia and the semi-autobiographical novels. For example, one woman described how "I was eating fruit and dry crispbreads, lettuce and celery and a very little lean meat. My diet was unvaried. Every day had to be the same. I panicked if the shop did not have exactly the brand of crispbread I wanted, I panicked if I could not eat, ritually, at the same time" (Lawrence, 1984, p. 124). Shute's novel *Life-size* (1992) described in detail an anorexic's eating: "peas were good because you could eat them one by one, spearing each on a single tine. Brussels sprouts were good, because you could unwrap them leaf by leaf and make them last forever. Corn could be nibbled, a few kernels at a time . . . Potatoes were evil. I would never eat one, no matter what . . ." (p. 125). Shute also provided insights into the other main aspect of anorexia, namely feeling fat. She wrote: "I knew I still had much to lose. There was still fat on my stomach, a handful above the navel and a roll below. I pinched it hard several times an hour to remind myself that it was there, that nothing mattered more than getting rid of it." She also stated: "one day I will be thin enough. Just the bones, no disfiguring flesh, just the pure, clear shape of me." Anorexia therefore involves a complex set of behaviors designed to reduce food intake and weight. This has many negative consequences.

What are the Consequences of Anorexia Nervosa?

Only about 50 percent of those diagnosed with anorexia attain normal body weight and re-establish their periods (Hsu, 1990). All anorexics suffer a range of problems resulting from their condition. The problems associated with anorexia nervosa can be understood in terms of physical and psychological complications, and are illustrated in figure 10.2.

Physical complications

Death

At the far end of the spectrum is death. The crude mortality rates for anorexia range from 3.3 percent in an 8-year follow-up study (Patton,

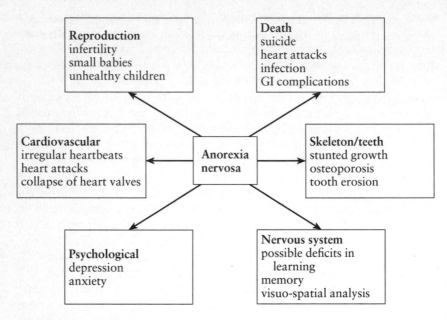

Figure 10.2   Possible consequences of anorexia nervosa

1988) and 5.1 percent in a cohort study of 246 eating disordered women (Herzog et al., 2000) to 18 percent in a 33-year outcome study (Nielsen et al., 1998). Mortality rates have also been developed in comparison with other populations. When compared to normal healthy populations matched for age, gender, and follow-up times, standardized mortality rates vary from 6.0 (Patton, 1988) to 12.82 (Eckert et al., 1995). Compared to other psychiatric problems, the mortality rate from anorexia is similar to that for schizophrenia, affective disorder, and personality disorder five years after a period of inpatient treatment (Zilber, Schufman, and Lerner, 1989) but lower than psychiatric problems complicated by alcohol and substance abuse. When compared to other women, anorexics are twice as likely to die from their problem than other female psychiatric inpatients (Sullivan, 1995). The most common causes of death are suicide, infection, gastrointestinal complications, and severe emaciation (W. Herzog et al., 1992). One study showed that an anorexic is 58.1 times more likely to commit suicide than an equivalent white healthy woman (Herzog et al., 2000). Therefore, anorexia is a high risk for mortality, particularly from suicide. For the majority of patients, however, it may not cause death but is associated with a wide range of either reversible or irreversible problems. The health effects of weight cycling are considered in chapter 9. The impact of anorexia on the skeleton and teeth, reproductive function, and the cardiovascular and nervous systems is considered below.

Skeleton and teeth

Adolescence is the key time for the development of bones, and malnutrition causes poor bone growth and decreased bone density. If anorexia develops at this time, the sufferer may be left with the irreversible problems of stunted growth and osteoporosis. Later-onset anorexia causes osteoporosis, but this may be reversed by dietary and hormonal supplements (Treasure and Szmukler, 1995). Teeth are also affected by anorexia, particularly if the sufferer vomits regularly, as this causes erosion of the tooth enamel which eventually results in exposure of the dentine making the teeth vulnerable to caries. Tooth erosion is sometimes the way in which persistent vomiting is recognized by health professionals.

Reproductive function

Starvation directly affects menstrual functioning, and the absence of menstrual periods is a key diagnostic criterion for anorexia. One study showed that of 69 women attending an infertility clinic, 16 percent (11 cases) fulfilled the criteria for an eating disorder (Stewart et al., 1990). Those women who do become pregnant while anorexic are more likely to have small babies, who may have complications such as respiratory distress and jaundice (Russell and Treasure, 1988). One of the largest studies of the reproductive effects of anorexia examined 140 patients over a period of 10 to 12 years. Of these women, 50 had had children (Brinch, Isager, and Tolstroop, 1988). The results showed that the rate of premature birth was twice the expected rate and the babies were six times more likely to die. Of the 86 children born, 79 were alive at follow-up, and 7 had died within the first week due to either prematurity, stillbirth, or hydrocephalus. Some research has also examined the health of children of anorexic mothers as they grow up. One study suggested that the infants show catch-up growth in infancy, therefore compensating for being small at birth (Russell and Treasure, 1988). However, other studies suggest that the children can develop a range of problems including stunted growth, poor nutrition, and social and emotional problems (Brinch, Isager, and Tolstroop, 1988; O'Donoghue, Treasure, and Russell, 1991).

The cardiovascular and nervous systems

Many deaths from anorexia are caused by heart attacks possibly caused by low levels of calcium or magnesium or a collapse of the mitral value in the heart (Treasure and Szmukler, 1995). Anorexia is also associated with changes in the nervous system. For example, brain scans have shown structural differences between the brains of anorexics compared to normal controls including reductions in pituitary size, changes in the midbrain area, widening of sulcal spaces, and cerebroventricular enlargement (Enzman and Lane, 1977; Palazidou, Robinson, and Lishman, 1990; Husain et al., 1992). It has been suggested that such changes in the central nervous system may be related to aspects of functioning such as deficits in attention, memory, visuo-spatial analysis, and learning (Szmukler et al., 1992). However, evidence for this remains weak and inconsistent.

Psychological complications

Depression is particularly common among sufferers of anorexia. For example, in a study of 41 anorexics between four and ten years after initial presentation, Morgan and Russell (1975) reported that 42 percent were depressed at presentation and 45 percent were depressed at follow-up. Similar rates of depression have also been reported by a range of subsequent researchers. For example, Cantwell et al. (1977) reported a rate of 45 percent, Toner, Garfinkel, and Garner (1988) reported a rate of 40 percent, and Halmi et al. (1991) reported a rate of 68 percent. It was consistently found in all these studies that the presence of depression was unrelated to the outcome of the anorexia, and there was a trend for depression to be higher among those anorexics who binged or purged (Halmi, 1995).

Anxiety disorders also co-occur alongside anorexia. For example, Halmi et al. (1991) reported a rate of 65 percent and Toner, Garfinkel, and Garner (1988) reported a rate of 60 percent in their patient populations. From these data the most common anxiety disorders are social phobia and obsessive compulsive behaviors.

Causes or consequences?

Most physical complications associated with anorexia can be analyzed as the consequences of the disorder. Starvation clearly causes skeletal and teeth problems and may ultimately cause death. The connection between anorexia and psychological problems is more complicated. Anorexics show both depression and anxiety, and this association has generated debates as to whether such psychological morbidity is a cause or a consequence of an eating disorder. Alternatively, depression and anxiety may be neither causes nor consequences but just manifestations of the problem itself. In fact, Crisp in 1967 conceptualized anorexia as a phobic disorder, and Brady and Rieger (1972) described an anxiety-reduction hypothesis which suggested that eating created anxiety in anorexics which was removed by food avoidance. Thus food avoidance and/or purging is reinforced through anxiety reduction. However, given that the rates of depression appear to remain constant throughout the treatment of anorexia, that depression is unrelated to recovery (Halmi, 1995), and that social phobia often precedes the onset of anorexia (Brewerton, Hand, and Bishop, 1993), these affective disorders are better considered secondary psychopathology rather than primary (Strober and Katz, 1987). They are therefore co-morbidities which may predispose an individual towards developing an eating disorder and may even perpetuate the problem, but do not cause it. Neither would their treatment result in a decline in the anorexia.

Bulimia Nervosa

The term "bulimia nervosa" was first used by Russell in 1979 to describe a variant of anorexia nervosa in 30 of his patients. He suggested that bulimia nervosa consisted of three factors: a powerful and intractable urge to eat resulting in episodes of overeating; avoidance of the fattening effects of food by inducing vomiting or abusing purgatives or both, and a morbid fear of becoming fat. Descriptions of bulimia nervosa focus on self-control but in contrast to anorexia nervosa the absence of this control is emphasized. For example, Cooper and Taylor (1988) stated that "episodes of excessive uncontrolled eating are a central feature" of bulimia, Cooper and Fairburn (1986) described bulimia as resulting from "a profound and distressing loss of control over eating," and "irresistible cravings for food" were central to the diagnostic criteria set by Russell (1979). Binge eating was similarly defined by Fairburn (1984) as "episodes of eating which are experienced as excessive and beyond the subject's control" (p. 235). DSM-IV's most recent description of bulimia nervosa characterizes it by the following (DSM-IV, 1994):

- Recurrent episodes of binge eating. An episode of binge eating is characterized by both 1) eating in a discrete period of time (e.g. in any two-hour period), an amount of food that is definitely larger than most people would eat in a similar period of time (taking into account time since last meal and social context in which eating occurred) and 2) a sense of lack of control over eating during the episodes (e.g. a feeling that one can't stop eating or control what or how much one is eating).

- Recurrent use of inappropriate compensatory behavior to avoid weight gain, e.g. self-induced vomiting.
- A minimum average of two episodes of binge eating and two inappropriate compensatory behaviors a week for at least three months.
- Self-evaluation unduly influenced by body shape and weight.
- The disturbance not occurring exclusively during episodes of anorexia nervosa.

DSM-IV recommends that bulimia nervosa be divided into two types: the purging type, to describe those who binge and purge using vomiting and/or laxatives, and the non-purging type, to describe those who binge only. This latter type mostly use excessive exercise or dieting as a means to compensate for food intake.

It is clear from this that the definition of bulimia nervosa is more ambiguous than that for anorexia and more open to interpretation based on an understanding of social norms. For example, what constitutes a binge to one person may not to another if they have a different sense of what is normal.

Who has it?

Many individuals who would fulfill the criteria for bulimia nervosa conduct their bulimic behavior in private and maintain apparently normal and functioning lives. They therefore do not come into contact with health professionals. Further, the course of bulimia is varied, with different symptoms peaking at different times. In addition there are no clear cut-off points for the severity of different symptoms, and definitions of the core clinical symptoms are dependent upon what is considered normal. Estimating the prevalence of bulimia nervosa is therefore problematic. Some popular literature claims that the majority of middle-class women are bulimic (Wolf, 1990). Similarly, studies using self-report measures among female student populations have reported the prevalence of bulimic episodes as being as high as 60 percent (Halmi, Falk, and Schwartz, 1981; Hart and Ollendick, 1985). Prevalence rates of bulimia nervosa as defined by DSM criteria have also been high. For example, Johnson, Lewis, and Hagman (1984) reported a rate of 8 percent among female American high-school students, Pope, Hudson, and

Yurgelun-Todd (1984) reported a rate of 14 percent, Hart and Ollendick (1985) reported a rate of 17 percent, and Halmi, Falk, and Schwartz (1981) reported a rate of 19 percent. More conservative estimates, however, are shown by community-based studies. For example, Pyle et al. (1983) used a questionnaire based upon DSM-III criteria and concluded that 4.5 percent of their large group of US female college students fulfilled the criteria for bulimia nervosa. In a similar vein, Cooper and Fairburn (1983) carried out a questionnaire survey of women attending a family planning clinic in southern England. They reported that 20.9 percent reported bulimic episodes as defined as episodes of "uncontrollable excessive eating" but that only 1.9 percent fulfilled the criteria for "probable bulimia nervosa" as defined as bulimic episodes, self-induced vomiting, and a morbid fear of fatness. This study was replicated in 1987 (Cooper, Charnock, and Taylor, 1987) and reported a comparable rate of 1.8 percent. In general, the prevalence of bulimia nervosa is accepted as being between 1 and 2 percent of the female population, with the peak age of onset being between 15 and 19 years. It is therefore twice as common as anorexia nervosa.

The change in incidence and prevalence since its description

Bulimia nervosa was first described in 1979. This raises the question "Has there been an increase in the incidence of bulimia nervosa from before to after the time of its description?" Two studies carried out since this time enable this question to be answered. The first was by Kendler et al. (1991), who interviewed 2,163 female subjects from a twin register in the US. Using DSM criteria they allocated a definite or probable diagnosis of bulimia to 60 individuals to enable the calculation of the proportion of individuals who could have received a diagnosis at any time in their life – the lifetime prevalence. They then examined this prevalence according to the age of the patients. This analysis showed that those born before 1950 were less likely to have had bulimia than those born after 1960. These data also indicated that the prevalence by the age of 25 for those born after 1959 was 4.6 times higher than for those born before 1950. The older patients may have been more likely to have forgotten their bulimia or to have been less aware of it due to the absence of any publicity about it at the time. Alternatively, these results could suggest that bulimia was very rare prior to its description in the late 1970s. This second explanation is supported by a study by Lucas and Soundy (1993). This study involved a retrospective analysis of cases

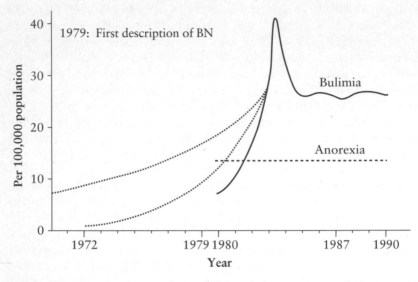

Figure 10.3   The changing incidence of bulimia nervosa since its description
(*Source*: after G.F.M. Russell, Anorexia nervosa through time, in G. Szmukler,
C. Dare, and J. Treasure (eds), *Handbook of Eating Disorders: Theory,
Treatment and Research*, New York: John Wiley and Sons, Inc., 1995, pp. 5–17)

that fulfilled the criteria for bulimia nervosa as recorded in the medical
database for the entire population of Rochester, Minnesota in the US
(about 60,000 in 1985). The analysis revealed only a very small number
of cases prior to 1979 but a very sharp increase in cases after the description of bulimia nervosa became formal. Russell (1995) reviewed the evidence for the change in incidence of bulimia before and after his original
description (see figure 10.3). He concluded that although there may have
been cases prior to this time, they were very rare. He also stated that the
increase in prevalence following this time could be due to the recognition
of clinical characteristics by health professionals. Furthermore, Russell
suggested that "the description of the disorder . . . encouraged the appearance of the key behaviors in vulnerable young women who consequently
acquired the illness as if by contagion" (Russell, 1995, p. 15).

The question also arises "Has there been an increase in the prevalence
of bulimia since it was first described?" One study carried out in the US
examined the prevalence of bulimia in 1983 and 1986 and reported a
threefold increase from 1 percent to 3.2 percent among female students
when using a strict criteria, involving bulimic episodes at least weekly,
and self-induced vomiting or laxative abuse (Pyle et al., 1983; Pyle and

Mitchell, 1986). In contrast to these results, Cooper and colleagues rep- licated their own 1983 study in 1986 and reported figures of 1.9 percent and 1.8 percent, indicating no change (Cooper and Fairburn, 1983; Cooper, Charnock, and Taylor, 1987). This may reflect different pat- terns of change between the UK and the US. Alternatively it may reflect different definitions and different tools of assessment. Therefore it would seem that bulimia was rare before the 1970s and has become much more common since this time. However, whether there has been an increase in its prevalence since its description remains unclear.

Demographic characteristics

The incidence of bulimia can also be considered in terms of the patient's demographic characteristics. About 90 percent of those with bulimia nervosa are young women (Gotesdam and Agras, 1995). They tend to be slightly older than anorexics, with the peak of onset being between 15 and 19 years (Lucas and Soundy, 1993). In terms of ethnicity and class the data for bulimia are as confusing as those for anorexia. For ethnicity, one study examined cases of bulimia in Arab female under- graduates in London and in Cairo and reported six cases in London and none in their home environment (Nasser, 1986). Another study com- pared Asian girls in the UK with an indigenous group of similarly aged girls and reported figures of 3.4 percent in the Asian girls compared to 0.6 percent in the indigenous population. Both these studies have been used to support the acculturation hypothesis also described in the con- text of anorexia, which suggests that eating disorders are higher in those populations which have moved from their own country to one where eating disorders are more common (Mumford, Whitehouse, and Platts, 1991). In terms of social class, bulimia nervosa appears to affect a broader spectrum of the population than anorexia nervosa, with patient popula- tions coming from a wider range of backgrounds (Gard and Freeman, 1996).

What do bulimics do?

Bulimic women are usually within the normal weight range and main- tain this weight through the processes of bingeing and purging. Bingeing involves eating a large amount of food in a discrete amount of time; foods eaten include sweet high-fat foods such as ice cream, doughnuts, pudding, chocolate, cookies, and cakes. Other foods eaten include breads and pasta, cheeses, meats, and snack foods such as peanuts and potato chips (e.g. Reiff, 1992). Kaye et al. (1992) measured the food intake of a group of normal-weight women with bulimia and reported an average food intake of 7,101 kcals during a bingeing episode compared to a daily intake of 1,844 kcals by normal-weight healthy women. Hetherington et al. (1994) also examined the eating behavior of ten bulimic women over a period of seven consecutive days and reported an average daily intake of 10,034 kcals. Such binges are accompanied by feelings of loss of control, are usually carried out in secret, involve very quick eating, and consist mainly of the foods that the patient is attempting to exclude from their diet. However, not all binges involve the consumption of enormous amounts of food. The core characteristic of a binge is that it is perceived by the individual to be a binge episode. Although there is substantial variability in the amounts eaten by bulimics, the patients themselves can clearly distinguish between normal and bulimic episodes of food intake (Abraham and Beumont, 1982). The consequences of a binge are described by Shute (1992): "my stomach, pressing painfully in all directions, could hold no more. I needed to collapse. Belching in rancid, vomity bursts, oozing oil from my pores, heavy and numb with self hatred . . . Avoiding the mirrors I pulled off my clothes, releasing an unrecognisable belly; my waistband left a vicious red stripe, but I only looked once" (p. 174).

Sufferers of bulimia nervosa also engage in compensatory behavior as a means to manage any weight gain caused by the binges. The most common form is self-induced vomiting, which usually occurs at the end of a binge but also after episodes of normal eating. One study reported that three-quarters of their bulimic sample vomited at least once a day and nearly half vomited twice a day (Fairburn and Cooper, 1984). This is usually achieved through the gag reflex using fingers, although many bulimics learn to vomit spontaneously. Vomiting is accompanied by feelings of self-disgust and loathing, is almost always secret, and may go undetected for years (Cooper and Cooper, 1987). Vomiting also provides a great sense of relief from the sense of distension caused by overeating and the fear of weight gain. It can therefore become habit-forming and encourages further overeating and further vomiting. In fact, although binge eating may start off as the primary behavior which causes vomiting, it has been argued that over time vomiting can start to drive the bingeing (Cooper and Cooper, 1987). Bulimics also use laxatives and diuretics as a means to compensate for bingeing. This behavior can also become habit-forming, particularly if the individual develops tolerance to the substances used and consequently increases their intake.

This cycle of bingeing and purging is accompanied by a set of beliefs and attitudes concerning food and weight. In particular, bulimics show overvalued ideas about the importance of attaining and or maintaining a specific body weight or shape, and report a "morbid fear of fatness" similar to that found in anorexics (Russell, 1979). Further, they show a considerable difference between their perceptions of their desired and actual size. Not all show a pathological desire to lose weight, but most show an extreme fear of weight gain. This is often reflected in a pre-occupation with weighing and awareness of every shift on the weighing scales' needle.

What are the Consequences of Bulimia Nervosa?

Long-term follow-ups of bulimics indicate that about 70 percent recover while about 10 percent stay fully symptomatic (Keel et al., 1999). The remaining 20 percent show great variability in their symptoms. Bulimia nervosa has a range of physical and psychological problems associated with it. Some of these are clearly consequences of the problem. For others it is unclear whether they are causes, consequences, or just co-occur. The potential consequences of bulimia nervosa are illustrated in figure 10.4.

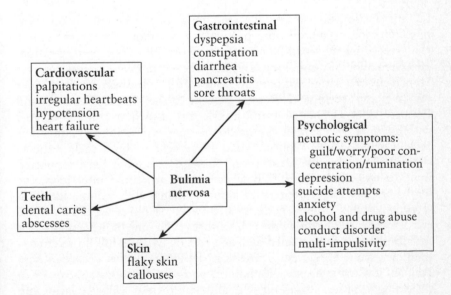

Figure 10.4   Possible consequences of bulimia nervosa

Physical complications

The mortality rate for bulimia is much lower than for anorexia and is estimated at between 1 and 3 percent (Keel and Mitchell, 1997). Those bulimics that do die from an eating-related disorder appear to have received a diagnosis of anorexia at some time in their history (Herzog et al., 2000). In the main, bulimia is not associated with mortality, but bulimics do suffer a wide range of physical complications. Many complications parallel those of anorexia and are due to nutritional deficits and the movement of stomach acid caused by the binge/purge cycle. Such problems are exacerbated by the disturbance of bodily fluids caused by laxative and diuretic abuse. For example, bulimics show cardiovascular problems such as palpitations, irregular and missed heartbeats, hypotension, and sometimes heart failure. They also suffer from gastrointestinal problems including dyspepsia, constipation, diarrhea, pancreatitis, may have sore throats, and often have dental caries and abscesses. They show muscle cramps and have skin problems such as dry flaky skin and callouses on the backs of their hands and fingers from induced vomiting (Treasure and Szmukler, 1995).

Psychological complications

Bulimia is also associated with a wide range of psychological complications. Neurotic symptoms are particularly common. For example, one study reported that pathological guilt, worrying, poor concentration, obsessional ideas, rumination, and nervous tension were present in over 80 percent of a sample of patients, and that hopelessness and inefficient thinking were present in over 60 percent of the sample (Fairburn and Cooper, 1984). Depression and anxiety are also frequently associated with bulimia. For example, in the original paper describing bulimia nervosa, Russell (1979) reported that 43 percent of his female patients showed signs of severe depression. Subsequent studies have supported this finding. Using larger sample sizes and structured interviews, the lifetime rate of major depression among patients with bulimia has been reported to range from 36 percent to 70 percent (Piran et al., 1985; Laessle et al., 1987). These studies also show that at the time of presentation for treatment between one-third and one-half of patients fulfill the criteria for depression. However, depression does not always co-occur with bulimia. It sometimes precedes bulimia and at times follows the onset of the eating disorder, suggesting that although there is a close relationship between bulimia and depression, neither is simply a secondary disorder to the other. Suicide attempts are also high among patients with bulimia. Of Russell's patients, 11 out of the 30 had made a suicide attempt, and Hatsukami et al. (1984) reported a suicide attempt rate of 16 percent. Actual suicide rates have also been shown to be higher than in the normal healthy population (Favaro and Santonastaso, 1997). In terms of anxiety, the majority of bulimic patients report anxiety symptoms (Fairburn and Cooper, 1984). However, many of these symptoms appear to be related to the specific psychopathology of bulimia. For example, bulimics feel anxious about eating in public and getting undressed in a communal area, and suffer anxiety-related symptoms when thinking about food, weight, or shape (Cooper and Cooper, 1987). Bulimia is also associated with other less common psychological problems. In particular, rates of alcohol and substance abuse are higher in bulimics than in control subjects (Hatsukami et al., 1984; Bulik, 1987), and bulimia is also associated with borderline personality disorder (D.B. Herzog et al., 1992), conduct disorder, and stealing (Rowston and Lacey, 1992). It has also been suggested that bulimia is related to poor impulse control and multi-impulsivity, which may explain some of the behaviors associated with this condition (Braun, Sunday, and Halmi, 1994).

In summary, bulimia is more common than anorexia and is less likely to cause death. It is, however, associated with a wide range of physical and psychological complications, some of which may precede the eating disorder, others of which may co-occur or follow after a diagnosis has been made. The next main question to be asked concerns the causes of both anorexia and bulimia. The causes of these two conditions are dealt with together, as most theories of causality do not distinguish between the two.

Causes of Eating Disorders

Since the increased interest in both anorexia and bulimia, theories of their causation have proliferated. This chapter provides an overview of the theories which currently have most academic credibility, and focuses on both physiological and psychological aspects of causation, illustrated in figure 10.5.

It explores the problems with the different models, with an emphasis on the extent to which they explain the epidemiology of eating disorders. Although these theories are presented individually it is generally now recognized that a multidimensional approach to understanding the causes of eating disorders is the most productive (Szmukler, Dare, and Treasure, 1995), although what such a model would look like remains unclear.

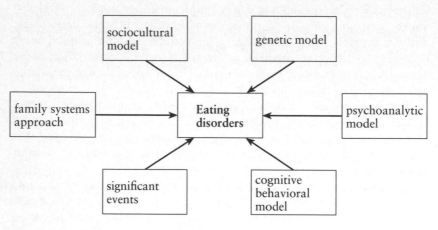

Figure 10.5 The causes of eating disorders

A genetic model of eating disorders

Some researchers have explored the genetic basis for eating disorders. This has involved an examination of family clusters and the use of twin studies.

Family clusters

Eating disorders appear to run in families. Strober et al. (1990) reported that female relatives of patients with anorexia nervosa were ten times more likely to develop an eating disorder than the control population. Strober et al. (1985) also reported that the risk of anorexia was increased among second-degree relatives of sufferers. Bulimia is also more common in families of patients with bulimia nervosa (Strober et al., 1990). Interestingly, the type of eating disorder appears to be specific, with anorexia being more common in families of anorexics and bulimia being more common in families of bulimics. Clustering within families suggests a role for genetics but cannot rule out the impact of a shared environment. Therefore, researchers have carried out twin studies using both monozygotic and dizygotic twins.

Twin studies

Twin studies are often presented as the "best case" method for determining the genetic basis to a given problem, as they purport to enable the separation of genetic and environmental factors. There are some problems which need to be considered. For example, zygosity needs to be determined accurately, the selection of twins is often difficult, particularly if the condition being studied is rare, and the sample selected must be deemed to be representative of twins in general rather than those twins with the condition under question. In addition, there remains the problem of the environment. It is assumed that the environment of identical twins is as similar as the environment for non-identical twins. However, it is possible that identical twins are treated in a more similar way than non-identical twins. Further, if adoptee studies are used it is possible that the environment of the adoptive family is still very similar to that of the biological family.

Given these methodological issues, research has addressed the role of genetics in the etiology of eating disorders. In terms of anorexia nervosa, research based in London using patients from two specialist eating disorders centers reported that 55 percent of identical twins were concordant for anorexia (9/16) whereas only 7 percent of non-identical twins were (1/14) (Holland et al., 1984; Crisp, Hall, and Holland, 1985). Further studies show concordance rates for identical twins of 57 percent (Schepank, 1992) and 45 percent (Treasure and Holland, 1989), and only 0 percent and 7 percent respectively for non-identical twins. This difference was even greater when the definition of anorexia was limited to restricting anorexia, thereby excluding those who showed bingeing behavior. For bulimia, the evidence for genetic factors is much weaker. For example, studies of bulimia have reported concordance rates for identical twins of 26 percent (Kendler et al., 1991) and 35 percent (Treasure and Holland, 1989), and 16 percent and 25 percent for non-identical twins respectively.

Therefore, the twin data provide some support for a genetic influence on anorexia, particularly restricting anorexia, but a much weaker role, if any, on the development of bulimia. How a genetic predisposition expresses itself remains unclear. Some researchers have addressed this issue and have pointed to the role of obsessive compulsive disorder, perfectionism, and body dissatisfaction as vulnerability traits (Treasure and Holland, 1995). This suggests that the genetic predisposition expresses itself in a greater tendency towards these factors, which then trigger anorexia. This conclusion remains tentative and as yet unsupported by an evidence base.

Problems with a genetic model

There are several problems with a genetic model of eating disorders which need to be considered:

- Eating disorders remain a problem of the West. A genetic model cannot explain why eating disorders do not occur in developing countries.
- Over the past few decades there has been an increase in the occurrence of eating disorders. This increase far outweighs any possible changes to the gene pool. A genetic model cannot explain this increase.
- The environmental differences for identical and non-identical twins is a problem for a genetic model.
- The environmental similarities for adoptee families and biological families is a problem for a genetic model.
- Eating disorders can be life-threatening problems. A genetic basis to a problem which can result in death does not fit in with the survival drive of either the individual or the gene which is central to genetics.
- A genetic model cannot explain how a genetic tendency is expressed.

A psychoanalytic model of eating disorders

There are many different psychoanalytic models of eating disorders. In general, such models do not aim to offer an all-encompassing model of causality to predict who will or will not develop an eating disorder, but offer a way of understanding the patient's experiences. Such models have two factors in common. First, they emphasize the meanings attached to the individual's symptoms and the function and need for such symptoms. Second, they emphasize the role of infancy and subsequent experiences in shaping the person, "so that when that person meets the possibility of being anorexic she clasps it to her emaciated breast and makes it her own" (Dare and Crowther, 1995b, p. 126).

The symbolic meaning of symptoms

The symptoms of eating disorders have been analyzed as being symbolically meaningful for the sufferer. Some work in this field has explored the interrelationship between the symptoms of eating disorders and aspects of sexuality. For example, vomiting has been considered an attempt to eliminate the unwanted penis of an traumatic sexual experience, fear of fatness has been analyzed as a rejection of pregnancy, and extreme thinness has been assessed as representing actual fear of death. Other theories address the meaning of food and hunger with an emphasis on control. For example, Dare and colleagues (Sandler and Dare, 1970;

Dare and Crowther, 1995b) argued that hunger reflects greed to the anorexic. They suggested that hunger is seen as an "invincible intrusive force" which must be resisted and that the more it is resisted the more it becomes desired and subsequently the more it is feared. Some theories also address the function of an eating disorder. For example, it has been argued that extreme food restriction functions to increase a sense of personal effectiveness by bringing about success in the area of food avoidance; and that weight loss functions to avoid the onset of sexuality by dieting away those aspects of the body associated with sexual functioning (Bruch, 1965, 1974). From a psychoanalytic perspective the avoidance of food has two central meanings. First it says "This is an area in which I am in control." Second it says "I am only a little child, I cannot live by myself, I have to be looked after" (Dare and Crowther, 1995b, p. 135).

The role of childhood

Some psychoanalytic theories have drawn upon a Freudian analysis of infancy and childhood. These have suggested that the preoccupation with food expressed through the preparation of meals for others and the ambivalent relationship with food reflect the oral sexual energies. More recent formulations of eating disorders have focused on parent–child relationships. For example, Bruch (1985) argued that children who are brought up to feel ineffectual may develop anorexia as a way to re-establish power within the family. Bruch suggested that this ineffectiveness may be particularly apparent in children whose mothers have anticipated their every need, have understood when the child was hungry, thirsty, or tired. Children brought up by apparently "perfect" mothers who are constantly aware of their child's needs may not be able to identify and understand their own internal states. Other research has argued that the binge/purge cycle shown by bulimics and some anorexics may represent a conflicting relationship between the sufferer and her mother, with the binge symbolizing the desire to be close to the mother and the purge reflecting a desire to reject her (Goodsitt, 1997).

In summary, a psychoanalytic approach emphasizes the function and symbolism of symptoms and the role of relationships developed in childhood.

Problems with a psychoanalytic model

There are the following problems with a psychoanalytic model of eating disorders:

- A psychoanalytic model can explain why those with eating disorders are predominantly women, and may explain why eating disorders are a problem for the West. These factors, however, are not explicitly addressed by the model.
- The model does not address what factors have changed over the past decade to result in the increased prevalence of eating disorders.
- Some psychoanalytic models describe symbolic meanings of symptoms which are considered to apply universally to all sufferers. For example, models which take a more Freudian analysis suggest that food means oral impregnation and fullness means pregnancy. This analysis does not allow for individual differences in the meaning of symptoms. More recent analyses, however, do emphasize personal rather than universal meanings.
- A psychoanalytic model explains the maintenance of a disorder but does not explain why childhood relationships are expressed through food avoidance. It is a model of perpetuating rather than causal factors.
- A psychoanalytic model is difficult to test and evaluate.
- The focus on the unconscious requires interpretation by the analyst. As with all therapies which involve interpretation, it remains unclear whether the psychoanalytic formulation is the therapist's or the patient's.

A cognitive behavioral model of eating disorders

Cognitive behavioral models of eating disorders draw on the central components of behaviorism such as classical and operant conditioning, and focus on concepts such as reinforcement, the stimulus-response process, and extinction. They then add the components central to cognitive theory such as beliefs, images, ideas, and attitudes. Models of anorexia and bulimia will be considered separately.

Anorexia nervosa

At their most basic, models of anorexia regard it as a behavior which has been learned and is maintained through a process of reinforcement. It is argued the individual reduces their food intake as a means to lose weight due to the social pressure to be thin. This behavior is then promoted by a wide variety of negative reinforcers. For example, being overweight or simply not being thin results in disapproval from others and a sense of unattractiveness, and food avoidance reduces the anxiety associated with eating and any accompanying weight gain. Aspects of food restriction have also been described as bringing positive consequences. For example, food avoidance produces attention, particularly from mothers (Ayllon, Haughton, and Osmond, 1964), having an empty stomach may be a pleasurable experience (Gilbert, 1986), starvation may result in the production of pleasurable brain chemicals (Szmukler and Tantam, 1984), and not eating may generate the positive state of feeling in control (Wyrwicka, 1984).

These essentially behaviorist models have been criticized for their focus on maintaining factors rather than causal factors and for the absence of antecedents (de Silva, 1995). Slade (1982) addressed the issue of antecedents and suggested a role for two important processes. The first involves a condition of dissatisfaction which derives from both interpersonal problems and conflicts within the family such as difficulties in establishing independence and autonomy, interpersonal anxiety, and the internal attribution of failure. According to Slade this dissatisfaction then combines with a perfectionistic tendency which reflects a desire for total control and total success. The two factors of dissatisfaction and perfectionism then trigger dieting behavior which is reinforced by praise and avoidance of eating-related anxiety as described above. This model addresses some of the problems with the behaviorist approaches. However, although cognitions are implicit within such models in the form of beliefs about weight and beliefs about the family, they have been criticized for omitting an explicit cognitive dimension (de Silva, 1995).

Researchers and clinicians such as Garner and Bemis (1982), Fairburn, Cooper, and Cooper (1986), and Bruch (e.g. 1974) include a more explicit role for cognitions. Central to these cognitive behavioral approaches to anorexia is their emphasis on the anorexic's faulty thinking about food, eating, weight, and shape which parallel Beck's work on depression (Beck, 1976). De Silva (1995) described the following cognitive dysfunctions as central to the development of anorexia:

- **Selective abstraction**, which involves focusing on selected evidence (e.g. "I am very special if I am thin"; "The only way I can be in control is through eating").
- **Dichotomous reasoning**, which involves thinking in terms of extremes (e.g. "If I am not in complete control I will lose all control"; "If I put on one pound I will become fat").
- **Overgeneralization**, which involves making conclusions from single events and then generalizing to all others (e.g. "I failed last night so I will fail today as well").

- **Magnification**, which involves exaggeration (e.g. "Gaining two pounds will push me over the brink").
- **Superstitious thinking**, which involves making connections between unconnected things (e.g. "If I eat this it will be converted into fat immediately").
- **Personalization**, which involves making sense of events in a self-centered fashion (e.g. "They were laughing, they must be laughing at me").

From this perspective the anorexic's food restriction is reinforced through pressures to be thin and the praise or concern that this brings. The high value placed on thinness and the fear of becoming fat is established and perpetuated through the anorexic's faulty thinking, which gets increasingly well established and is challenged less and less as the anorexic becomes more socially isolated. Within this analysis, anorexia is seen as a behavior which is learned through reinforcement and association, and established and perpetuated by cognitive dysfunctions.

Bulimia nervosa

Concepts from behaviorism have also been applied to bulimia in ways which parallel the models of anorexia. For example, anxiety-reduction models (Mowrer, 1960; Rosen and Leitenberg, 1982) suggested that vomiting and purging reduce anxiety, which reinforces this compensatory behavior. Like behavioral models of anorexia, this approach has been criticized for explaining only the maintenance and not the cause of the problem and for including cognitions only implicitly (de Silva, 1995). The first model to provide a coherent cognitive behavioral formulation of bulimia nervosa was by Fairburn, Cooper, and Cooper (1986), who described the following factors as central: low self-esteem, overconcern about shape and weight, extreme dieting, binge eating, compensatory self-induced vomiting or laxative use. The model was then extended in Wilson's cognitive-social learning model (1989). Wilson's analysis described the following five factors:

- **Cognitions** about weight, shape, and food, and dysfunctional thinking
- **Fear** of weight gain and becoming fat
- **Binge eating** followed by periods of food restriction which are facilitated by low mood, anger, or stress
- **Purging** involving vomiting, laxative abuse, or periods of excessive food denial

- **Post-purge psychological effects** involving two stages. First the individual feels both physical and psychological relief. Second they feel worry about the psychological and physical consequences, make promises never to do it again ("purification promise"), and then increase their dietary restraint.

This model parallels that of dietary restraint, described in detail in chapter 7, which emphasized the central place of periods of food restriction followed by violation of dietary rules (Herman and Polivy, 1975). It is also reflected in the "spiral model of eating disorders" (Heatherton and Polivy, 1991) which described the transition from dieting to dis-ordered eating through dietary failure, reduced self-esteem, and lowered mood.

The transition from dieting to eating disorders is illustrated by the bestselling *The Beverly Hills Diet* (Mazel, 1981), which described how Judy Mazel started dieting when she was eight years old and how by the time she was at high school she was "on everything; thyroid pills, diet pills, laxatives." Mazel developed an obsession with diuretics which could determine whether she gained or lost up to ten pounds in one day. She then discovered that eating only fruit could have a very similar effect, which forms the core of her diet. She advised: "Buy enough . . . five pounds of grapes on a grape day is not excessive," and boasted that "I can peel and eat a mango while driving a standard shift car wearing a white dress." However, these episodes of starvation existed purely to compensate for the inevitable binges: "I still eat a triple order of potato pancakes without choking, an entire roast beef without blinking an eye, a whole, extra rich cheese cake without a single gasp . . . so can you." Therefore, a diet aimed to cause weight loss was designed as a fruit diet punctuated by episodes of bingeing: "If you have loose bowel movements, hooray! Keep in mind that pounds leave your body in two ways – bowel movements and urination. The more time you spend on the toilet the better." As Wooley and Wooley (1982) stated, "The Beverly Hills diet marks the first time an eating disorder – anorexia nervosa – has been marketed as a cure for obesity." Further they said: "That training in anorexic psychopathology is selling so well holds a message . . . the figures mean that women are so afraid of fat they are no longer willing to wait for a safe, scientific method of weight control . . . the prevailing belief is that nothing is worse than being fat; that no price is too high for thinness, including health."

In summary, cognitive behavioral approaches have been used to explain both anorexia and bulimia. At their most basic they emphasize how the core behaviors of these eating disorders are established through the processes of positive and negative reinforcement. The more complex models include descriptions of antecedents, and some explicitly describe the individual's cognitive state.

Problems with a cognitive behavioral model

Cognitive behavioral models describe both cognitive and reinforcement factors as being important, and have face validity. There is also some empirical evidence to support aspects of faulty thinking and the effectiveness of treatment based on these models (e.g. Fairburn, 1981; see chapter 11 below). There are several problems with a cognitive behavioral approach to eating disorders, as follows:

- The behavioral models cannot explain how the eating disorder is caused, only how it is maintained.
- These models only describe cognitions implicitly.
- Many women show poor self-esteem, engage in dieting, and value thinness. Many women also show dysfunctional cognitions. A small minority develop an eating disorder. Cognitive behavioral theories can explain why eating disorders are mainly a female problem. They can also explain why they are a problem for the West, and why the prevalence has increased over recent years. They cannot explain why so few individuals develop eating disorders.

A family systems model of eating disorders

A family systems approach to eating disorders considers the family as a complex social system. It does not see the family as the cause of an eating disorder; rather, it emphasizes the family as the context within which the eating disorder is embedded (Eisler, 1995). Causality is seen as a circular rather than linear process, as the eating disorder not only develops within the context of a particular set of family relationships but also becomes part of these relationships (Eisler, 1993). Family systems theory has been informed by two main schools of thought, the "strategic approach" which draws on the work of Erikson (1964, 1975), and the "structural approach," which is based on the work of Minuchin (e.g. Minuchin, Rosman, and Baker, 1978). Although these two schools of thought emphasize different aspects of the family system and recommend different approaches to family therapy, they have the following four central tenets in common.

Symptoms as communicative acts

According to systems theory, symptoms arise out of disturbances within relationships (either a couple or a family) and are regarded as communicative acts between members of the system. Specifically, the symptoms are considered statements that something is wrong and are attempts to change any existing difficulty. Haley (1973) stated that a symptom appears when a person "is in an impossible situation and is trying to break out of it" (p. 44). The symptom replaces verbal language within the system.

The homeostatic family

The second basic tenet is that of homeostasis and the importance of equilibrium within the family system. The symptoms expressed by members of this system are regarded as mechanisms to maintain this balance. The problem is not, therefore, the symptom per se, but the difficulties that have arisen within the family system, generating a need for the symptom to re-establish balance.

Boundaries

A family systems approach also emphasizes the importance of boundaries between individuals within the family which are described in terms of proximity and distance. These boundaries denote "who participates and how" in the family, and delineate each member's "turf." They also indicate coalitions within the family in terms of close associations between individual parents and children.

Conflict avoidance

The final tenet of a systems approach is the role of conflict avoidance. It is argued that some families avoid conflict, and that symptoms may arise within such families as a means to distract from any ongoing conflict and to facilitate conflict avoidance as the family's way of functioning. Research has addressed the issue of conflict within the context of "expressed emotion," which has been mainly used within the literature on psychosis. It has been argued that low levels of critical comments within the family may be a reflection of lowered expressed emotion (e.g. Dare et al., 1994).

These four components of family systems theory have been applied to eating disorders. For example, Selvini Palazzoli described how the anorexic family is often extremely close, with blurred intergenerational boundaries (e.g. Selvini Palazzoli, 1974). She also described how the family avoids conflict and has a need for a compliant perfect child. Within this framework the symptoms of anorexia are regarded as expressions of the conflict within the family and an attempt to resolve the family's problems. Minuchin also applied family systems theory to eating disorders. He described the "psychosomatic family" and suggested that anorexia nervosa is a prime example of such a system (Minuchin, Rosman, and Baker, 1978). Minuchin's model of eating disorders has three factors:

- The child is physiologically vulnerable (although this is unspecified).
- The family has four essential characteristics: enmeshment (an extreme form of overinvolvement and intimacy), overprotectiveness (an extreme level of concern), rigidity (a determination to maintain the status quo), and a lack of conflict resolution (families avoid conflict or are in a permanent state of chronic conflict).
- The anorexic child plays an important role in conflict avoidance, which reinforces the child's symptoms.

In line with this a child may develop anorexia within a family which has blurred boundaries and which shows conflict avoidance as a means of maintaining the homeostasis of the family system.

Problems with a family systems model

There are several problems with a family systems analysis, as follows:

- Clinicians and researchers working from a family systems perspective state that they do not blame the family for the development of an eating disorder. Implicit within this approach, however, is a sense that the problem was caused by the way in which the family functions. Further, therapy based on this analysis focuses on changing the way the family functions as a means to reduce the anorexic's symptoms. Blame and responsibility may be detrimental to the patient's health.
- A family systems approach is useful for explaining the onset of eating disorders during adolescence when the individual is still embedded within her family, but some cases of anorexia and many cases of bulimia start after the individual has left home and has

established herself as an independent adult. A family systems approach is less effective at explaining later-onset problems.

• The central tenets of a family systems approach explain why an individual may develop psychological problems. They do not, however, explain why an individual develops an eating disorder rather than depression, or anxiety-related problems.

• A family systems approach can explain why most individuals with eating disorders are women and why this is a problem for the West. It does not explain what has changed over the past few decades to result in the increased prevalence of eating disorders.

A sociocultural model of eating disorders

A sociocultural model of eating disorders places the anorexic or bulimic patient within their social context and analyzes eating disorders as an expression of social values. Some writers in this field draw upon the work of Yap (1951) and Devereux (1980a and b), and describe eating disorders as a "culture bound syndrome" or an "ethnic disorder." From this perspective, eating disorders are considered expressions of anxieties and unresolved problems within a given culture, and as described by Gordon (2000) "one cannot understand the proliferation of these conditions in the contemporary era without an analysis of the broader sociocultural framework in which they occur" (p. vi). This approach also reflects the work of psychotherapists and writers who draw upon a feminist perspective. Such work focuses its explanation on why those with eating disorders are mostly young women and emphasizes the role of women within society. A sociocultural model regards eating disorders as the product of a series of conflicts which are expressed through a socially sanctioned pathway relating to the meanings of size and food. This is illustrated in figure 10.6.

Gender

The main conflict considered to contribute to the development of eating disorders is the conflict between a traditional female gender role of nurturer, mother, and carer, and the expectations placed upon a woman in a modern society. In line with this, Gordon (2000) argued that "anorexia nervosa expresses symptomatically the contradictions of female identity of the present" (p. 12) and that "the politics of eating disorders ultimately revolves around the politics of gender" (p. 214). He also

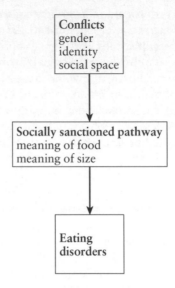

Figure 10.6   A sociocultural model of eating disorders

stated that "It is the multiplicity of role demands, many of which seem to conflict with one another, which makes the contemporary situation for women so difficult" (p. 111). Some empirical work has addressed this conflict. At times this work has suggested that adopting a traditionally feminine role may be protective. For example, Silverstein, Peterson, and Perdue (1986) showed that women with non-traditional sex-role aspirations were twice as likely to binge or purge as their more traditional counterparts. In direct contrast, however, Klingenspor (1994) reported that disordered eating was associated with low scores for psychological masculinity, and Brown, Cross, and Nelson (1990) concluded that bulimic behaviors were associated with femininity. Some researchers have therefore argued that it is not ignoring the conflict and being either feminine or masculine which relates to eating disorders, but an awareness of the conflict and a resulting tension and stress. For example, Thornton, Leo, and Alberg (1991) concluded from their study of undergraduates in the US that "superwoman syndrome," which describes attempts to conform to both traditional and non-traditional stereotypes, was predictive of disordered eating. Similarly, Martz, Handley, and Eisler (1995) found that women with disordered eating reported feeling both committed to a feminine gender role and dissatisfied that they were not meeting their own expectations. From this perspective the conflict between attempting to conform to a traditional gender role and fulfilling the expectations of living in a more modern world may contribute to the development of an eating disorder.

The role of gender has also been addressed by the feminist and psychotherapeutic literature. For example, Orbach (1986) stated that "A dominant motif for all the anorexic women I have worked with is thinness as ultra feminine and at the same time, thinness as a rejection of femininity. In other words two exaggerated and oppositional responses, each representing an attempt to negotiate an individual's identity, operate simultaneously" (p. 85).

Identity

Closely related to the conflict over gender is one relating to a sense of identity. This encompasses conflicts concerning being an adult versus being a child, and being dependent versus being independent. These conflicts can occur across the lifespan, when children leave home, or when career decisions need to be made, but most often occur in young adulthood, the time when the onset of eating disorders is most common. Erikson (1964) described identity as a sense of self-cohesion and the sense of continuity and sameness in time. In line with this analysis, Gordon (2000) argued that the "process of identity formation is particularly susceptible to disruption by radical changes in social roles or cultural expectations" and that the changes in cultural expectations which have affected women over the past few decades make them "highly susceptible to epidemic symptoms of identity confusion" (p. 96). Lawrence (1984) also focused on the importance of identity and described the role of "identity crises" and conflicts concerned with the development of a sense of self. She argued that "an identity crisis occurs when we feel in a great deal of conflict about who we are both as individual separate people and about where we stand in relation to other people" (p. 49). She then provided examples from several women with whom she has worked who had developed anorexia. For example, Suzanne "no longer had the demands of a young family to cope with and had to confront herself for the first time as an adult in her own right." She therefore "distinguished herself only by the fact that she was exceptionally thin" (p. 48). In parallel, Marjorie had been a success at college but when she left college "she had a real crisis about her own autonomy and felt completely unable to lead an independent and grown up life" (p. 48). Marjorie's eating rituals are described as giving "her days a kind of focus which they seemed to lack without them" (p. 48). From this analysis, the conflict over identity can result in identity crises and feelings of being out of control, which are expressed in a drive for thinness and the rejection of food.

Space and invisibility

The next conflict which has been hypothesized to relate to eating disorders is one between space and invisibility. Orbach (1978, 1986) argued that "a smaller body size for women was being proposed just at that moment in history when women were . . . 'demanding more space' " (p. 75). She also suggested that becoming smaller can actually create a sense of power. For example, she cited the case of a nurse called Audrey, for whom "the slimness she achieved with her anorexia made her feel that she was presenting the image of someone who was just a 'slip of a thing'," and described how this contrasted with an ability to disarm the "bureaucratic and thoughtless" hospital authorities: "They never anticipated that this urchin like figure would be tough and demanding" (p. 85). Audrey "looked impish, even childlike, but she was strong" (p. 85). Orbach therefore argued that the eating disorder was an expression of the conflict between taking up space and becoming invisible, which results in a sense of control over the outside and inside world.

In summary, from a sociocultural perspective eating disorders are seen as an expression of a series of conflicts concerning gender, identity, and social space. The consequence of these conflicts is a sense of loss of control which expresses itself in thinness and the rejection of food. This process of expression is through the socially sanctioned pathway offered by the meanings of size and food.

The socially sanctioned pathway

Conflicts over gender, identity, and space result in a sense of loss of control, and could be expressed in a variety of ways. They could make an individual depressed, withdrawn, and isolated, or anxious and having panic attacks, or angry and frustrated. So why would they stop eating and want to become thin? From a sociocultural perspective these conflicts express themselves in ways which are meaningful and can be understood within a given culture. Using the analysis of an ethnic disorder, Devereux stated that patterns of psychopathology within a culture are "patterns of misconduct" which are socially understood. He argued that a culture says "Don't go crazy, but if you do, you must behave as follows" (1980a, p. 42). Likewise, Gordon (2000) argued that "the deviant behaviour patterns that become prevalent in a society tend to follow particular models or templates that are immediately and widely recognized by members of the culture" (p. 166). In line with this analysis, conflicts of gender, identity, and social space are expressed through disordered eating because of the social meanings associated with thinness and food. The media representations of women, with their emphasis on thinness as attractiveness and the associated meanings of control, freedom, and success, provide a forum for expression of these conflicts (see chapter 5). As Dana argued (1987), "being a certain body size means something very important in a woman's inner world. It expresses for her messages she is unable to express in words" (p. 46). Acquiring a thin body allows the conflicts to be expressed. Furthermore, the central part that food plays in women's lives, with its associated meanings of conflict, power, love, pleasure, and caring, provides the vehicle through which the conflicts can be managed and thinness can be attained (see chapters 4 and 5). In refusing food, Dana (1987) argued, "the anorexic woman has totally abolished the needy part of her. She pretends it does not exist: she does not need people, she does not need relationships . . . She does not even need food" (p. 58); the "refusal of food symbolises a much larger statement she is making which is the only way she [has] found to say 'no'" (p. 57). Food refusal and becoming thin express the conflicts in a way that has been socially sanctioned by the social meanings attached to size and food. As Gordon (2000) stated, becoming thin and food avoidance are the "vocabulary of discomfort" (p. 214) for women at this time.

In summary, a sociocultural model of eating disorders places the individual suffering from either anorexia or bulimia within their social context, with a particular emphasis on the conflicts arising from their environment. In particular, it argues that individuals experience a series of conflicts concerned with gender, identity, and social space which generate a sense of being out of control. It also indicates that these conflicts are expressed through the socially sanctioned pathway offered by the meanings of thinness and food.

Problems with a sociocultural model

A sociocultural model of eating disorders makes intuitive sense, as it can explain why most individuals with eating disorders are female and why onset is usually during late adolescence. It can also explain why eating disorders have become more common over recent years and why they remain a Western problem. There are some problems with this analysis.

- Most women in the West are confronted with conflicts concerning their gender, identity, and social space.
- They are also exposed to images of thin women and have a complex relationship with food.
- A sociocultural model can explain why so many women diet (see chapter 7).
- It can also explain why so many women are dissatisfied with their body shape (see chapter 6).
- The main problem with this analysis is that it cannot explain why only a minority of women develop eating disorders.

Significant events as a trigger

Some researchers have explored the extent to which specific life events can act as triggers to the development of an eating disorder. The two most commonly studied life events which will be considered here are childhood sexual abuse and parental loss.

Childhood sexual abuse

Many patients with eating disorders disclose sexual abuse during the treatment process. The publication of case studies on individual patients reporting sexual abuse led to the study of the possible role of childhood sexual abuse in triggering eating disorders (Crisp, 1984; Goldfarb, 1987). This literature was reviewed by Connors and Morse (1993). They examined clinic-based studies, and reported rates of sexual abuse in eating disordered patients of 29.5 percent (Oppenheimer et al., 1985), 28.5 percent (Root and Fallon, 1988), 34.4 percent (Bulik, Sullivan, and Rorty, 1989), 50 percent (Hall et al., 1989), and 30 percent (Steiger and Zanko, 1990). They also reviewed community-based studies and reported rates of 58 percent (Calan and Slade, 1989), 13 percent (Bailey and Gibbons, 1989), and 23 percent (Smolak, Levine, and Sullins, 1990). These studies used a range of definitions of sexual abuse and defined eating disorders using different assessment tools. Following their analysis of the data, Connors and Morse (1993) concluded that about 30 percent of individuals with an eating disorder have been sexually abused in childhood. They suggested that this prevalence is similar to that found in non–eating-disordered women, but lower than that reported by other psychiatric patients. Connors and Morse (1993) concluded that "child sexual abuse is neither necessary nor sufficient for the development of an eating disorder" (p. 9), but suggested that childhood sexual abuse is "best considered a risk factor in a biopsychosocial etiological model of eating disorders" (p. 1).

Parental loss

Research has also addressed the extent to which parental loss through either separation or death can trigger an eating disorder. Most research, however, indicates that although such a theory of etiology has face validity, it is not supported by the evidence. For example, Rastam and Gillberg (1991) explored the prevalence of death or family break-up in the families of eating disordered patients compared to controls and found no difference. This was supported by the findings of Dolan, Lacey, and Evans (1990) and Kendler et al. (1992). In contrast to these results, Schmidt, Tiller, and Treasure (1993) reported an association between loss and the development of bulimia (not anorexia) if the meaning of loss was expanded to include parental separation, death of a parent, or being sent to boarding school. Rastam and Gillberg (1991) also reported a relationship between loss and the development of an eating disorder, in this case anorexia, if the definition of loss was expanded to include deaths in the immediate family, including those that had happened prior to the onset of the disorder. The authors suggested that the mechanism for this may be unresolved grief; however, the study did not test this hypothesis.

Research has, therefore, addressed the extent to which childhood sexual abuse may trigger the onset of an eating disorder, and provides no support for this association. There is some tentative support for the role of parental loss if an expanded definition is used.

Problems for a significant events theory

There are several problems with this analysis, as follows:

- The evidence for individual triggers of eating disorders remains weak.
- This analysis cannot explain why eating disorders are a problem for women in the West and why they are more common now.
- It cannot explain why such triggers are translated into food avoidance and the desire to be thin.
- It cannot explain why many individuals experience triggers such as sexual abuse and parental loss and do not develop an eating disorder.

Conclusion

Anorexia and bulimia nervosa have received much attention over recent years from both the popular and academic worlds. Anorexia is characterized by weight loss and is associated with a high mortality rate and a range of psychological and physical problems. Most anorexics receive help in some form or another, as the problem is easily recognized. Bulimia is more common than anorexia, although how common is unclear since many bulimics remain unrecognized as the behavior can be carried out in private and may not result in any observable changes. Bulimia is also associated with a range of psychological and physical problems, although the mortality rate is lower than for anorexia.

Many theories have been developed to describe the causes of eating disorders, which vary in their emphasis. Genetic models focus on the physiological triggers to eating disorders, while a family systems approach, a cognitive behavioral approach, a sociocultural model, and a significant events model place the individual within their social context. For a family systems approach the most important context is the family, whereas for other psychological models the broader context consisting of social meanings and norms is also relevant. To date there is no one comprehensive theory which can explain the etiology of eating disorders. In particular, they have yet to satisfactorily address why most sufferers are young women, and even when they do focus on age and gender, they cannot explain why so few women become eating disordered.

Towards an integrated model of diet

Choosing a healthy diet is made complex by the social meanings of size and food which can result in weight concern. In particular, many women are dissatisfied with their body size and shape, resulting in dieting and subsequent episodes of overeating. Eating behavior is related to several problems. This chapter has explored disordered eating in the form of anorexia and bulimia. The treatment of these problems is the focus of the next chapter.

chapter eleven

Treating Eating Disorders

The previous chapter described the etiology of anorexia and bulimia in terms of six different theoretical perspectives. These were a genetic model, a psychoanalytic model, a cognitive behavioral model, a family systems model, a sociocultural model, and one focusing on significant events. At times models of etiology translate into a treatment perspective. For example, a psychoanalytic theory of the etiology of eating disorders forms the basis of psychoanalytic psychotherapy, a cognitive formulation results in cognitive behavioral treatment, and a family systems analysis results in family therapy. This chapter first describes the individual perspectives of these three treatment perspectives. Some etiological theories, however, do not translate into a treatment approach, and most treatment approaches involve an integration of the different perspectives. In addition, some individuals with anorexia are in a critical state and need treatment to get them back to a physically stable state. This chapter illustrates how inpatient treatment offers an integrated approach to the treatment of anorexia. Self-help groups for bulimia are also available, which draw on a range of the different theoretical perspectives described below. Other treatment interventions such as drug treatments and, more controversially, surgery are sometimes used, but are not commonplace and are not covered here.

This chapter covers:

- Psychoanalytic psychotherapy
- Cognitive behavioral therapy (CBT)
- Family therapy
- Inpatient treatment
- An integrated approach to treatment

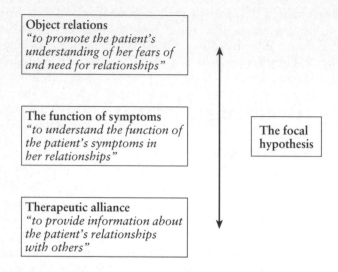

Figure 11.1   Focal psychoanalytic psychotherapy

Psychoanalytic Psychotherapy

The two core themes of a psychoanalytic model of eating disorders were described in chapter 10 as the role of childhood and the symbolic nature of symptoms. Dare and Crowther (1995a) have developed a form of "focal psychoanalytic psychotherapy" specifically for eating disorders, which is time-limited, standardized, and addresses these two core themes. This approach involves giving no advice about the individual's eating problems but focuses on the development of "the focal hypothesis" which hypothesizes an association between three factors' object relations, the function of symptoms, and the therapeutic alliance (Dare and Crowther, 1995a) (see figure 11.1).

Object relations

The term "object relations" is used within psychoanalytic psychotherapy to describe the "patient's internalised representations of the significant people in her past, and her relationships with them, these being, for the most part, family members" (Dare and Crowther, 1995a, p. 298). This therefore addresses the role of childhood. It is argued that patients with eating disorders often have a pivotal time-point when their relationships with others changed (this may be real or perceived), and that their inner world of object relations generates a fear of becoming close to others. Sufferers of eating disorders are also described as having a longing for an ideal relationship. This results in a conflict between wanting and not wanting closeness. The role of the therapist is to facilitate the patient's understanding of her relationships. The therapist aims to provide a forum for the patient to express her conscious thoughts and feelings and also to identify her unexpressed attitudes, feelings, fears, and wishes.

The function of symptoms

The second component of the "focal hypothesis" is the function of symptoms, and it is argued that the therapy should focus on "the use the patient makes of the symptoms in current personal relations" (Dare and Crowther, 1995a, p. 298). This addresses the second core theme of the symbolic nature of symptoms. It is argued that the symptoms of food avoidance and weight loss function to control and modulate the patient's relationships with other people. For example, the symptoms can transform the patient into a dependent needy person, one who cannot be expected to fulfill the normal expectations and demands made on a healthy person. The patient therefore fears weight gain, as it brings with it an expectation of coping and the assumption that emotional problems have been dealt with. The body is therefore used by the patient as her only form of communication to express her feelings. The role of the therapist is to be aware of these communications, to understand the function of the symptoms and their symbolic value, and to help the patient to find a way of putting these feelings into words. The patient is therefore encouraged to face her own feelings and describe them in words rather than to express her feelings through a degradation of her body (Dare and Crowther, 1995a).

The therapeutic alliance

Psychoanalytic psychotherapy therefore examines the role of childhood in terms of the early relationships with significant others, and focuses on "object relations." It also explores the function of symptoms in terms of their symbolic meaning and their impact on current relationships. Both of these factors are addressed with the context of the third component of the focal hypothesis, which is the relationship between the patient and therapist. This therapeutic alliance is central to any psychoanalytic approach, as it is assumed that "the patient's use of the therapy relationship will resemble her relationships outside the therapy room" (Dare and Crowther, 1995a, p. 298). This is described as "transference and counter transference."

Transference

The patient's internal object relations and the function of her symptoms impact on all of the patient's relationships, which includes her relationship with the therapist. The term "transference" describes the patient's feelings, attitudes, and behaviors towards the therapist. Transference for the anorexic patient can involve fear and suspicion of the therapist's proffered closeness, as the patient prefers the sensation of loneliness to neediness because the latter brings with it a fear of losing self-control and a sense of being taken over (Dare and Crowther, 1995a).

Counter transference

In response to this transference the therapist will experience his or her own emotions to the patient, known as "counter transference." As Dare and Crowther (1995a) described, these feelings often involve a desire to protect, indulge, and nurture the patient rather than "facing her up to harsh reality" (p. 304).

The two processes of transference and counter transference provide the therapist with information about the patient. The transference provides the therapist with an insight into the patient's relationships in the past and the function of her symptoms. The counter transference provides the therapist with information concerning how the patient has made others react to her and how she would prefer them to act. As the therapeutic alliance and the processes of transference and counter transference take place, the focal hypothesis concerning the patient's object relations and the function of her symptoms is tested, refuted, and embellished. This is considered the conscious part of the therapist's work. In addition, the therapeutic alliance also involves the development of a empathic, involved, and trusting relationship. The goal of psychoanalytic psychotherapy is, therefore, to encourage the patient to understand which feelings are being expressed through her bodily symptoms, to understand how her past relationships have influenced her desire not to express her feelings in words, and to facilitate the expression of her feelings in words rather than through her body.

Effectiveness of psychoanalytic psychotherapy

Psychoanalytic psychotherapy is often the main type of therapy offered to anorexics and some bulimics both through hospitals and therapy centers such as the Women's Therapy Centers in the UK (see Orbach, 1978, 1986; Lawrence, 1984, 1987). To date, however, there is only one small-scale study which has evaluated its effectiveness. This study involved a randomized control trial carried out at the Maudsley Hospital in the UK and compared focal psychoanalytic psychotherapy with family therapy, cognitive analytic therapy (CAT), and low-contact "routine" treatment (Dare et al., 2001). Patients were included in the trial if they were 18 years or older and fulfilled DSM-IV criteria for anorexia. They were excluded if they fulfilled the criteria for hospital admission (see section below on inpatient treatment). Of those recruited into the study (n = 84), 54 completed the full year of treatment (focal = 12; family therapy = 16; CAT = 13; routine = 13). The results showed that most patients had improved at the one-year follow-up, although some were still severely undernourished. In addition, those who received either focal psychoanalytic therapy or family therapy fared better than the control group who received routine care in terms of weight gain and the DSM-IV criteria for anorexia. This suggests that focal psychoanalytic psychotherapy can be used for the effective treatment of later-onset anorexics.

Problems with psychoanalytic psychotherapy for eating disorders

The problems with this approach are as follows:

- The treatment of anorexic patients using this approach does not always match up to the standards set by psychoanalytic psychotherapy. For example, some patients will have been committed under the Mental Health Act and therefore have had their freedom to choose the type of therapy removed. If the therapy is being offered as part of a hospital-based trial, then the therapist will also have had their right to choose patients removed. Furthermore, if the therapy is part of an outpatients clinic then it is likely that the room will not always be private, the phone might ring, and intrusions are likely. Finally, if the patient is still losing weight or at a low weight, her weight will need to be taken at the start of each therapy session, which may feel inappropriate to the patient given the therapeutic emphasis on her relationships and psychological well-being.

- Central to anorexia is a fear of relationships and closeness. Psychoanalytic therapy requires a close relationship between therapist and patient. This can cause patients to react against their therapist and refuse to engage in the therapy session.
- The therapeutic approach requires the patient to be motivated to engage with the therapist. Some anorexics have been committed under the Mental Health Act and they have therefore not volunteered for therapy.
- Anorexics see their food refusal and weight loss as the solution to their problem. Therapy aimed at food acceptance and weight gain (even if this is unstated) can feel more like another problem to the patient than like a solution.
- Ending psychoanalytic therapy can be difficult for the patient. If the patient has learned to trust the therapist and to believe that closeness need not lead to a loss of control, ending the therapy sessions can be perceived by the patient as yet another rejection, confirming her beliefs that relationships cause pain and are not worth engaging in.
- Evaluating the effectiveness of this approach is time-consuming, expensive, and difficult but a recent trial indicates that it is more effective than "routine" nonspecific care for adult anorexics.

In summary, focal psychoanalytic psychotherapy focuses on the role of family relationships with its emphasis on object relations and the function of symptoms. In addition, it explores how object relations and symptoms are expressed and integrated within the context of the therapeutic alliance between therapist and patient. There is some evidence that it is effective for adult anorexics, particularly when compared to routine nonspecific care.

Cognitive Behavioral Therapy (CBT)

A cognitive behavioral formulation of eating disorders involves two core themes. The first is the process of learning via reinforcement, which is reflected in the patient's behavior, and the second is the formation of dysfunctional cognitions about body weight and self-esteem. Cognitive behavioral therapy (CBT) is used extensively with bulimia nervosa and addresses the two central themes of behavior and thoughts. It has been used less widely with anorexia nervosa. Freeman (1995) described CBT for eating disorders in terms of a series of stages which apply to both group and individual therapy. These are parallel to those developed by Fairburn (1985) and Fairburn et al. (1986), and are synthesized below.

Stage 1: Assessment

The assessment stage involves taking a full history, making any phys-ical investigations, and excluding patients who have a marked suicidal intent or severe physical illness. Extreme emaciation will also preclude a patient from CBT, which may be offered once weight gain has started.

Stage 2: Introducing the cognitive and behavioral approaches

This stage addresses both the cognitive and behavioral components of eating disorders.

The cognitive model

The therapist will describe the basics of the cognitive component of CBT. Freeman (1995) described this in terms of:

- The link between thoughts and feelings
- Therapy as a collaboration between patient and therapist
- The patient as scientist and the role of experimentation
- The importance of self-monitoring
- The importance of regular measurement
- The idea of an agenda for each session set by both patient and therapist
- The idea that treatment is about learning a set of skills
- The idea that the therapist is not the expert who will teach the patient how to get better
- The importance of regular feedback by both patient and therapist.

The behavioral model

The therapist will describe the basics of the behavioral model in terms of three factors:

- **Breaking the cycle:** A discussion will be held concerning the cycle of dieting and bingeing, the psychological triggers to bingeing, the importance of eating regularly and frequently, and the cycle of purging and bingeing.
- **Principles of normal eating:** This involves a discussion of the nature of healthy eating, the importance of regular meals, the role of eating in company, planning meals, reducing weighing, and using distraction.

- **Diary keeping:** Diary keeping and self-monitoring is central to the CBT approach. This can be used to record food eaten and the time and place of any binges, and to monitor mood and feelings of control.

Stage 3: Cognitive restructuring techniques

Central to a cognitive behavioral approach to eating disorders is the role of dysfunctional cognitions. These take the form of automatic thoughts and automatic schemata. Cognitive restructuring addresses these cognitions. This involves:

- Explaining that "automatic thoughts" are automatic, frequent, believed to be true by the patient, and can influence mood and behavior. An example is "If I cannot stick to my diet I am a complete failure."
- Helping the patient to catch and record her thoughts in her diary.
- Challenging these thoughts and replacing them with more helpful ones. This involves the therapist asking "Socratic questions" such as "What evidence do you have to support your thoughts?" and "How would someone else view this situation?" The therapist can use role play and role reversal.
- Introducing the concept of automatic schemata, which refers to deeper layers of thinking around themes such as control, perfectionism, self-indulgence, and guilt.
- Challenging the basic automatic schemata using role play and Socratic questions.

Stage 4: Relapse prevention

This stage involves emphasizing that the skills learned during therapy can be used when therapy has finished, and that if relapse should happen the patient now has new skills to manage it. Further, in line with Marlatt and Gordon's model of relapse prevention (1985), the patients are taught to expect relapse and to plan for it by developing effective coping strategies.

Stage 5: Follow-up

The CBT described by Freeman (1995) involves 18 sessions of therapy with top-up sessions at 1, 3, 6, and 12 months. In addition, once CBT has finished patients are encouraged to continue some form of help, either in terms of self-help groups or group therapy through organizations such as The Women's Therapy Centre or the Eating Disorders Association.

Effectiveness of CBT

For bulimia nervosa

Most studies of CBT have explored its impact on bulimia, and the results show that it is more effective than drug treatment (Mitchell et al., 1990), more effective than cognitive restructuring on its own without the behavioral component (Wilson et al., 1986), and sometimes, but not always, more effective than behavioral therapy on its own without the cognitive component (Fairburn et al., 1993). It is not clear whether it is more effective than interpersonal psychotherapy. CBT seems to be more effective in the short term but not at the longer term follow-up (Fairburn et al., 1993). In general the results show that following about 20 sessions of CBT lasting up to four months, about 80 percent of patients show a reduction in the frequency of binges and about 35 percent have stopped bingeing completely.

For anorexia nervosa

There is very little evidence for the effectiveness of CBT for this problem. One study (Freeman and Newton, 1992) randomly allocated 32 patients with severe anorexia (BMI under 14) to receive CBT either as a day patient or during inpatient treatment. At three-year follow-up those who had been day patients had had fewer relapses, fewer readmissions, showed a more stable weight pattern, and reported better social functioning. This could indicate the effectiveness of CBT for anorexia. However, Freeman (1995) argued that "so many other factors were involved in the treatment packages that formal CBT may have been irrelevant" (p. 329). He therefore concluded that further research is needed.

Problems with CBT for eating disorders

The problems with CBT for eating disorders are as follows:

- Although it works well for bulimia it requires major changes before it can be applied to anorexia nervosa.

- CBT requires patients to be motivated to change and to engage actively in therapy by keeping diaries and providing feedback. Anorexic patients may be being treated against their will and may be poorly motivated.
- For anorexics, their emaciation is seen as the solution to their problems. A therapist who is attempting to facilitate eating and weight gain can be seen as another problem, not a solution.
- Anorexics have the automatic schemata addressed by CBT, but they may be so entrenched that the use of Socratic questions may not shift them.
- CBT does not address the role of family relationships and the impact of such relationships on current functioning to the same extent as psychoanalytic psychotherapy.

In summary, cognitive behavioral therapy addresses both the patient's cognitions through cognitive restructuring, and their behavior through the use of self-monitoring and information. It is assumed that changed cognitions will result in a subsequent change in behavior. It is also believed that behavior change will also promote a shift in cognitions. It has been shown to be particularly effective for bulimia but to date there is no substantive evidence supporting its use with anorexia.

Family Therapy

A family systems analysis of eating disorders emphasizes four central components: symptoms as communicative acts, the homeostatic family, the role of boundaries, and conflict avoidance. Family therapy addresses these factors by emphasizing the symptoms and the family dynamics. It does this using both individual and family sessions depending upon the age of the patient, and is mainly used for anorexic rather than bulimic patients.

The symptoms

During the early stages of family therapy the therapist will emphasize the dangers of food restriction and weight loss, insist that problems such as continued starvation, bingeing, and vomiting are self-perpetuating, and assert that such symptoms must eventually be eliminated (Dare and Eisler, 1995). In addition, for younger patients much family therapy involves asking the parents to oppose the abnormal eating patterns, to take control of the patient's calorie intake and bulimic symptoms, and to develop a feeding regimen that "compels the patient to eat more than her disorder would dictate" (Dare and Eisler, 1995, p. 345). This can be facilitated by describing how nurses bring about a change in eating behavior when patients are in hospital, and by emphasizing the problems which would arise if the patient were admitted into hospital. This approach can at times make the parents feel that they are being blamed for their child's problem, but it is argued that it can succeed in bringing about change "by a mixture of intensely focused sympathy, specific knowledge of the eating disorders and a powerful, sustained insistence that somehow, something must change" (Dare and Eisler, 1995, p. 346). These interventions address the problem of the symptoms and have been described as the "problem solving" component of family therapy.

Family dynamics

Family therapy also addresses family dynamics. At times relationships within the families of anorexics can be enmeshed and overinvolved. For older patients particularly, the therapist will encourage a change in these relationships and suggest that the patient become more independent by finding new interests outside the family. In addition, the symptoms of the eating disorder can come to dominate the family, creating a focus for the family and diminishing the role of other potential points of contact. Specifically, the symptoms can be seen as a "common concern" which holds the family together. A remission in the symptoms can feel threatening to the family as they have to learn new ways of interacting. The family therapist can address these issues by announcing any change in the place of the symptoms and encouraging the family to fill any opening space with new activities and new ways of relating to each other. Specific interventions used as part of family therapy include instructions, interpretations, and the facilitation of negotiations between the parents and between parents and children. Further, the therapist can facilitate a change in the dynamics by challenging and blocking any unhelpful interactions which occur within the family during therapy, supporting particular family members, and pointing out new ways of interacting. The aim of such interventions is described by Dare and Eisler (1995, p. 339) as the following:

- The clarification of roles and of communication
- The establishment of age-appropriate hierarchical organizations and boundaries within the family
- The encouragement of a clear alliance between the adults in the family for the sake of effective parenting.

This component of family therapy has been described as the "family systems" component.

Effectiveness of family therapy

The effectiveness of family therapy has been assessed involving patients who vary in the severity of their problem, and in comparison with a range of other interventions. One trial involved 80 patients (57 with anorexia and 23 with bulimia) who were randomly allocated to receive either family therapy or individual supportive therapy just before discharge from an inpatient unit. The results showed that family therapy fared better than individual supportive therapy for patients who had developed anorexia before 19 years of age and had had it for less than three years (Russell et al., 1987; Dare et al., 1990). This difference persisted at the five-year follow-up (Eisler et al., 1997). A further study showed that family therapy was more effective than individual therapy for severely ill patients a third of whom had been ill for ten years or more and who had an average age of 26 at assessment (Dare and Eisler, 1995). In addition, family therapy has also been shown to be more effective than routine nonspecific care for adult anorexics (Dare et al., 2001). An additional study, however, indicated that family therapy was not as effective as family counseling (reported in Dare and Eisler, 1995). Family therapy has therefore been shown to be effective for young and older patients with both anorexia and bulimia.

Problems with family therapy for eating disorders

The potential problems with family therapy are as follows:

- A referral for family therapy can be understood as a diagnosis which blames the family for the problem. Both patients and their families can be reluctant to accept such an approach.
- Patients may see the problem as their own, not the family's. They may see no need for their family to be involved in treatment.
- Parents are often keen to help in whatever way they can but may fear that the therapy will find them culpable.
- At times family therapy requires the patient to challenge existing ways of relating to and supporting individual family members as a means to shift the homeostasis within the family system. This can be experienced as threatening by the family and patient and if not carried out professionally can result in hostility to the therapist.

- For very ill, emaciated patients there may not be enough time to encourage them into family therapy, and hospital admission may be necessary.
- Some family boundaries may be so enmeshed and the family so overinvolved with the problem that time away from the family can be helpful.

In summary, family therapy addresses the patient's symptoms through information, problem solving, and family dynamics, using the strategies of family systems theory. These include being challenging, and blocking and facilitating communication. Getting patients and their families to agree to family therapy can be problematic, as it is often regarded as a diagnosis that the family was to blame. Evidence, however, indicates that it can be a successful approach for treating both adolescent and adult anorexics.

This chapter has explored the ways in which individual theories of etiology can be translated into treatment approaches. These approaches are mostly carried out without the patient being admitted to a hospital. At times, however, individuals become so emaciated, dehydrated, and ill that admission to a hospital is necessary. This chapter will now explore the processes involved in the inpatient treatment of anorexia nervosa, which often reflects an integration of several aspects of the treatment approaches described above.

Inpatient Treatment

The main reason for treating eating-disordered patients as inpatients is weight restoration. The large majority of inpatients, therefore, are anorexic rather than bulimic, although many also show bulimic symptoms. Treasure, Todd, and Szmukler (1995) described the grounds for admission to a hospital as including the following physical indications:

- BMI below 13.5 or a rapid decrease in weight of more than 20 percent in six months
- Lowered blood sugars
- Cardiac irregularities
- Muscle weakness
- Impaired blood clotting
- Risk of suicide
- Intolerable family situation
- Social isolation
- Failure of outpatient treatment.

Fewer patients are currently admitted to a hospital than ten years ago, but inpatient treatment is still regarded as necessary if weight restoration is essential.

Central to the inpatient treatment of anorexia is nursing care which focuses on two factors: the development of a therapeutic alliance between nurse and patient, and weight restoration. Inpatient treatment draws on aspects of the therapeutic perspectives described in the previous sections.

The therapeutic alliance

Patients with anorexia have an overwhelming desire to lose weight and to avoid eating even though their bodies are telling them to eat. Given that the main goal of inpatient treatment is weight restoration, developing a therapeutic relationship between patient and nurse can be difficult. Central to this relationship is the establishment of trust, a belief by the patient that the nurse is on their side, and a sense that the relationship is about collaboration. This is developed by the nurse asking respectful questions of the patient, keeping the patient informed about the aims and structure of the ward, and by the nurse interpreting any deceit and aggression as part of the illness, not as a personal assault. The nurse also needs to be firm and consistent in the insistence that the patient's behavior must change. Once a trusting relationship has been developed, this alliance can be used as the forum for some of the therapeutic interventions described in the previous sections. For example, the nurse may use cognitive restructuring skills such as searching for evidence and asking Socratic questions of the patients. It is also becoming common for nurses to use motivational interviewing, which is derived from Stages of Change theory (Prochaska and DiClemente, 1984). This theory describes individuals as being in a particular stage in their determination to change their behavior, and is a dynamic model as it illustrates how people move from stage to stage both away and towards behavior change (see figure 11.2). Using a stages of change approach involves the nurse eliciting where the patient is in terms of their desire to change their behavior, accessing the patient's perceived obstacles to changing their behavior, and asking them about the pros and cons of not eating and eating. In particular, within the context of both cognitive restructuring and motivational interviewing the nurse may address the meanings associated with food avoidance, being thin, and the implications of weight gain.

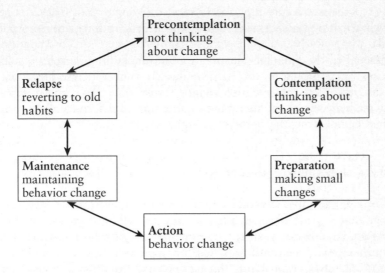

Figure 11.2   The Stages of Change model (*Source*: after J.O. Prochaska and C.C. DiClemente, *The Transtheoretical Approach: Crossing Traditional Boundaries of Therapy*, Homewood, IL: Dow Jones Irwin, 1984)

Weight restoration

Starvation brings with it a preoccupation with food and cognitive distortions. It is also life threatening. Weight restoration is therefore essential to the health of the patient and to their ability to engage in other forms of therapy. Inpatient weight restoration involves encouraging the patient to eat regularly, to eat small meals and snacks, and to limit exercise. Food intake usually starts at about 1,000 kcals a day which is gradually increased to 3,000 kcals, and a target weight range is set according to the patient's premorbid weight, taking into account their age of illness onset. A weight increase of 1–2 kg per week is usually the aim, which results in an average admission period of between 12 and 14 weeks.

The process of weight restoration is achieved by utilizing many of the strategies described by the behavioral components of CBT. For example, meals are taken at a table with other patients and with the nurses. This provides the patient with support from their peers and enables the nurses to provide reinforcement in the form of verbal encouragement and praise. It also provides a forum for the patient to re-learn the pleasures of social eating and to model the normal eating behavior of the nurses. Communal eating also enables patients who are further down the recovery path to support the newer patients, which can facilitate self-esteem in the healthier patients and provide additional peer reinforcement for the less well individuals. It also enables the nurses to observe and comment upon abnormal eating behaviors such as rumination, cutting up food into tiny pieces, and counting food, and provides a forum for these problems to be discussed. Patients are also weighed regularly. Some clinics tell the patient their weight, which aims to build trust and active collaboration. Other clinics keep the patients' weight from a patient to minimize a preoccupation with weight and reduce any anxiety caused by weight gain. There is no evidence for the relative effectiveness of these two practices for anorexic patients (see chapter 9 for a discussion of weighing in general).

The structure of the eating regimen also helps towards restructuring the patient's cognitions. On admission to the ward the nurses will take complete responsibility for the patient's choice of food and the amount eaten. Negotiations about food will be kept to a minimum and nurses will take control of a patient's eating behavior. Many patients are determined not to eat but are being told to eat by their bodies. Handing over responsibility for eating to the nurses enables the patient to eat without feeling the panic of losing control. They can therefore continue in their belief that they are solving their problems and keeping control of their lives by not eating, while at the same time consuming food. Gradually, control over food intake is handed back to the patient once the patient begins to see that eating and any accompanying weight gain does not bring with it the anticipated catastrophic consequences. Accordingly, changes in the patients' behavior precede changes in their cognitions.

For a small minority of patients, behavioral strategies are not sufficient to motivate the patient to eat, which has triggered a debate concerning the right of the patient to refuse treatment and the use of forced refeeding. For example, some units resort to intravenous feeding or tube feeding, while others pursue the less coercive process of assisted feeding, which involves spoon-feeding a patient while she is restrained and comforted by a nurse. It is argued by some that anorexia is a conscious "hunger strike" (Orbach, 1986), a political statement and/or a way of coping within the family, and that the patient is therefore making a conscious choice not to eat. Within this framework it is seen as abusive to disregard this right and impose forced or coerced feeding. In contrast, the refusal to eat is considered by others to be part of the illness which increases with starvation, and the UK Court of Appeal ruled in 1992 in a case concerning a young girl, "anorexia . . . destroyed the ability of the sufferer to make a rational decision and Lord Justice Nolan said that the court had an inescapable responsibility to overrule J's wishes" (Roberts,

1992). For most specialized inpatient units the question of force feeding is avoided by effective nursing and the power of behavioral strategies. At times inpatient units may use more controversial techniques, particularly if there is a life-threatening medical emergency.

Effectiveness of inpatient treatment

The primary aim of inpatient treatment is weight restoration, and studies of its effectiveness indicates that inpatient treatment in a specialist unit is more effective than in a nonspecialized unit (Royal College of Psychiatrists, 1992), with an average weight gain of 12.7 kg versus 5.9 kg. Likewise, Crisp et al. (1992) reported that the standardized mortality for patients seen at a specialized inpatient unit was 136 compared to 471 for patients seen in an area without specialized units. Specialised inpatient treatment would seem to be effective in terms of weight gain and mortality. However, McKensie and Joyce (1992) reported from their five-year follow-up study of 112 patients in New Zealand that 48 percent were readmitted to hospital on more than one occasion after their first admission, and that those aged under 16 were even more likely to be readmitted. Crisp et al. (1991) also reported the results from a randomized control trial which allocated patients to receive either inpatient treatment, outpatient-based family and individual therapy, outpatient group therapy, or one outpatient assessment. Of the 80 patients recruited into the trial, only 59 patients took up their treatment, and the results showed no differences between the four groups in terms of global measures of outcome. Treasure, Todd, and Szmukler (1995) analyzed these negative findings and suggested that "A cynical interpretation would be that specialist treatment is unnecessary" (p. 278), but argued that the poor uptake rate makes the results difficult to interpret and that "randomised studies with minimal selection bias are required to establish good clinical practice" (p. 289).

Problems with inpatient treatment for eating disorders

The problems with inpatient regimens for eating disorders are as follows:

- Unless the patient is committed under the Mental Health Act, admission into an inpatient ward is voluntary. Patients who see their thinness as the solution to their problems will resist the offered treatment as it will be seen as a problem, not a solution.

- Inpatient treatments are useful for weight restoration when a patient is critically ill. Relapse rates are high once the patient leaves the hospital unless intensive follow-up outpatient care is given.
- It has been suggested that inpatient weight restoration may lead to depression and suicide if the weight gain is not accompanied by a sufficient change in cognition.
- It has also been argued that weight restoration might lead to the development of bulimia if weight is gained in response to nurse and peer pressure, as bulimic symptoms can enable the external appearance of recovery to be maintained.
- It is possible that prolonged inpatient treatment can provide a social network for the patient which is lost once they recover and leave the hospital. This may motivate weight loss to gain readmission.
- Inpatient care removes the patient from their family. If the patient's relationships with the family are not changed, then once the patient returns to their family these relationships may trigger relapse.

In summary, inpatient treatment for eating disorders mainly applies to patients with anorexia, and focuses on the development of a therapeutic relationship between nurse and patient and aims to restore weight. It draws on many different theoretical perspectives and although the therapy offered is not as intensive as CBT or psychotherapy, aspects of these approaches can be seen to permeate the practice of an inpatient unit both in terms of the therapeutic alliance and the strategies used to promote weight gain. In terms of effectiveness some evidence indicates that it is more effective when offered in specialist units, although to date there is a scarcity of research.

An Integrated Approach to Treatment

Some theories of the etiology of eating disorders can be translated into their treatment. For example, a psychoanalytic approach translates into psychoanalytic psychotherapy. This focuses on the role of childhood relationships and the function of symptoms within the context of the therapeutic alliance between therapist and patient. Likewise, a cognitive formulation translates into CBT with its emphasis on changing behavior through self-monitoring and feedback and changing cognitions through cognitive restructuring. Similarly, a family systems analysis results in family therapy, which emphasizes the symbolic role of symptoms and family dynamics. However, not all theories of etiology result in treatment.

Furthermore, most treatments involve a combination of treatment approaches. In addition, while the above interventions are mainly carried out on an outpatient basis, some patients require inpatient treatment. This focuses on the development of an alliance between patient and nurse and aims to restore weight. Some patients will, however, be exposed to a range of therapies as their problem persists. For example, given the high relapse rates and the prolonged nature of the condition some patients will have both outpatient and inpatient treatments, will receive both individual and group therapy, and will also become involved in self-help groups. At times therapy will be given as a means to keep the patient alive without any real hope of a complete cure. At other times the treatment approach will appear to be the one which has been given to the right patient at the right time and they will recover. Most patients therefore receive an integrated approach to their problem. For some this may be integrated in terms of the ranges of treatments given at any one time, but many will receive an integration of different treatments given across different times.

Towards an integrated model of diet

Choosing healthy food is a complicated process due to the social meanings of size and food. This can result in eating-related problems. Weight concern is one such problem, which takes the form of body dissatisfaction and dieting, and these contribute to both lowered self-esteem and overeating. They illustrate problems of a less severe nature which affect some men and the majority of women at some point in their life. Obesity is more problematic and is associated with a range of psychological and physical consequences, and although it is much less common than weight concern its incidence is on the increase. Much evidence suggests that obesity is not solely a disorder of eating. Bulimia and anorexia represent patterns of disordered eating which are of greater clinical significance and have more serious implications for morbidity and mortality. They remain, however, problems for the minority. This book has described the spectrum of eating behavior from healthy to disordered eating and has explored a range of factors which influence how and why an individual eats what they eat. Many common themes have run through the different theories and the different chapters. An integration of these different themes is the focus for the final chapter.

chapter twelve

An Integrated Model of Diet

Most areas of diet-related research are studied by different researchers, published in different outlets, and examined from different theoretical perspectives. This book has provided a detailed map of this vast literature and has described the spectrum of eating behavior from healthy eating through to eating disorders. To do so it has drawn upon disciplines such as psychology, nutrition, medicine, and sociology, and used both empirical and clinical evidence. This final chapter first provides a summary of the literature covered and presents an overview of the ways in which these different areas of diet relate to each other. Secondly, the chapter explores the themes and constructs which are common to the different theories, models, and studies which have been presented. Finally, the chapter examines the ways in which these common themes interrelate, and offers an integrated model of diet.

This final chapter covers:

- A summary of the literature on diet
- Common themes across the literature on eating behavior
- An integrated model of diet

A Summary of the Literature on Diet

The research and theories presented in this book could have been grouped in a variety of different ways. This book presented the work using a spectrum from healthy to disordered eating. This spectrum involved a progression in terms of two main factors. First, the areas covered reflected an increase in significance in terms of mortality and impact on

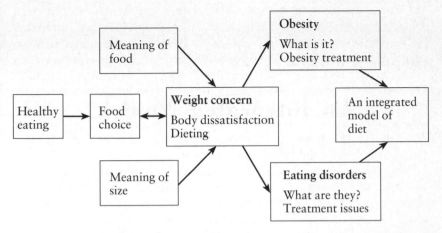

Figure 12.1   From healthy to disordered eating: A spectrum of diet

psychological and physical morbidity. In line with this, weight concern is more problematic than healthy eating but is less problematic than eating disorders. This does not mean that dieting does not have serious consequences, nor does it mean that body dissatisfaction is not unpleasant. But the spectrum used reflects an increase in clinical significance. Second, the spectrum reflects an increasingly problematic model of food intake, with an increasingly important role for the social context. Accordingly, the literature on healthy eating emphasizes health as the motivator, while the models of dieting and eating disorders emphasize the importance of the meanings of food and size. The spectrum is shown in figure 12.1.

The different areas of research and chapters of this book can be summarized as follows.

Healthy eating can be understood in terms of five food groups and is important for promoting good health, and treating ill health, after a diagnosis has been made. Much research shows that many people do not eat a sufficiently healthy diet. The research on food choice has been developed to try to understand why people eat what they eat. This research includes three major overarching perspectives. First, a developmental perspective emphasizes the role of learning through exposure, social learning, and associative learning. This literature emphasizes that although there are some basic inherent food preferences, food choice is the result of reinforcement and association, and given the right environment food choice can be modified and re-learned. Second, a cognitive perspective emphasizes an individual's beliefs and suggests that these beliefs predict behavioral intentions which in turn predict behavior. Important beliefs include behavioral control, subjective norms, and attitudes. The third perspective emphasizes an individual's physiology. Such an approach highlights the role for neurochemicals in hunger and satiety, chemical senses in food preferences, the psychophysiological responses to certain food, and the role of stress in eliciting food intake or food avoidance. These three perspectives are essential to understanding eating behavior. However, although at times they place the individual within their social context, they neglect the complex meanings associated with food and body shape and therefore cannot explain why food intake is so unpredictable and why it is associated with so many problems.

Food plays a central role within any culture and is loaded with a multitude of meanings. For example, it can express self-identity in terms of gender, sexuality, conflicts, and self-control. It can act as a form of social interaction and communicate love, power, and conflicts concerning health and pleasure; it can also communicate cultural norms in the form of religion or social power, and can delineate culture and nature. Body size is also associated with a range of meanings. For example, in Western culture while obesity means unattractiveness, lethargy, a lack of self-control, and low status, thinness means success, psychological stability, and control. Given this range of meanings, food choice becomes complex, as the decision to eat or not eat is influenced by the meaning of food and the meaning of any potential changes in body size. In line with this, many people show weight concern in the form of body dissatisfaction. In particular, many women are dissatisfied with their body size and shape; this may come from social factors such as the media, ethnicity, class, and the family which are translated into body dissatisfaction via a range of beliefs and the need for control. For many, body dissatisfaction results in dieting which, although aimed at eating less, often leads to overeating, weight variability, and weight gain. Explanations of the association between dieting and overeating have focused on the role of boundaries, mood, cognitions, and a reaction to denial. Weight concern in the form of body dissatisfaction and dieting illustrate eating-related problems which affect a majority of the population. Although they often cause lowered mood and self-esteem and may trigger overeating, for the majority they do not have clinically significant consequences. The problems of body dissatisfaction and weight concern illustrate how attempting to eat a healthy diet is more complicated than simply knowing what is healthy, and how the meanings associated with food and size can undermine any good intentions.

Obesity is another eating-related problem which does have clinically significant consequences, and although it still only affects a minority its incidence is on the increase. There is evidence for a strong genetic basis for obesity, but inheritance is not the complete story. There is also an important role for both diet and exercise. Although obesity is a common problem and interventions have been designed by a range of clinicians, the effectiveness of obesity treatments remain poor. In particular, although dieting can result in weight loss in the short term, weight regain is common. While exercise may not be as effective as dieting at promoting initial weight loss, it has greater overall benefits to health and may be more predictive of long-term weight loss and maintenance. Drug therapy and surgery may result in more success but can be accompanied by unpleasant side-effects. Success may also be predicted by the individual's beliefs about what obesity is. The problem of obesity exemplifies how healthy eating is made difficult by the context in which food in consumed.

Anorexia and bulimia are eating disorders at the far end of the spectrum. Although much rarer than weight concern and obesity, anorexia in particular has more serious implications for mortality and morbidity. Theories of what causes eating disorders highlight a role for genetics, family relationships, the function of symptoms, the role of learning and dysfunctional cognitions, conflicts arising from the modern world, and the need for control. Treatment perspectives address these aspects of etiology where possible. Eating disorders illustrate how attempts to eat healthily can be sabotaged by a range of factors and how the meanings associated with food and size impinge on an individual's eating behavior in the extreme.

From this analysis, therefore, diet can be understood on a continuum from healthy to disordered eating which increasingly places food intake within its social context. Common themes emerge across these different aspects of diet-related research. These will now be considered.

Common Themes across the Literature on Eating Behavior

Many themes have emerged throughout the literature on diet which are common across disciplines, areas of study, and the aspect of food intake being considered. These are described below.

Control

The theme of control permeates much of the literature on diet. At times attempted control is the solution to eating problems, and at others it is the core component of their cause.

- The food-choice literature shows that parental control over food can result in children preferring the very foods they are being denied.
- Attempting to limit food intake can result in stress, leading to overeating.
- Food results in a conflict for women between its preparation and consumption versus its denial.
- Food is used as a statement of self-control.
- Food is used as a statement of social control and a means to regain power.
- Being overweight represents being out of control while thinness signifies self-control.
- Body dissatisfaction is translated into dieting, as it is believed that the body is a controllable object.
- Dieting is the latest form of attempts to control the female body.
- Dieting aims for food control but paradoxically sometimes leads to overeating and loss of control.
- Eating control is presented as the solution to obesity.
- Imposing control over eating is the central problem for patients with eating disorders.

Family

Eating behavior takes place within a variety of contexts. One of these is the family setting. The theme of the family is apparent within a range of literatures.

- Food preferences are transmitted within the family from parent to child.
- Providing healthy and pleasurable food for the family symbolizes love and caring.
- The allocation of food within the family communicates the power relations and hierarchy within the family.
- Becoming thin can be read as a rejection of the family and of the desire to reproduce.
- Obesity runs in families, and prevention programs are being developed to target at-risk children.
- Not eating and thinness can be used to express problems within the family.
- The symptoms of eating disorders can function to keep the family together and avoid family conflict.

Cognitions

An individual's thoughts, beliefs, and attitudes are described throughout the literature on eating behavior.

- From a social-cognition perspective an individual's beliefs about food contribute towards their intentions to eat a particular diet, which in turn affects their eating behavior.
- Individuals hold a range of beliefs about the meaning of food.
- Individuals also hold a range of beliefs about the meaning of body size and shape.
- People believe that body shape can be changed and that dieting can bring about weight loss.
- Beliefs that dieting is an "all or nothing" phenomenon may contribute towards overeating.
- Overeating may be triggered by shifts in a cognitive set, with eating being either a passive behavior or an active rebellion against food deprivation.
- Many people show negative stereotypes of the obese and the overweight.
- People hold beliefs about obesity. Such beliefs may contribute towards the success of obesity treatment.
- Obesity treatment focuses on changing beliefs about food as a means to change behavior. In particular it uses cognitive restructuring.
- Distorted cognitions about weight, shape, and food may contribute to the cause and perpetuation of disordered eating.
- Treatment for eating disorders challenges distorted cognitions using Socratic questions.

Conflict

Eating behavior relates to many different conflicts. These conflicts both contribute to and result from eating-related problems.

- Food sets up a conflict between the pleasure of eating and the subsequent guilt.
- Food results in a conflict between eating food and denying food as a means to remain thin.

- Food results in a conflict for the providers between offering unhealthy food which is often desired the most, and healthy food which can be rejected.
- Eating disorders can be seen as an expression of gender-related conflicts between conforming to a traditional gender role or adopting a more modern gender identity.
- Eating disorders can be seen as resulting from conflicts concerning identity in terms of being either dependent or independent, or a child or adult.
- Eating disorders can be seen as reflecting a conflict over space in terms of being small or taking up social space.
- Eating disorders may be an expression of conflict avoidance with the family and function as a way to maintain the status quo.

Gender

Many aspects of eating behavior are gender related. At times gender issues can contribute to eating-related problems. Gender differences also highlight some of the mechanisms central to eating behavior.

- Women are the main providers of food for the family.
- Gender is central to many of the conflicts surrounding food, such as health versus pleasure, eating versus denial, and guilt versus pleasure.
- Women are portrayed differently from men in the media, with a greater emphasis on their bodies and less emphasis on their faces.
- Women show more body dissatisfaction than men, and size is more important to women's self-esteem than it is to men's.
- Women's body dissatisfaction mainly leads to dieting, whereas men take up exercise.
- Obesity is related to ill health, particularly if the fat is located around the abdomen. Most women's fat is located around their thighs and bottom, which has less serious health implications.
- The large majority of individuals with either anorexia or bulimia are women.
- The ways in which women are expected to look and behave may lead to weight loss and food avoidance being reinforced by others, thereby perpetuating disordered eating.
- A sociocultural model of eating disorders focuses on why it is so gender specific, and highlights a conflict over gender identity as core.

Social norms

Eating behavior takes place within a social context which offers a strong basis for what is considered normal and abnormal. These social norms are central to the creation and perpetuation of many eating-related attitudes and behaviors.

- Food choice and preferences are influenced by the eating behavior of important others such as parents, peers, and media images.
- Media norms of attractiveness influence what is considered the desirable body size and shape, and may result in body dissatisfaction.
- Family and cultural norms of both body size and eating behavior influence body dissatisfaction.
- Dieting has become the acceptable solution to body dissatisfaction through the impact of the media and the dieting industry. This norm perpetuates dieting behavior.
- Social norms of attractiveness contribute towards the discrimination and negative stereotypes of the obese and overweight.
- Media images of the obese contribute to the belief that obesity is a self-inflicted state which is caused by overeating. This perception influences the stigma both felt and enacted towards the obese.
- Peer influence and social support can be used to modify eating behavior in the obese.
- Thinness is a socially desirable state. Reinforcement of weight loss through praise and attention can perpetuate food avoidance in those with a tendency towards disordered eating.
- Food avoidance can be both a socially normal and abnormal state. Reinforcement can also perpetuate behavior in those with a tendency towards disordered eating.
- Peer influence and social support can be used to re-establish normal eating patterns in those with eating disorders.
- Modeling of nurses' normal behavior is used in the inpatient treatment of anorexics to encourage healthy eating behavior and attitudes.

Biology

Biological factors are central to many explanations of eating and eating-related problems. Biology influences eating behavior, health, and illness.

- Food is central to survival. A healthy diet consisting of the correct balance between the five food groups contributes towards good health, while malnutrition or an imbalance can cause illness.
- Dietary change is central to the treatment of illnesses such as coronary heart disease and diabetes.
- A preference for sweet foods and a dislike of bitter foods has been shown in newborn babies, suggesting that it is innate.
- The physiological consequences of eating, such as pleasure or illness, can influence subsequent food preferences.
- The chemical senses such as salt, bitter, and sweet impact upon food choice.
- Neurochemicals such as the catecholamines and serotonin influence hunger and satiety.
- Hunger and satiety are also affected by drugs.
- Foods such as carbohydrates and chocolate have an impact upon mood and cognitions.
- Stress can elicit eating behavior, perhaps via changes in stress-induced chemicals.
- Dieting can cause overeating, which results in changes in body weight and weight variability.
- Weight variability has been linked with coronary heart disease.
- Obesity is associated with illnesses such as coronary heart disease, diabetes, and cancer.
- There is evidence for a genetic basis for obesity. This might express itself through metabolic rate, fat cells, or appetite regulation.
- Drugs can be used to treat obesity by either reducing fat absorption or changing hunger.
- Research has highlighted a role for genetics in a predisposition towards anorexia.

Communication

Communication plays a central role in many aspects of eating.

- Food can be read as a statement about the self, as a form of social interaction, or as a symbol of culture.
- Thinness can be read as a statement of success, control, and psychological stability.
- Refusing to eat is a strong statement of power.
- Obesity and overweight are read as a sign of being out of control, a lack of success, and as illustrative of psychological problems.

- The symptoms of food avoidance and thinness are seen by a family systems theory perspective as a communication about a problem.
- From a psychoanalytic perspective thinness and food avoidance can be read as expressions of the need for control and feelings of neediness.
- The symptoms of eating disorders can be seen as an expression of a range of conflicts resulting from a modern society.

An Integrated Model of Diet

The literature on diet can therefore be understood in terms of a range of themes which permeate research on different aspects on diet, from different theoretical perspectives, and derived using different methodologies. These themes can be conceptualized in terms of an integrated model of diet which is illustrated in figure 12.2.

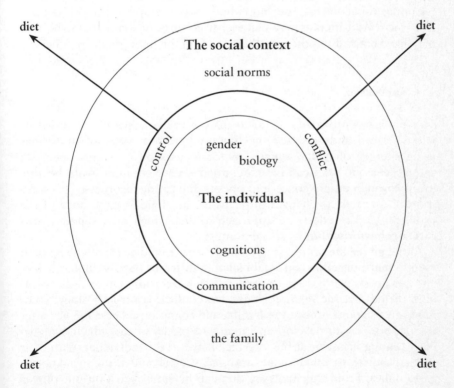

Figure 12.2   An integrated model of diet

Using this analysis the individual with their cognitions, gender, and biology are located at the core of the model and placed within the broader context of social norms and the family. In the interface between the individual and the broader context lie the themes of control, conflict, and communication, as these issues arise as the individual interacts with and is produced from their social world. This interface is central to the understanding of eating behavior. Food intake is not an individual behavior which occurs in isolation form the outside world. Nor is it driven solely by social norms and the family. Eating can be conceptualized as a product of the interface between the individual and their social world which manifests itself through the themes of communication, conflict, and control. In particular, as the individual interacts with their social world, food acts as a forum for communication about who they are and how they lie in relation to others. Food also generates conflicts for the individual and can be used to express conflicts to others. Finally, as the individual behaves and thinks within their social context they can experience feelings of being out of control, and food offers a forum for regaining this control. The individual may attempt to impose control over their food intake, may experience feelings of loss of control, and may have control imposed on their food intake upon them by others.

Conclusion

This book has provided a detailed map of the vast literature on diet. It has described and analyzed the literature from a range of disciplines using a range of methodologies which focuses on different aspects of eating behavior. Diet can be understood on a continuum from healthy eating through weight concern to obesity and eating disorders. This spectrum of diet reflects changes in terms of the clinical significance of the problem. It also reflects an approach to diet which increasingly places eating behavior within its social context.

Although the literatures, studies, and theories on diet are often explored by different researchers and published in different outlets, many themes and constructs can be seen to permeate this literature. On analysis, common themes emerge relating to gender, conflict, control, biology, communication, social norms, the family, and cognitions. These themes offer the opportunity to develop an integrated model of diet. Such a model places eating behavior at the interface between the individual (with their gender, cognitions, and biology) and their social context (the social norms and family). From this analysis, diet can be seen as arising out of this interface through the themes of control, conflict, and communication.

References

Abraham, S.F. and Beumont, P.J.V. 1982: How patients describe bulimia or binge eating. *Psychological Medicine*, 12, 625–35.

Abrams, K., Allen, L., and Gray, J. 1992: Disordered eating attitudes and behaviours, psychological adjustment and ethnic identity: A comparison of black and white female college students. *International Journal of Eating Disorders*, 14, 49–57.

Ahmed, S., Waller, G., and Verduyn, C. 1994: Eating attitudes among Asian school girls: The role of perceived parental control. *International Journal of Eating Disorders*, 15, 91–7.

Ajzen, I. 1985: From intention to actions: A theory of planned behavior. In J. Kuhl and J. Beckman (eds), *Action-Control: From Cognition to Behavior*, Heidelberg: Springer, 11–39.

Ajzen, I. and Fishbein, M. 1970: The prediction of behaviour from attitudinal and normative beliefs. *Journal of Personality and Social Psychology*, 6, 466–87.

Akan, G.E. and Grilo, C.M. 1995: Sociocultural influences on eating attitudes and behaviours, body image, and psychological functioning: A comparison of African-American, Asian-American and Caucasian college women. *International Journal of Eating Disorders*, 18, 181–7.

Alderson, T. and Ogden, J. 1999: What mothers feed their children and why. *Health Education Research: Theory and Practice*, 14, 717–27.

Allied Dunbar 1992: Allied Dunbar National Fitness Survey. A report on activity patterns and fitness levels. London: Sports Council and Health Education Authority.

Allison, D.B. (ed.) 1995: *Handbook of Assessment Methods for Eating Behaviours and Weight-Related Problems: Measures Theory and Research*, Newbury Park, CA: Sage.

Allison, D.B., Kaprio, J., Korkeila, M., Neale, M.C., and Hayakawa, K. 1996: The heritability of body mass index among an international sample of monozygotic twins reared apart. *International Journal of Obesity*, 20, 501–6.

Allon, N. 1982: The stigma of overweight in everyday life. In B.B. Wolman (ed.), *Psychological Aspects of Obesity: A Handbook*, New York: Van Nostrand, 130–74.

Anon. 1997: The prevention and treatment of obesity. *Effective Health Care*, 3, 1–12.

Archer, D., Iritani, B., Kimes, D.D., and Barrios, M. 1983: Face-ism: Five studies of sex differences in facial prominence. *Journal of Personality and Social Psychology*, 45, 725–35.

Arens, W. 1979: *The Man-Eating Myth: Anthropology and Anthropophagy*. New York: Oxford University Press.

Ashton, W., Nanchahal, K., and Wood, D. 2001: Body mass index and metabolic risk factors for coronary heart disease in women. *European Heart Journal*, 22, 46–55.

Astrup, A., Brunwald, G.K., Melanson, E.L., Saris, W.H., and Hill, J.O. 2000: The role of low-fat diets in body weight control: A meta-analysis of ad libitum dietary intervention studies. *International Journal of Obesity and Related Metabolic Disorders*, 24, 1545–52.

Attie, I. and Brooks-Gunn, J. 1989: Development of eating problems in adolescent girls: A longitudinal study. *Developmental Psychology*, 25, 70–9.

Axelson, M.L., Brinberg, D., and Durand, J.H. 1983: Eating at a fast-food restaurant – a social-psychological analysis. *Journal of Nutrition Education*, 15, 94–8.

Ayllon, T., Haughton, E., and Osmond, H.P. 1964: Chronic anorexia: A behaviour problem. *Canadian Psychiatric Association Journal*, 9, 147–57.

Bailey, C.A. and Gibbons, S.J. 1989: Physical victimization and bulimic-like symptoms: Is there a relationship? *Deviant Behavior*, 10, 335–52.

Baker, C.W., Whisman, M.A., and Brownell, K.D. 2000: Studying intergenerational transmission of eating attitudes and behaviors: Methodological and conceptual questions. *Health Psychology*, 19, 376–81.

Baker, P. 1994: Under pressure: What the media is doing to men. *Cosmopolitan*, November, 129–32.

Ballor, D.L. and Poehlman, E.T. 1994: Exercise-training enhances fat-free mass preservation during diet-induced weight loss: A meta-analytical finding. *International Journal of Obesity*, 18, 35–40.

Barker, D.J.P. (ed.) 1992: *Fetal and Infant Origins of Adult Disease*. London: BMJ Books.

Barthes, R. 1961: Towards a psycho sociology of contemporary food consumption. In R. Forster and O. Ranum (eds), *Annales ESC*, 16, 977–86.

Bates, C.J., Prentice, A., Cole, T.J., van der Pols, J.C., Doyle, W., Finch, S., Smithers, G., and Clarke, P.C. 1999: Micronutrients: Highlights and research challenges from the 1994–5 National Diet and Nutrition Survey of people aged 65 years and over. *British Journal of Nutrition*, 82, 7–15.

Bates, C.J., Prentice, A., and Finch, S. 1999: Gender differences in food and nutrient intakes and status indices from the National Diet and Nutrition Survey of people aged 65 years and over. *European Journal of Clinical Nutrition*, 53, 694–9.

Beauchamp, G.K. and Moran, M. 1982: Dietary experience and sweet taste preference in human infants. *Appetite*, 3, 139–52.

Beck, A.T. 1976: *Cognitive Therapy and Emotional Disorders*. New York: International Universities Press.

Beck, D., Casper, R., and Anderson, A. 1996: Truly late onset of eating disorders: A study of 11 cases averaging 60 years of age at presentation. *International Journal of Eating Disorders*, 20, 389–95.

Becker, M.H. and Rosenstock, I.M. 1984: Compliance with medical advice. In A. Steptoe and A. Mathews (eds), *Health Care and Human Behaviour*, London: Academic Press Inc.

Beecher, H.K. 1959: *Measurement of Subjective Responses*. New York: Oxford University Press.

Beeney, L.J. and Dunn, S.M. 1990: Knowledge improvement and metabolic control in diabetes education: Approaching the limits? *Patient Education and Counselling*, 16, 217–29.

Ben-Tovim, D.I. and Walker, M.K. 1991a: The development of the Ben-Tovim Walker Body Attitudes Questionnaire (BAQ), a new measure of women's attitudes towards their own bodies. *Psychological Medicine*, 21, 775–84.

Ben-Tovim, D.I. and Walker, M.K. 1991b: Women's body attitudes: A review of measurement techniques. *International Journal of Eating Disorders*, 10, 155–67.

Bennett, P., Moore, L., Smith, A., Murphy, S., and Smith, C. 1995: Health locus of control and value for health as predictors of dietary behaviour. *Psychology and Health*, 10, 41–54.

Beren, S., Hayden, H., Wilfley, D., and Grilo, C. 1996: The influence of sexual orientation on body dissatisfaction in adult men and women. *International Journal of Eating Disorders*, 2, 135–41.

Berenson, G.S., Srinivasan, S.R., Bao, W., Newman, W.P. III, Tracy, R.E., and Wattigney, W.A. 1998: Association between multiple cardiovascular risk factors and atherosclerosis in children and young adults. *New England Journal of Medicine*, 338, 1650–6.

Beumont, P.J.V., Beardwood, C.J., and Russell, G.F.M. 1972: The occurrence of the syndrome of anorexia nervosa in male subjects. *Psychological Medicine*, 2, 216–31.

Birch, L.L. 1980: Effects of peer models' food choices and eating behaviors on preschoolers' food preferences. *Child Development*, 51, 489–96.

Birch, L.L. 1989: Developmental aspects of eating. In R. Shepherd (ed.), *Handbook of the Psychophysiology of Human Eating*, London: Wiley, 179–203.

Birch, L.L. 1999: Development of food preferences. *Annual Review of Nutrition*, 19, 41–62.

Birch, L.L., Birch, D., Marlin, D., and Kramer, L. 1982: Effects of instrumental eating on children's food preferences. *Appetite*, 3, 125–34.

Birch, L.L. and Deysher, M. 1986: Caloric compensation and sensory specific satiety: Evidence for self-regulation of food intake by young children. *Appetite*, 7, 323–31.

Birch, L.L. and Fisher, J.O. 2000: Mothers' child-feeding practices influence daughters' eating and weight. *American Journal of Clinical Nutrition*, 71, 1054–61.

Birch, L.L., Gunder, L., Grimm-Thomas, K., and Laing, D.G. 1998: Infant's consumption of a new food enhances acceptance of similar foods. *Appetite*, 30, 283–95.

Birch, L.L. and Marlin, D.W. 1982: I don't like it; I never tried it: Effects of exposure on two-year-old children's food preferences. *Appetite*, 23, 353–60.

Birch, L.L., Marlin, D., and Rotter, J. 1984: Eating as the "means" activity in a contingency: Effects on young children's food preference. *Child Development*, 55, 431–9.

Birch, L.L., McPhee, L., Shoba, B.C., Pirok, E., and Steinberg, L. 1987: What kind of exposure reduces children's food neophobia? Looking vs tasting. *Appetite*, 9, 171–8.

Birch, L.L., Zimmerman, S., and Hind, H. 1980: The influence of social affective context on preschool children's food preferences. *Child Development*, 51, 856–61.

Blackburn, G.L. and Kanders, B.S. 1987: Medical evaluation and treatment of the obese patient with cardiovascular disease. *American Journal of Cardiology*, 60, 55–8.

Blair, S.N. 1993: Evidence for success of exercise in weight loss and control. *Annals of Internal Medicine*, 199, 702–6.

Blair, S.N., Ellsworth, N.M., Haskell, W.L., Stern, M.P., Farquhar, J.W., and Wood, P.D. 1981: Comparison of nutrient intake in middle aged men and women runners and controls. *Medicine, Science and Sports and Exercise*, 13, 310–15.

Blair, S.N., Kampert, J.B., Kohl, H.W. et al. 1996: Influences of cardiorespiratory fitness and other precursors on cardiovascular disease and all-cause mortality in men and women. *Journal of the American Medical Association*, 276, 205–10.

Blair, S.N., Kohl, H.W., Barlow, C.E., Paffenbarger, R.S. Jr, Gibbons, L.W., and Macera, C.A. 1995: Changes in physical fitness and all-cause mortality: A prospective study of health and unhealthy men. *Journal of the American Medical Association*, 273, 1093–8.

Blair, S.N., Kohl, H.W., Paffenbarger, R.S., Clark, D.G., Cooper, K.H., and Gibbons, L.W. 1989: Physical fitness and all-cause mortality: A prospective study of healthy men and women. *Journal of the American Medical Association*, 262, 2395–2401.

Blaxter, M. 1978: Diagnosis as category and process: The case of alcoholism. *Social Science and Medicine*, 12, 9–17.

Blundell, J.E. and Hill, A.J. 1987: Influence of tryptophan on appetite and food selection in man. In S. Kaufman (ed.), *Amino Acids in Health and Disease: New Perspectives*, New York: Alan Liss, 403–19.

Blundell, J.E. and Hill, A.J. 1988: On the mechanisms of action of desfenfluramine: Effect on alliesthesia and appetite motivation in lean and obese subjects. *Clinical Neuropharmacology*, 11, S121–S134.

Blundell, J.E., Hill, A.J., and Lawton, C.L. 1989: Neurochemical factors involved in normal and abnormal eating in humans. In R. Shepherd (ed.), *Handbook of the Psychophysiology of Human Eating*, London: Wiley, 85–112.

Blundell, J.E., Lawton, C.L., Cotton, J.R., and Macdiarmid, J.I. 1996: Control of human appetite: Implications for the intake of dietary fat. *Annual Review of Nutrition*, 16, 285–319.

Blundell, J.E. and Macdiarmid, J. 1997: Fat as a risk factor for over consumption: Satiation, satiety and patterns of eating. *Journal of the American Dietetic Association*, 97, 563–9.

Bolton-Smith, C. and Woodward, M. 1994: Dietary composition and fat to sugar ratios in relation to obesity. *International Journal of Obesity*, 18, 820–8.

Bordo, S. 1990: Reading the slender body. In M. Jacobus, E.F. Keller, and S. Shuttleworth (eds), *Body/Politics: Women and the Discourses of Science*, New York: Routledge.

Bouchard, C., Trembley, A., Despres, J.P., Nadeu, A., Dupien, P.J., and Formet, G. 1990: The response to long term overfeeding in identical twins. *New England Journal of Medicine*, 322, 1477–82.

Brabant, S. and Mooney, L. 1986: Sex role stereotyping in the Sunday comics: Ten years later. *Sex Roles*, 14, 141–8.

Bradley, P.J. 1985: Conditions recalled to have been associated with weight gain in adulthood. *Appetite*, 6, 235–41.

Brady, J.P. and Rieger, W. 1972: Behaviour treatment of anorexia nervosa. In *Proceedings of the International Symposium of Behaviour Modification*, New York: Appleton Century Croft, p. 57.

Brand, P., Rothblum, E., and Soloman, L. 1992: A comparison of lesbians, gay men, and heterosexuals on weight and restricted eating. *International Journal of Eating Disorders*, 11, 253–9.

Braun, D.L., Sunday, S.R., and Halmi, K.A. 1994: Psychiatric comorbidity in patients with eating disorders. *Psychological Medicine*, 24, 859–67.

Bray, G.A. 1986: Effects of obesity on health and happiness. In K.D. Brownell and J.P. Foreyt (eds), *Handbook of Eating Disorders: Physiology, Psychology and Treatment of Obesity, Anorexia and Bulimia*, New York: Basic Books.

Breckler, S.J. 1994: A comparison of numerical indexes for measuring attitude ambivalence. *Educational and Psychological Measurement*, 54, 350–65.

Brewerton, T.D., Hand, L.D., and Bishop, E.R. Jr 1993: The Tridimensional Personality Questionnaire in eating disorder patients. *International Journal of Eating Disorders*, 14, 213–18.

Brinch, M., Isager, T., and Tolstroop, K. 1988: Anorexia nervosa and motherhood: Reproduction pattern and mothering behavior of 50 women. *Acta Psychiatrica Scandinavica*, 77, 98–104.

Brodie, D.A., Slade, P.D., and Riley, V.J. 1991: Sex differences in body image perceptions. *Perceptual and Motor Skills*, 72, 73–4.

Brodie, D.A., Slade, P.D., and Rose, H. 1989: Reliability measures in disturbed body image. *Perceptual and Motor Skills*, 69, 723–32.

Broverman, I.K., Vogel, S.R., Broverman, D.M., Clarkson, F.E., and Rosenkrantz, P.S. 1972: Sex-role stereotypes: A current appraisal. *Journal of Social Issues*, 28, 59–78.

Brown, J.A., Cross, H.J., and Nelson, J.M. 1990: Sex role identity and sex role ideology in college women with bulimic behaviour. *International Journal of Eating Disorders*, 9, 571–5.

Brown, T.A., Cash, T.F., and Mikulka, P.J. 1990: Attitudinal body-image assessment: Factor analysis of the Body-Self Relations Questionnaire. *Journal of Personality Assessment*, 55, 135–44.

Brownell, K.D. 1989: Weight control and your health. In *World Book Encyclopedia*.

Brownell, K.D. 1990: *The LEARN Programme for Weight Control*. New Haven: Yale University Press.

Brownell, K.D. 1991a: Dieting and the search for the perfect body: Where physiology and culture collide. *Behavior Therapy*, 22, 1–12.

Brownell, K.D. 1991b: Personal responsibility and control over our bodies: When expectation exceeds reality. *Health Psychology*, 10, 303–10.

Brownell, K.D. 1995: Exercise and obesity treatment: Psychological aspects. *International Journal of Obesity and Related Metabolic Disorders*, Suppl. 4, S122–5.

Brownell, K.D. 1998: Diet, exercise and behavioural intervention: The nonpharmacological approach. *European Journal of Clinical Investment*, Suppl. 2, 19–21.

Brownell, K.D. 1999: The central role of lifestyle change in long-term weight management. *Clinical Cornerstone*, 2, 43–51.

Brownell, K.D., Greenwood, M.R., Stellar, E., and Shrager, E.E. 1986: The effects of repeated cycles of weight loss and regain in rats. *Physiology and Behaviour*, 38, 459–64.

Brownell, K.D., Marlatt, G.A., Lichtenstein, E., and Wilson, G.T. 1986: Understanding and preventing relapse. *American Psychologist*, 41, 765–82.

Brownell, K.D. and Napolitano, M.A. 1995: Distorting reality for children: Body size proportions of Barbie and Ken dolls. *International Journal of Eating Disorders*, 3, 295–8.

Brownell, K.D. and Wadden, T.A. 1991: The heterogeneity of obesity: Fitting treatments to individuals. *Behaviour Therapy*, 22, 153–77.

Brownell, K.D. and Wadden, T.A. 1992: Etiology and treatment of obesity: Understanding a serious, prevalent and refractory disorder. *Journal of Consulting and Clinical Psychology*, 60.

Brownmiller, S. 1984: *Femininity*. London: Paladin Grafton Books.

Bruch, H. 1965: Anorexia nervosa and its differential diagnosis. *Journal of Nervous and Mental Disease*, 141, 556–66.

Bruch, H. 1974: *Eating Disorders: Obesity, Anorexia and the Person Within*. New York: Basic Books.

Bruch, H. 1985: Four decades of eating disorders. In D.M. Garner and P.E. Garfinkel (eds), *Handbook of Psychotherapy for Anorexia Nervosa and Bulimia*, New York: Guilford Press.

Brumberg, J.J. 1988: *Fasting Girls: The Emergence of Anorexia Nervosa as a Modern Disease*. Cambridge, MA: Harvard University Press.

Bryant-Waugh, R. and Lask, B. 1991: Anorexia nervosa in a group of Asian children living in Britain. *British Journal of Psychiatry*, 158, 229–33.

Buckley, P., Freyne, A., and Walsh, N. 1991: Anorexia nervosa in males. *Irish Journal of Psychological Medicine*, 8, 15–18.

Bulik, C. 1987: Drug and alcohol abuse by bulimic women and their families. *American Journal of Psychiatry*, 144, 1604–6.

Bulik, C.M., Sullivan, P.F., and Rorty, M. 1989: Childhood sexual abuse in women with bulimia. *Journal of Clinical Psychiatry*, 50, 460–4.

Bull, R.H., Engels, W.D., Engelsmann, F., and Bloom, L. 1983: Behavioural changes following gastric surgery for morbid obesity: A prospective, controlled study. *Journal of Psychosomatic Research*, 27, 457–67.

Bullen, B.A., Reed, R.B., and Mayer, J. 1964: Physical activity of obese and non-obese adolescent girls appraised by motion picture sampling. *American Journal of Clinical Nutrition*, 4, 211–33.

Burnett, J. 1989: *Plenty and Want: A Social History of Food in England from 1815 to the Present Day*. 3rd edition. London: Routledge.

Buttriss, J. 1995: *Nutrition in General Practice*, vol. 2: *Promoting Health and Preventing Disease*. London: Royal College of General Practitioners.

Calan, R.M. and Slade, P.D. 1989: Sexual experiences and eating problems in female undergraduates. *International Journal of Eating Disorders*, 8, 391–7.

Cannon, G. and Einzig, H. 1983: *Dieting Makes you Fat*. London: Century Publishing Co. Ltd.

Cantor, M.G. 1987: Popular culture and the portrayal of women: Content and control. In B.B. Hess and M.M. Ferree (eds), *Analyzing Gender*, Newbury Park, CA: Sage, 190–214.

Cantwell, D.P. et al. 1977: Anorexia nervosa: An affective disorder? *Archives of General Psychiatry*, 34, 1087–93.

Casey, R. and Rozin, P. 1989: Changing children's food preferences: Parents' opinions. *Appetite*, 12P, 171–82.

Cash, T.F. and Pruzinsky, T. (eds) 1990: *Body Images: Development, Deviance and Change*. New York: Guilford Press.

Cash, T., Winstead, B., and Janda, L. 1986: The great American shape-up: Body image survey report. *Psychology Today*, 20, 30–7.

Cecil, D. 1929: *The Stricken Deer; or, The Life of Cowper*. London: Constable.

Central Statistical Office 1994: Social trends 24. London: HMSO.

Chaiken, S. and Pliner, P. 1987: Women but not men are what they eat: The effect of meal size and gender on perceived femininity and masculinity. *Personality and Social Psychology Bulletin*, 13, 166–76.

Chan, J.M., Rimm, E.B., Colditz, G.A., Stampfer, M.J., and Willett, W.C. 1994: Obesity, fat distribution, and weight gain as risk factors for clinical diabetes in men. *Diabetes Care*, 17, 961–9.

Charles, N. and Kerr, M. 1986: Eating properly: the family and state benefit. *Sociology*, 20, 412–29.

Charles, N. and Kerr, M. 1987: Just the way it is: Gender and age differences in family food consumption. In J. Brannen and G. Wilson (eds), *Give and Take in Families: Studies in Resource Distribution*, London: Allen and Unwin.

Charnock, D.J. 1989: A comment on the role of dietary restraint in the development of bulimia nervosa. *British Journal of Clinical Psychology*, 28, 329–40.

Chavez, D. 1985: Perpetuation of gender inequality: A content analysis of comic strips. *Sex Roles*, 13, 93–102.

Chernin, K. 1992: Confessions of an eater. In D.W. Curtin and L.M. Heldke (eds), *Cooking, Eating, Thinking: Transformative Philosophies of Food.* Indianapolis: Indiana University Press, 56–67.

Chinn, S. and Rona, R.J. 2001: Prevalence and trends in overweight and obesity in three cross-sectional studies of British children, 1974–94. *British Medical Journal*, 322, 24–6.

Choudry, I.Y. and Mumford, D.B. 1992: A pilot study of eating disorders in Mirpur (Pakistan) using an Urdu version of the Eating Attitudes Test. *International Journal of Eating Disorders*, 11, 243–51.

Clark, M. and Hampson, S. 2001: Implementing a psychological intervention to improve lifestyle self management in patients with Type 2 Diabetes. *Patient Education and Counselling*, 42, 247–56.

Clubley, M., Bye, C.E., Henson, T.A., Peck, A.W., and Riddington, C.J. 1979: Effects of caffeine and cyclizine alone and in combination on human performance, subjective effects and EEG activity. *British Journal of Clinical Pharmacology*, 7, 157–63.

Coates, T.J., Jeffrey, R.W., and Wing, R.R. 1978: The relationship between a person's relative body weights and the quality and quantity of food stored in their homes. *Addictive Behaviour*, 3, 179–84.

Cogan, J.C., Bhalla, S.K., Sefa-Dedeh, A., and Rothblum, E.D. 1996: A comparison study of United States and African students on perceptions of obesity and thinness. *Journal for Cross Cultural Psychology*, 27, 98–113.

Cole, S. and Edelmann, R. 1988: Restraint, eating disorders and the need to achieve in state and public school subjects. *Personality and Individual Differences*, 8, 475–82.

Coleman, V. 1990: *Eat Green – Lose Weight.* London: Angus and Robertson.

Colvin, R.H. and Olson, S.B. 1983: A descriptive analysis of men and women who have lost significant weight and are highly successful at maintaining the loss. *Addictive Behaviour*, 8, 287–95.

Comfort, A. 1974: *The Joy of Sex: A Gourmet Guide to Lovemaking.* London: Quartet.

Conley, R. 1989: *Rosemary Conley's Complete Hip and Thigh Diet.* London: Arrow Books.

Conley, R. 1991: *Metabolism Booster Diet.* London: Arrow Books.

Conley, R. 1996: *Complete Flat Stomach Plan.* London: Arrow Books.

Conner, M., Fitter, M., and Fletcher, W. 1999: Stress and snacking: A diary study of daily hassles and between meal snacking. *Psychology and Health*, 14, 51–63.

Conner, M., Martin, E., Silverdale, N., and Grogan, S. 1996: Dieting in adolescence: An application of the theory of planned behaviour. *British Journal of Health Psychology*, 1, 315–25.

Conner, M. and Norman, P. 1996: *Predicting Health Behaviours*. Buckingham, UK: Open University Press.

Connors, M.E. and Morse, W. 1993: Sexual abuse and eating disorders: A review. *International Journal of Eating Disorders*, 13, 1–11.

Considine, R.V., Considine, E.L., Williams, C.J. et al. 1995: Evidence against either a premature stop codon or the absence of obese gene mRNA in human obesity. *Journal of Clinical Investigation*, 95, 2986–8.

Contento, I.R., Basch, C., Shea, S., Gutin, B., Zybert, P., Michela, J.L., and Rips, J. 1993: Relationship of mothers' food choice criteria to food intake of pre-school children: Identification of family subgroups. *Health Education Quarterly*, 20, 243–59.

Cools, J., Schotte, D.E., and McNally, R.J. 1992: Emotional arousal and overeating in restrained eaters. *Journal of Abnormal Psychology*, 101, 348–51.

Cooper, P.J. and Charnock, D. 1990: From restraint to bulimic episodes: A problem of some loose connections. *Appetite*, 14, 120–2.

Cooper, P.J., Charnock, D.J., and Taylor, M.J. 1987: The prevalence of bulimia nervosa. *British Journal of Psychiatry*, 151, 684–6.

Cooper, P.J. and Cooper, Z. 1987: The nature of bulimia nervosa. *Pediatric Rev. Commun*, 1, 217–37.

Cooper, P.J. and Fairburn, C.G. 1983: Binge eating and self-induced vomiting in the community: A preliminary study. *British Journal of Psychiatry*, 142, 139–44.

Cooper, P.J. and Fairburn, C.G. 1986: The depressive symptoms of bulimia nervosa. *British Journal of Psychiatry*, 148, 268–74.

Cooper, P.J. and Taylor, M.J. 1988: Body image disturbance in bulimia nervosa. *British Journal of Psychiatry*, 153, 32–6.

Cooper, P.J., Taylor, M.J., Cooper, Z., and Fairburn, C.G. 1987: The development and validation of the Body Shape Questionnaire. *International Journal of Eating Disorders*, 6, 485–94.

Cosford, P.A. and Arnold, E. 1992: Eating disorders in later life: A review. *International Journal of Geriatric Psychiatry*, 7, 491–8.

Counts, C.R. and Adams, H.E. 1985: Body image in bulimic, dieting and normal females. *Journal of Psychopathology and Behavioural Assessment*, 7, 289–300.

Cox, B.D., Huppert, F.A., and Whichelow, M.J. (eds) 1993: *The Health and Lifestyle Survey: Seven Years On*. Aldershot, UK: Dartmouth.

Crisp, A.H. 1967: Anorexia nervosa. *Hospital Medicine*, 1, 713–18.

Crisp, A.H. 1984: The psychopathology of anorexia nervosa: Getting the "heat" out of the system. In A.J. Stunkard and E. Stellar (eds), *Eating and Its Disorders*, New York: Raven Press, 209–34.

Crisp, A.H., Callender, J.S., Halek, C., and Hsu, L.K.G. 1992: Long-term mortality in anorexia nervosa: A twenty-year follow-up of the St George's and Aberdeen cohorts. *British Journal of Psychiatry*, 161, 104–7.

Crisp, A.H., Hall, A., and Holland, A.J. 1985: Nature and nurture in anorexia nervosa: A study of 34 pairs of twins, one pair of triplets and an adoptive family. *International Journal of Eating Disorders*, 4, 5–27.

Crisp, A.H., Hsu, L., Harding, B., and Hartshorn, J. 1980: Clinical features of anorexia. A study of consecutive series of 102 female patients. *Journal of Psychosomatic Research*, 24, 179–91.

Crisp, A.H., Norton, K.R.W., Gower, S., Halek, C., Bowyer, C., Yeldham, D., Levett, G., and Bhat, A. 1991: A controlled study of the effect of therapies aimed at adolescent and family psychopathology in anorexia nervosa. *British Journal of Psychiatry*, 159, 325–33.

Crisp, A., Palmer, R., and Kalucy, R. 1976: How common is anorexia nervosa? A prevalence study. *British Journal of Psychiatry*, 128, 549–54.

Crisp, A.H., Queenan, M., Sittampaln, Y., and Harris, G. 1980: "Jolly fat" revisited. *Journal of Psychosomatic Research*, 24, 233–41.

Daly, M. 1978: *Gyn/Ecology: The Metaethics of Radical Feminism*. London: The Women's Press.

Dana, M. 1987: Boundaries: One way mirror to the self. In M. Lawrence (ed.), *Fed Up and Hungry*. London: The Women's Press.

Dare, C. and Crowther, C. 1995a: Living dangerously: Psychoanalytic psychotherapy of anorexia nervosa. In G. Szmukler, C. Dare, and J. Treasure (eds), *Handbook of Eating Disorders: Theory, Treatment and Research*. London: Wiley, 293–307.

Dare, C. and Crowther, C. 1995b: Psychodynamic models of eating disorders. In G. Szmukler, C. Dare, and J. Treasure (eds), *Handbook of Eating Disorders: Theory, Treatment and Research*. London: Wiley, 125–39.

Dare, C. and Eisler, I. 1995: Family therapy. In G. Szmukler, C. Dare, and J. Treasure (eds), *Handbook of Eating Disorders: Theory, Treatment and Research*, London: Wiley, 333–49.

Dare, C., Eisler, I., Russell, G.F.M., and Szmukler, G. 1990: Family therapy for anorexia nervosa: Implications from the results of a controlled trial of family and individual therapy. *Journal of Marital and Family Therapy*, 16, 39–57.

Dare, C., Le Grange, D., Eisler, I., and Rutherford, J. 1994: Redefining the psychosomatic family: Family process of 26 eating disorder families. *International Journal of Eating Disorders*, 16, 211–26.

Dare, C., Russell, G., Treasure, J., and Dodge, L. 2001: Psychological therapies for adults with anorexia nervosa. *British Journal of Psychiatry*, 178, 216–21.

Davis, C. 1928: Self selection of diets by newly weaned infants. *American Journal of Disease of Children*, 36, 651–79.

Davis, C. 1939: Results of the self selection of diets by young children. *The Canadian Medical Association Journal*, 41, 257–61.

Davis, K. 1995: Reshaping the female body: The dilemma of cosmetic surgery. London: Routledge.

de Groot, C.P.G.M., van Staveren, W.A., and Hautvast, J.G.A.J. (eds) 1991: EURONUT-SENECA. Nutrition and elderly in Europe, *European Journal of Clinical Nutrition*, 45 (Suppl. 3), 1–196.

de Groot, L.C.P.G.M. and van Staveren, W.A. 2000: SENECA's accomplishments and challenges. *Nutrition*, 16, 541–3.

de Silva, P. 1995: Cognitive-behavioral models of eating disorders. In G. Szmukler, C. Dare, and J. Treasure (eds), *Handbook of Eating Disorders: Theory, Treatment and Research*, London: Wiley, 141–53.

De Vries, J. 1989: *Realistic Weight Control*. Edinburgh: Mainstream.

Deaux, K., Kite, M.E., and Lewis, L.L. 1985: Clustering and gender schemata: An uncertain link. *Personality and Social Psychology Bulletin*, 11, 387–97.

Deaux, K. and Lewis, L.L. 1984: The structure of gender stereotypes: Interrelationships among components and gender labels. *Journal of Personality and Social Psychology*, 46, 991–1004.

Dejong, W. 1980: The stigma of obesity: The consequences of naive assumptions concerning the causes of physical deviance. *Journal of Health and Social Behaviour*, 21, 75–87.

Delphy, C. 1979: Sharing the same table: Consumption and the family. In C. Harris (ed.), *The Sociology of the Family: New Directions for Britain*. Sociological Review Monograph 28, Keele, UK: University of Keele.

Denton, D. 1982: *The Hunger for Salt*. Berlin: Springer Verlag.

Department of Health 1991: *Dietary Reference Values for Food Energy and Nutrients for the United Kingdom*. Report on Health and Social Subjects, no. 41. London: HMSO.

Department of Health 1995: *Obesity: Reversing an Increasing Problem of Obesity in England. A Report from the Nutrition and Physical Activity Task Forces*. London: HMSO.

Desor, J.A., Maller, O., and Turner, R.E. 1973: Taste and acceptance of sugars by human infants. *Journal of Comparative and Physiological Psychology*, 84, 496–501.

Despres, J.-P., Lemieux, I., and Prud'homme, D. 2001: Treatment of obesity: Need to focus on high risk abdominally obese patients. *British Medical Journal*, 322, 716–20.

Devereux, G. 1980a: Normal and abnormal. In *Basic Problems of Ethnopsychiatry*, Chicago: University of Chicago Press, 3–71.

Devereux, G. 1980b: Schizophrenia: An ethnic psychosis, or schizophrenia without tears. In *Basic Problems of Ethnopsychiatry*, Chicago: University of Chicago Press, 214–36.

DiNicola, V.F. 1990: Anorexia multiforme: Self starvation in historical and cultural context. Anorexia as a culture reactive syndrome. *Transcultural Psychiatric Research Review*, 27, 245–86.

Dirren, H., Decarli, B., Lesourd, B., Schlienger, J.L., Deslypere, J.P., and Kiepurski, A. 1991: Nutritional status: Haematology and albumin. *European Journal of Clinical Nutrition*, 45 (Suppl. 3), 43–52.

Dishman, R.K. 1982: Compliance/adherence in health-related exercise. *Health Psychology*, 1, 237–67.

Dishman, R.K., Sallis, J.F., and Orenstein, D.M. 1985: The determinants of physical activity and exercise. *Public Health Reports*, 100, 158–72.

Dolan, B., Lacey, J., and Evans, C. 1990: Eating behaviour and attitudes to weight and shape in British women from three ethnic groups. *British Journal of Psychiatry*, 157, 523–8.

Doll, R. and Peto, R. 1981: *The Causes of Cancer*. New York: Oxford University Press.

Dornbusch, S., Carlsmith, J., Duncan, P. et al. 1984: Sexual maturation, social class and the desire to be thin among adolescent females. *Developmental and Behavioural Paediatrics*, 5, 475–82.

Douglas, M. 1966: *Purity and Danger: An Analysis of the Concepts of Pollution and Taboo*. London: Routledge and Kegan Paul.

Douglas, M. 1975: *Implicit Meanings*. London: Routledge.

Dowey, A.J. 1996: *Psychological Determinants of Children's Food Preferences*. Unpublished PhD Dissertation, University of Wales, Bangor.

Drenowski, A., Kurt, C., and Krahn, D. 1994: Body weight and dieting in adolescence: Impact of socioeconomic status. *International Journal of Eating Disorders*, 16, 61–5.

Dritschel, B., Cooper, P.J., and Charnock, D. 1993: A problematic counter regulation experimental implications for the link between dietary restraint and overeating. *International Journal of Eating Disorders*, 13, 297–304.

DSM-IV 1994: *Diagnostic and Statistical Manual*. Washington, DC: American Psychiatric Association.

Duncker, K. 1938: Experimental modification of children's food preferences through social suggestion. *Journal of Abnormal Social Psychology*, 33, 489–507.

Durnin, J.V.G.A., Lonergan, M.E., Good, J., and Ewan, A. 1974: A cross sectional nutritional and anthropometric study with an interval of 7 years on 611 young adolescent school children. *British Journal of Nutrition*, 32, 169–79.

Dusseldorp, E., van Elderen, T., Maes, S., Meulman, J., and Kraaij, V. 1999: A meta-analysis of psychoeduational programs for coronary heart disease patients. *Health Psychology*, 18, 506–19.

Earle, E. 1995: *Bikini Diet*. London: Boxtree.

Eckert, E., Halmi, K.A., Marchi, P., Grove, E., and Crosby, R. 1995: Ten year follow up of anorexia nervosa: Clinical course and outcome. *Psychological Medicine*, 25, 143–56.

Edholm, O.G., Fletcher, J.G., Widdowson, E.M., and McCance, R.A. 1955: The food intake and individual expenditure of individual men. *British Journal of Nutrition*, 9, 286–300.

Eisler, I. 1993: Families, family therapy and psychosomatic illness. In S. Moorey and M. Hodes (eds), *Psychological Treatments in Human Disease and Illness*, London: Gaskill.

Eisler, I. 1995: Family models of eating disorders. In G. Szmukler, C. Dare, and J. Treasure (eds), *Handbook of Eating Disorders: Theory, Treatment and Research*, London: Wiley, 293–307.

Eisler, I., Dare, C., Russell, G.F., Szmukler, G., le Grange, D., and Dodge, E. 1997: Family and individual therapy in anorexia nervosa: A five-year follow up. *Archives of General Psychiatry*, 54, 1025–30.

Eisler, I. and Szmukler, G. 1985: Social class as a confounding variable in the eating attitudes test. *Journal of Psychiatric Research*, 19, 171–6.

Emmons, R.A. 1996: Strivings and feeling: Personal goals and subjective well-being. In P.M. Gollwitzer and J.A. Bargh (eds), *The Psychology of Action: Linking Cognition and Motivation to Behavior*, New York: Guilford Press, 313–37.

Enzman, D.R. and Lane, B. 1977: Cranial computed tomography findings in anorexia nervosa. *Journal of Computer Assisted Tomography*, 1, 410–14.

Epel, E., Lapidus, R., McEwen, B., and Brownell, K. 2001: Stress may add bite to appetite in women: A laboratory study of stress-induced cortisol and eating behavior. *Psychoneuroendocrinology*, 26 (1), 37–49.

Epel, E.S., McEwen, B., Seeman, T., Matthews, K., Castellazzo, G., Brownell, K.D., Bell, J., and Ickovics, J.R. 2000: Stress and body shape: Stress-induced cortisol secretion is consistently greater among women with central fat. *Psychosomatic Medicine*, 62, 623–32.

Epel, E.S., Spanakos, A., Kasl-Godley, J., and Brownell, K.D. 1996: Body shape ideals across gender, sexual orientation, socioeconomic status, race, and age in personal advertisements. *International Journal of Eating Disorders*, 19, 265–73.

Epstein, L.H., Valosky, A., Wing, R.R., and McCurley, J. 1994: Ten year outcomes of behavioural family-based treatment for childhood obesity. *Health Psychology*, 13, 373–83.

Erikson, E.H. 1964: *Identity, Youth and Crisis*. New York: W.W. Norton.

Erikson, E.H. 1975: *Life History and the Historical Moment*. New York: W.W. Norton.

Etter-Lewis, G. 1988: Power and social change: Images of Afro-American women in the print media. Paper presented at the annual meeting of the National Women's Studies Association, Minneapolis, MN.

Eyton, A. 1982: *The F Plan Diet*. London.

Fairburn, C. 1981: A cognitive-behavioural approach to the management of bulimia. *Psychological Medicine*, 11, 697–706.

Fairburn, C.G. 1984: Bulimia: Its epidemiology and management. *Res Publ Assoc Res Nerv Ment Dis.*, 62, 235–58.

Fairburn, C.G. 1985: Cognitive-behavioural treatment for bulimia. In D.M. Garner and P.E. Garfinkel (eds), *Handbook of Psychotherapy for Anorexia Nervosa and Bulimia*, New York: Guilford Press, 160–92.

Fairburn, C.G. and Cooper, P.J. 1984: The clinical features of bulimia nervosa. *British Journal of Psychiatry*, 144, 238–46.

Fairburn, C., Cooper, Z., and Cooper, P.J. 1986: The clinical features and maintenance of bulimia nervosa. In K.D. Brownell and J. Foreyt (eds), *Physiology, Psychology and Treatment of Eating Disorders*, New York: Basic Books.

Fairburn, C.G., Jones, R., Peveler, R.C., Hope, R.A., and O'Connor, M. 1993: Psychotherapy and bulimia nervosa: Longer-term effects of interpersonal psychotherapy behavior therapy, and cognitive behavior therapy. *Archives of General Psychiatry*, 50, 419–28.

Fairburn, C.G., Kirk, J., O'Connor, M., and Cooper, P.J. 1986: A comparison of two psychological treatments for bulimia nervosa. *Behaviour Research and Therapy*, 24, 629–43.

Fallon, A, 1990: Culture in the mirror: Sociocultural determinants of body image. In T. Cash and T. Pruzinski (eds), *Body Images: Development, Deviance and Change*, New York: Guilford Press, 80–109.

Fallon, A. and Rozin, P. 1985: Sex differences in perceptions of desirable body shape. *Journal of Abnormal Psychology*, 94, 102–5.

Farooqi, I.S., Jebb, S.A., Cook, G. et al. 1999: Effects of recombinant leptin therapy in a child with leptin deficiency. *New England Journal of Medicine*, 16, 879–84.

Favaro, A. and Santonastaso, P. 1997: Suicidality in bulimia nervosa: Clinical and psychological correlates. *Acta Psychiatrica Scandinavica*, 95, 508–14.

Fedoroff, I.C., Polivy, J., and Herman, C.P. 1997: The effect of pre-exposure to food cues on the eating behavior of restrained and unrestrained eaters. *Appetite*, 28, 33–47.

Fehily, A. 1999: Epidemiology of obesity in the UK. In *Obesity: The Report of the British Nutrition Foundation Task Force*. Oxford: Blackwell Science, 23–36.

Ferron, F., Considine, R.V., Peino, R., Lado, I.G., Dieguez, C., and Casanueva, F.F. 1997: Serum leptin concentrations in patients with anorexia nervosa, bulimia nervosa and non specific eating disorders correlate with body mass index but are independent of the respective disease. *Clinical Endocrinology*, 46, 289–93.

Ferster, C.B., Nurnberger, J.I., and Levitt, E.B. 1962: The control of eating. *Journal of Mathetics*, 1, 87–109.

Fichter, M., Elton, M., Sourdi, L., Weyerer, S. et al. 1988: Anorexia nervosa in Greek and Turkish adolescents. *European Archives of Psychiatry and Neurological Sciences*, 237, 200–8.

Fiddes, N. 1990: *Meat: A Natural Symbol*. London: Routledge.

Fieldhouse, P. 1986: *Food and Nutrition: Customs and Culture*. London: Croom Helm.

Fishbein, M. and Ajzen, I. 1975: *Belief, Attitude, Intention, and Behavior: An Introduction to Theory and Research*. Reading, MA: Addison-Wesley.

Fisher, J.O. and Birch, L.L. 1999: Restricting access to a palatable food affects children's behavioral response, food selection and intake. *American Journal of Clinical Nutrition*, 69, 1264–72.

Fisher, J.O., Birch, L.L., Smiciklas-Wright, H., and Piocciano, M.F. 2000: Breastfeeding through the first year predicts maternal control in feeding and subsequent toddler energy intakes. *Journal of the American Dietetic Association*, 100, 641–6.

Flegal, K.M., Harlan, W.R., and Landis, J.R. 1988: Secular trends in body mass index and skinfold thickness with socioeconomic factors in young adult women. *American Journal of Clinical Nutrition*, 48, 535–43.

Ford, E., Williamson, D., and Liu, S. 1997: Weight change and diabetes incidence: Findings from a national cohort of US adults. *American Journal of Epidemiology*, 146: 214–22.

Foreit, K.G., Agor, A.T., Byers, J., Larue, J., Lokey, H., Palazzini, M., Patterson, M., and Smith, L. 1980: Sex bias in the newspaper treatment of male-centred and female-centred news stories. *Sex Roles*, 6, 465–80.

Formon, S.J. 1974: *Infant Nutrition*. 2nd edition. Philadelphia: W.B. Saunders.

Fossarelli, P.D. 1984: Television and children: A review. *Journal of Deviative Behaviour and Paediatrics*, 5, 30–7.

Fox, K. 1999: Treatment of obesity III: Physical activity and exercise. In *Obesity: The Report of the British Nutrition Foundation Task Force*, Oxford: Blackwell Science, 165–74.

Franzoi, S.L. and Shields, S.A. 1984: The body esteem scale: Multidimensional structure and sex differences in a college population. *Journal of Personality Assessment*, 48, 173–8.

Freedman, R. 1986: *Beauty Bound*. Lexington, MA: D.C. Heath.

Freeman, C. 1995: Cognitive therapy. In G. Szmukler, C. Dare, and J. Treasure (eds), *Handbook of Eating Disorders: Theory, Treatment and Research*, London: Wiley, 309–31.

Freeman, C.P.F. and Newton, J.R. 1992: Anorexia nervosa: What treatments are most effective? In K. Hawton and P. Cowan (eds), *Practical Problems in Clinical Psychiatry*, Oxford: Oxford University Press.

Freeman, R.F., Thomas, C.D., Solyom, L., and Hunter, M.A. 1984: A modified video camera for measuring body image distortion: Technical description and reliability. *Psychological Medicine*, 14, 411–16.

French, S.A. and Jeffrey, R.W. 1997: Current dieting, weight loss history and weight suppression: Behavioural correlates of three dimensions of dieting. *Addictive Behaviour*, 22, 31–44.

French, S.A., Jeffrey, R.W., Forster, J.L., McGovern, P.G., Kelder, S.H., and Baxter, J.R. 1994: Predictors of weight change over two years among a population of working adults: The healthy worker project. *International Journal of Obesity*, 18, 145–54.

Friedman, L.A. and Kimball, A.W. 1986: Coronary heart disease mortality and alcohol consumption in Framingham. *American Journal of Epidemiology*, 124, 481–9.

Furnham, A. and Greaves, N. 1994: Gender and locus of control correlates of body image dissatisfaction. *European Journal of Personality*, 8, 183–200.

Garcia, J., Hankisn, W.G., and Rusiniak, K. 1974: Behavioral regulation of the milieu intern in man and rat. *Science*, 185, 824–31.

Gard, M.C.E. and Freeman, C.P. 1996: The dismantling of a myth: A review of eating disorders and socioeconomic status. *International Journal of Eating Disorders*, 20, 1–12.

Gardner, R.M., Martinez, R., and Sandoval, Y. 1987: Obesity and body image: An evaluation of sensory and non sensory components. *Psychological Medicine*, 17, 927–32.

Garfinkel, P.E. and Garner, D.M. 1986: *Anorexia Nervosa: A Multidimensional Perspective*. New York: Brunner Mazel.

Garn, S.M., Bailey, S.M., Solomon, M.A., and Hopkins, P.J. 1981: Effects of remaining family members on fatness prediction. *American Journal of Clinical Nutrition*, 34, 148–53.

Garner, D.M. and Bemis, K.M. 1982: A cognitive-behavioural approach to anorexia nervosa. *Cognitive Therapy and Research*, 6, 123–50.

Garner, D., Garfinkel, P., Schwartz, D., and Thomson, M. 1980: Cultural expectations of thinness among women. *Psychological Reports*, 47, 483–91.

Garner, D.M., Olmsted, M.P., and Polivy, J. 1981: The eating disorder inventory: A measure of cognitive behavioural dimensions of anorexia nervosa and bulimia. In P.L. Darby, P.E. Garfinkel, D.M. Garner, and D.V. Coscina (eds), *Anorexia Nervosa: Recent Developments in Research*, New York: Liss.

Garner, D.M. and Wooley, S.C. 1991: Confronting the failure of behavioral and dietary treatments of obesity. *Clinical Psychology Review*, 6, 58–137.

Garrow, J. 1974: *Energy Balance and Obesity in Man*. New York: Elsevier.

Garrow, J.S. 1987: Energy expenditure in man – an overview. *Americal Journal of Clinical Nutrition*, 45, 1114–19.

Garrow, J.S. 1994: Should obesity be treated? Treatment is necessary. *British Medical Journal*, 309, 654–5.

Garrow, J.S. and Summerbell, C.D. 1995: Meta-analysis: Effect of exericise, with or without dieting, on body composition of overweight subjects. *European Journal of Clinical Nutrition*, 49, 1–10.

Garrow, J.S. and Webster, J.D. 1985: Are pre-obese people energy thrifty? *Lancet*, 2, 670–1.

Geldard, F.A. 1972: *The Human Senses*. New York: Wiley.

General Household Survey 1992: London: OPCS.

General Household Survey 1994: London: OPCS.

Gettelman, T.E. and Thompson, J.K. 1993: Actual differences and stereotypical perceptions in body image and eating disturbance: A comparison of male and female heterosexual and homosexual samples. *Sex Roles*, 29, 545–62.

Gilbert, S. 1986: *Pathology of Eating*. London: Routledge.

Gleghorn, A.A., Penner, L.A., Powers, P.S., and Schulman, D. 1987: The psychometric properties of several measures of body image. *Journal of Psychopathology and Behavioural Assessment*, 9, 203–18.

Glynn, S.M. and Ruderman, A.J. 1986: The development and validation of an Eating Self Efficacy Scale. *Cognitive Therapy and Research*, 10, 403–20.

Goldfarb, L. 1987: Sexual abuse antecedent to anorexia nervosa, bulimia, and compulsive overeating: Three case reports. *International Journal of Eating Disorders*, 6, 675–80.

Gollwitzer, P.M. 1993: Goal achievement: The role of intentions. In W. Stroebe and M. Hewstone (eds), *European Review of Social Psychology*, 4, 141–85.

Goodsitt, A. 1997: Eating disorders: A self psychological perspective. In D.M. Garner and P.E. Garfinkel (eds), *Handbook of Treatment for Eating Disorders*, New York: Guilford Press, 205–28.

Gordon, R.A. 2000: *Eating Disorders: Anatomy of a Social Epidemic*. 2nd edn. Oxford: Blackwell.

Gortmaker, S.L., Must, A., Sobol, A.M., Peterson, K., Colditz, G.A., and Dietz, W.H. 1996: Television viewing as a cause of increasing obesity among children in the United States: 1986–1990. *Archives of Pediatric Adolescent Medicine*, 150, 356–62.

Gotesdam, K.G. and Agras, W.S. 1995: General population based epidemiological survey of eating disorders in Norway. *International Journal of Eating Disorders*, 18, 119–26.

Gray, J., Ford, K., and Kelly, L. 1987: The prevalence of bulimia in a black college population. *International Journal of Eating Disorders*, 6, 733–40.

Greene, G.W., Smiciklas-Wright, H., Scholl, T.O., and Karp, R.J. 1988: Postpartum weight change: How much of the weight gained in pregnancy will be lost after delivery? *Obstetrics and Gynecology*, 71, 701–7.

Greeno, C.G. and Wing, R.R. 1994: Stress-induced eating. *Psychological Bulletin*, 155, 444–64.

Greer, G. 1970: *The Female Eunuch*. London: Grafton Books.

Grilo, C.M., Shiffman, S., and Wing, R.R. 1989: Relapse crisis and coping among dieters. *Journal of Consulting and Clinical Psychology*, 57, 488–95.

Grogan, S. 1999: *Body Image: Understanding Body Dissatisfaction in Men, Women and Children*. London: Routledge.

Grogan, S. and Wainwright, N. 1996: Growing up in the culture of slenderness: Girls' experiences of body dissatisfaction. *Women's Studies International Forum*, 19: 665–73.

Grogan, S., Williams, Z., and Conner, M. 1996: The effects of viewing same gender photographic models on body satisfaction. *Women and Psychology Quarterly*, 20, 569–75.

Grunberg, N.E., Bowen, D.J., and Morse, D.E. 1984: Effects of nicotine on body weight and food consumption in rats. *Psychopharmacology*, 83, 93–8.

Gull, W.W. 1874: Anorexia nervosa (apepsia hysterica, anorexia hysterica). *Transactions of the Clinical Society of London*, 7, 22–8.

Haapenen, N., Miilunpalo, S., Pasenen, M., Oja, P., and Vuori, I. 1997: Association between leisure time physical activity and ten year body mass change among working aged men and women. *International Journal of Obesity*, 21, 288–96.

Hales, C.N. et al. 1991: Fetal and infant growth and impaired glucose tolerance at age 64. *British Medical Journal*, 303, 1019–22.

Haley, J. 1973: *Uncommon Therapy: The Psychiatric Techniques of Milton H. Erickson, M.D.* MA: W.W. Norton and Co.

Hall, A. and Brown, L.B. 1982: A comparison of the attitudes of young anorexia nervosa patients and non patients with those of their mothers. *British Journal of Psychology*, 56, 39–48.

Hall, R.C.W., Tice, L., Beresford, T.P., Wooley, B., and Hall, A.K. 1989: Sexual abuse in patients with anorexia nervosa and bulimia. *Psychosomatics*, 30, 73–9.

Halmi, K.A. 1995: Current concepts and definitions. In G. Szmukler, C. Dare, and J. Treasure (eds), *Handbook of Eating Disorders: Theory, Treatment and Research*, London: Wiley, 29–42.

Halmi, K.A., Eckert, E., Marchi, P.A. et al. 1991: Comorbidity of psychiatric diagnoses in anorexia nervosa. *Archives of General Psychiatry*, 48, 712–18.

Halmi, K.A., Falk, J.R., and Schwartz, E. 1981: Binge-eating and vomiting: A survey of a college population. *Psychological Medicine*, 11, 697–706.

Halmi, K.A., Stunkard, A.J., and Mason, E.E. 1980: Emotional responses to weight reduction by three methods: Diet, jejunoileal bypass, and gastric. *American Journal of Clinical Nutrition*, 33, 446–51.

Hamilton, K. and Waller, G. 1993: Media influences on body size estimation in anorexia and bulimia: an experimental study. *British Journal of Psychiatry*, 162, 837–40.

Hamm, P.B., Shekelle, R.B., and Stamler, J. 1989: Large fluctuations in body weight during young adulthood and twenty-five year risk of coronary death in men. *American Journal of Epidemiology*, 129, 312–18.

Han, T.S., Richmond, P., Avenell, A., and Lean, M.E.J. 1997: Waist circumference reduction and cardiovascular benefits during weight loss in women. *International Journal of Obesity*, 21, 127–34.

Harris, M.B., Harris, R.J., and Bochner, S. 1982: Fat, four eyed and female: Stereotypes of obesity, glasses and gender. *Journal of Applied Psychology*, 100, 78–83.

Hart, K.J. and Ollendick, T.H. 1985: Prevalence of bulimia in working and university women. *American Journal of Psychiatry*, 142, 851–4.

Hatsukami, D.K. et al. 1984: Affective disorder and substance abuse in women with bulimia. *Psychological Medicine*, 14, 701–4.

Haus, G., Hoerr, S.L., Mavis, B., and Robinson, J. 1994: Key modifiable factors in weight maintenance: Fat intake, exercise and weight cycling. *Journal of the American Diet Association*, 94, 409–13.

Heatherton, T.F. and Baumeister, R.F. 1991: Binge eating as an escape from self awareness. *Psychological Bulletin*, 110, 86–108.

Heatherton, T.F., Herman, C.P., and Polivy, J. 1991: Effects of physical threat and ego threat on eating behavior. *Journal of Personality and Social Psychology*, 60, 138–43.

Heatherton, T.F., Herman, C.P., Polivy, J.A., King G.A., and McGree, S.T. 1988: The (mis)measurement of restraint: An analysis of conceptual and psychometric Issues. *Journal of Abnormal Psychology*, 97, 19–28.

Heatherton, T.F. and Polivy, J. 1991: Chronic dieting and eating disorders: A spiral model. In J.H. Crowther, S.E. Hobfall, M.A.P. Stephens, and D.L. Tennenbaum (eds), *The Etiology of Bulimia: The Individual and Familial Context*. Washington, DC: Hemisphere Publishers.

Heatherton, T.F., Polivy, J., and Herman, C.P. 1991: Restraint, weight loss and variability of body weight. *Journal of Abnormal Psychology*, 100, 78–83.

Heatherton, T.F., Polivy, J., Herman, C.P., and Baumeister, R.F. 1993: Self-awareness, task failure, and disinhibition: How attentional focus affects eating. *Journal of Personality and Social Psychology*, 61, 49–61.

Heinberg, L.J. and Thompson, J.K. 1995: Body image and televised images of thinness and attractiveness: A controlled laboratory investigation. *Journal of Social and Clinical Psychology*, 14, 325–38.

Heitmann, B.L. and Lissner, L. 1995: Dietary underreporting by obese individuals – is it specific or non-specific? *British Medical Journal*, 311, 986–9.

Helman, C.G. 1984: *Culture, Health and Illness: An Introduction for Health Professionals*. London: Wright.

Herman, C.P. and Mack, D. 1975: Restrained and unrestrained eating. *Journal of Personality*, 43, 646–60.

Herman, C.P. and Polivy, J. 1975: Anxiety, restraint and eating behavior. *Journal of Abnormal Psychology*, 84, 666–72.

Herman, C.P. and Polivy, J. 1980: Restrained eating. In A.J. Stunkard (ed.), *Obesity*, Philadelphia, London, Toronto: W.B. Saunders, 208–25.

Herman, C.P. and Polivy, J.A. 1984: A boundary model for the regulation of eating. In A.J. Stunkard and E. Stellar (eds), *Eating and its Disorders*, New York: Raven Press, 141–56.

Herman, C.P. and Polivy, J.A. 1988: Restraint and excess in dieters and bulimics. In K.M. Pirke and D. Ploog (eds), *The Psychobiology of Bulimia*, Berlin: Springer-Verlag.

Herman, C.P., Polivy J.A., and Esses, V.M. 1987: The illusion of counterregulation. *Appetite*, 9, 161–9.

Herzog, D.B., Greenwood, D.N., Dorer, D.J., Flores, A.T., Ekeblad, E.R., Richards, A., Blais, M.A., and Keller, M.B. 2000: Mortality of eating disorders, a descriptive study. *International Journal of Eating Disorders*, 28, 20–6.

Herzog, D.B., Keller, M.B., Sacks, N.R., Yeh, C.J., and Lavori, P.W. 1992: Psychiatric co-morbidity in treatment seeking anorexics and bulimics. *Journal of the American Academy for Child and Adolescent Psychiatry*, 32, 835–42.

Herzog, W., Deter., H.C., Schellberg, D., Seilkopf, S., Sarembe, E., Kroger, F., Minne, H., Mayer, H., and Petzold, S. 1992: Somatic findings at 12 year follow up of 103 anorexia nervosa patients: Results of the Heidelberg-Mannheim follow up. In W. Herzog, H.C. Deter, and W. Vanderyken (eds), *The Comprehensive Medical Text*, Berlin: Springer-Verlag.

Hetherington, M., Altemus, M., Nelson, M.L., Bernat, A.S., and Gold, P.W. 1994: Eating behaviour in bulimia nervosa: Multiple meal analysis. *American Journal of Clinical Nutrition*, 60, 864–73.

Hetherington, M.M. and Macdiarmid, J.I. 1993: "Chocolate addiction": A preliminary study of its description and its relationship to problem eating. *Appetite*, 21, 233–46.

Hibscher, J.A. and Herman, C.P. 1977: Obesity, dieting, and the expression of "obese" characteristics. *Journal of Comparative Physiological Psychology*, 91, 374–80.

Hill, A.J. and Bhatti, R. 1995: Body shape perception and dieting in preadolescent British Asian girls: Links with eating disorders. *International Journal of Eating Disorders*, 17, 175–83.

Hill, A.J. and Blundell, J.E. 1986: Model system for investigating the actions of anorectic drugs: Effect of d fenfluramine on food intake, nutrient selection, food preferences, meal patterns hunger and satiety in healthy human subjects. *Advances in the Bioscience*, 60, 377–89.

Hill, A.J., Draper, E., and Stack, J. 1994: A weight on children's minds: Body shape dissatisfactions at 9 years old. *International Journal of Obesity*, 18, 383–9.

Hill, A.J., Oliver, S., and Rogers, P.J. 1992: Eating in the adult world: The rise of dieting in childhood and adolescence. *British Journal of Clinical Psychology*, 31, 95–105.

Hill, A.J., Weaver, C., and Blundell, J.E. 1990: Dieting concerns of 10 year old girls and their mothers. *British Journal of Clinical Psychology*, 29, 346–8.

Hirsch, J. 1975: Cell number and size as a determinant of subsequent obesity. In: M. Winick (ed.), *Childhood Obesity*, New York: John Wiley, 15–22.

Hirsch, J. 1998: Magic bullet for obesity. *British Medical Journal*, 317, 1136–8.

Hoiberg, A.M., Berard, S., Watten, R.H., and Caine, C. 1994: Correlates of weight loss in treatment and at follow up. *International Journal of Obesity*, 8, 457–65.

Holden, N.L. and Robinson, P.H. 1988: Anorexia nervosa and bulimia nervosa in British Blacks. *British Journal of Psychiatry*, 152, 544–9.

Holland, A.J., Murray, R., Russell, G.F.M., and Crisp, A.H. 1984: Anorexia nervosa: A study of 34 pairs of twins and one set of triplets. *British Journal of Psychiatry*, 145, 414–19.

Hollister, L.E. 1971: Hunger and appetite after single doses of marihuana, alcohol, and dextroamphetamine. *Clinical Pharmacology and Therapeutics*, 12, 44–9.

Hopkinson, G. and Bland, R.C. 1982: Depressive syndromes in grossly obese women. *Canadian Journal of Psychiatry*, 27, 213–15.

Horm, J. and Anderson, K. 1993: Who in America is trying to lose weight? *Annals of Internal Medicine*, 1, 119 (7 Pt 2), 672–6.

Hsu, L.K.G. 1987: Are the eating disorders becoming more common in Blacks? *International Journal of Eating Disorders*, 6, 113–25.

Hsu, L.K.G. 1990: *Eating Disorders*. New York: Guilford Press.

Hsu, L.K.G. and Lee, S. 1993: Is weight phobia always necessary for a diagnosis of anorexia nervosa? *American Journal of Psychiatry*, October.

Hunt, S.C., Daines, M.M., Adams, T.D., Heath, E.M., and Williams, R.R. 1995: Pregnancy weight retention in morbid obesity. *Obesity Research*, 3, 121–30.

Hursti, U.K.K. and Sjoden, P.O. 1997: Food and general neophobia and their relationship with self-reported food choice: Familial resemblance in Swedish families with children of ages 7–17 years. *Appetite*, 29, 89–103.

Husain, M.M., Black, K.J., Doraiswamy, P.M., Shah, S.A., Rockwell, W.J.K., Ellinwood, E.H., and Krishman, R.R. 1992: Subcortical brain anatomy in anorexia and bulimia. *Biological Psychology*, 31, 735–8.

Institute of Medicine 1995: Committee to develop criteria for evaluating the outcomes of approaches to prevent and treat obesity. In *Weighing the Options – Criteria for Evaluating Weight-Management Programs*. Washington, DC: National Academy Press.

Intersalt Cooperative Research Group 1988: Intersalt: An international study of electrolyte excretion and blood pressure. Results for 24 hour urinary sodium and potassium excretion. *British Medical Journal*, 297, 319–28.

Jacobs, A.H. 1958: Masai age-groups and some functional tasks. *East African Institute of Social Research Conference Proceedings*, Makerere.

James, W.P.T., Avenell, A., Broom, J., and Whitehead, J. 1997: A one year trial to assess the value of orlistat in the management of obesity. *International Journal of Obesity*, 21 (Suppl. 3), S24–S30.

Jebb, S.A., Prentice, A.M., Goldberg, G.R., Murgatroyd, P.R., Black, A.E., and Coward, W.A. 1996: Changes in macronutrient balance during over feeding and under feeding assessed by 12 day continuous whole body calorimetry. *American Journal of Clinical Nutrition*, 64, 259–66.

Jeffrey, R.W., Adlis, S.A., Forster, J.L. 1991: Prevalence of dieting among working men and women: The healthy worker project. *Health Psychology*, 10, 274–81.

Jeffrey, R.W., Gray, C.W., French, S.A. et al. 1995: Evaluation of weight reduction in a community intervention for cardiovascular disease risk: Changes in body mass index in the Minnesota Heart health program. *International Journal of Obesity*, 19, 30–9.

Johnson, C., Lewis, C., and Hagman, J. 1984: The syndrome of bulimia. Review and synthesis. *Psychiatr Clin North Am*, 7, 247–73.

Jones, D.J., Fox, M.M., Babigian, H.M., and Hutton, H.E. 1980: Epidemiology of anorexia nervosa in Monroe County, New York: 1960–1976. *Psychosomatic Medicine*, 42, 551–8.

Kafatos, A., Schlienger, J.L., Deslypere, J.P., Ferro-Luzzi, A., and Amorim Cruz, J.A. 1991: Nutritional status: Serum lipids. *European Journal of Clinical Nutrition*, 45 (Suppl. 3), 53–61.

Kalat, J.W. and Rozin, P. 1973: "Learned safety" as a mechanism in long-delay taste-aversion learning in rats. *Journal of Comparative and Physiological Psychology*, 83, 198–207.

Kalucy, R.S., Crisp, A.H., and Harding, B. 1977: A study of 56 families with anorexia nervosa. *British Journal of Medical Psychology*, 50, 381–95.

Kaplan, S.P. 1984: Rehabilitation counselling students' perceptions of obese male and female clients. *Dissertation Abstracts International*, 42, 214.

Katahn, M. 1982: The 200 calorie solution: How to stop dieting forever. London: Arlington Books.

Kaye, W.H., Weltzin, T.E., McKee, M., McConaha, C., Hansen, D., and Hsu, L.K.G. 1992: Laboratory assessment of feeding behaviour in bulimia nervosa and healthy women. Methods for developing a human feeding laboratory. *American Journal of Clinical Nutrition*, 55, 372–80.

Kayman, S., Bruvold, W., and Stern, J.S. 1990: Maintenance and relapse after weight loss in women: Behavioural aspects. *American Journal of Clinical Nutrition*, 52, 800–7.

Keel, P.K. and Mitchell, J.E. 1997: Outcome in bulimia nervosa. *American Journal of Psychiatry*, 154, 313–21.

Keel, P.K., Mitchell, J.E., Miller, K.B., Davis, T.L., and Crow, S.J. 1999: Long-term outcome of bulimia nervosa. *Archives of General Psychiatry*, 56, 63–9.

Kelder, S.H., Perry, C.L., Klepp, K.-I., and Lytle, L.L. 1994: Longitudinal tracking of adolescent smoking, physical activity, and food choice behaviours. *American Journal of Public Health*, 84, 1121–6.

Kendell, R.E., Hall, D.J., Hailey, A., and Babig, H.M. 1973: The epidemiology of anorexia nervosa. *Psychological Medicine*, 3, 200–3.

Kendler, K.S., Maclean, C., Neale, M., Kessler, R., Heath, A., and Eaves, L. 1991: The genetic epidemiology of bulimia nervosa. *American Journal of Psychiatry*, 148, 1627–37.

Kendler, K.S., Meale, M.C., Kessler, R.C., Heath, A.C., and Eaves, L.J. 1992: Childhood parental loss and adult psychopathology in women. *Archives of General Psychiatry*, 49, 109–16.

Kerr, M. and Charles, N. 1986: Servers and providers: The distribution of food within the family. *Sociological Review*, 34 (1), 115–57.

Keys, A., Brozek, J., Henscel, A., Mickelson, O., and Taylor, H.L. 1950: *The Biology of Human Starvation*. Minneapolis, MN: University of Minnesota Press.

Kiernan, M., King, A.C., Kraemer, H.C., Stefanick, M.L., and Killen, J.D. 1998: Characteristics of successful and unsuccessful dieters: An application of signal detection methodology. *Annals of Behavioural Medicine*, 20, 1–6.

Kilbourne, J. 1994: Still killing us softly: Advertising and the obsession with thinness. In P. Fallon, M.A. Katzman, and S.C. Wooley (eds), *Feminist Perspectives on Eating Disorders*, New York: Guilford Press, 395–418.

King, G.A., Herman, C.P., and Polivy, J. 1987: Food perception in dieters and non-dieters. *Appetite*, 8, 147–58.

King, M.B. and Bhugra, D. 1989: Eating disorders: Lessons from a cross-cultural study. *Psychological Medicine*, 19, 955–8.

King, N.A., Blundell, J.E., and Tremblay, A. 1997: Effects of exercise on appetite control: Implications for energy balance. *Medicine and Science in Sports and Exercise*, 29, 1076–89.

Kirkley, B.G., Burge, J.C., and Ammerman, M.P.H. 1988: Dietary restraint, binge eating and dietary behaviour patterns. *International Journal of Eating Disorders*, 7, 771–8.

Kissileff, H.R., Pi-Sunyer, F.X., Thornton, J., and Smith, G.P. 1981: C-terminal octapeptide of cholecystokin decreases food intake in man. *American Journal of Clinical Nutrition*, 34, 154–60.

Klem, M.L., Wing, R.R., McGuire, M.T., Seagle, H.M., and Hill, J.O. 1997: A descriptive study of individuals successful at long term maintenance of substantial weight loss. *American Journal of Clinical Nutrition*, 66, 239–46.

Klem, M.L., Wing, R.R., McGuire, M.T., Seagle, H.M., and Hill, J.O. 1998: Psychological symptoms in individuals successful at long-term maintenance of weight loss. *Health Psychology*, 17, 336–45.

Klesges, R.C., Isbell, T.R., and Klesges, L.M. 1992: Relationship between dietary restraint, energy intake, physical activity, and body weight: A prospective analysis. *Journal of Abnormal Psychology*, 101, 668–74.

Klesges, R.C., Klem, M.L., Hanson, C.L., Eck, L.H., Ernst, J., O'Laughlin, D., Garrott, A., and Rife, R. 1990: The effects of applicants' health status and qualifications on simulated hiring decisions. *International Journal of Obesity*, 14, 527–35.

Klesges, R.C. and Klesges, L. 1988: Cigarette smoking as a dieting strategy in a university population. *International Journal of Eating Disorders*, 7, 413–19.

Klesges, R.C., Mizes, J.S., and Klesges, L.M. 1987: Self help dieting strategies in college males and females. *International Journal of Eating Disorders*, 6, 409–17.

Klesges, R.C., Stein, R.J., Eck, L.H., Isbell, T.R., and Klesges, L.M. 1991: Parental influences on food selection in young children and its relationships to childhood obesity. *American Journal of Clinical Nutrition*, 53, 859–64.

Klingenspor, B. 1994: Gender identity and bulimic eating behaviour. *Sex Roles*, 31, 407–31.

Kopelman, P.G. 1997: The effects of weight loss treatments on upper and lower body fat. *International Journal of Obesity*, 21, 619–25.

Kopelman, P. 1999a: Aetiology of obesity II: Genetics. In *Obesity: The Report of the British Nutrition Foundation Task Force*, Oxford: Blackwell Science, 39–44.

Kopelman, P. 1999b: Treatment of obesity V: Pharmacotherapy for obesity. In *Obesity: The Report of the British Nutrition Foundation Task Force*, Oxford: Blackwell Science, 182–6.

Kornhaber, A. 1970: The stuffing syndrome. *Psychosomatics*, 11, 580–4.

Kral, J.G. 1995: Surgical interventions for obesity. In K.D. Brownell and C.G. Fairburn (eds), *Eating Disorders and Obesity*, New York: Guilford Press, 510–15.

Kuczmarski, R.J., Flegal, K.M., Campbell, S.M., and Johnson, C.I. 1994: Increasing prevalence of overweight among US adults: The national health and nutrition examination surveys, 1960 to 1991. *Journal of the American Medical Association*, 272, 205–11.

Lacey, J.H. and Dolan, B.M. 1988: Bulimia in British Blacks and Asians: A catchment area study. *British Journal of Psychiatry*, 152, 73–9.

Laessle, R., Kittl, S., Fichter, M. et al. 1987: Major affective disorder in anorexic nervosa and bulimia. *British Journal of Psychiatry*, 151, 785–9.

Laessle, R.G., Tuschl, R.J., Kotthaus, B.C., and Pirke, K.M. 1989: Behavioural and biological correlates of dietary restraint in normal life. *Appetite*, 12, 83–94.

Lamb, C.S., Jackson, L., Cassiday, P., and Priest, D. 1993: Body figure preferences of men and women: A comparison of two generations. *Sex Roles*, 28, 345–58.

Larkin, J.C. and Pines, H.A. 1979: No fat persons need to apply: Experimental studies on the overweight sterotype and hiring preference. *Sociology of Work and Occupations*, 6, 312–27.

Lasegue, C. 1873: De l'anorexie hysterique. *Archives Generale de Medicine*, 21 (April), 385–403.

Lask, B. and Bryant-Waugh, R. 1992: Early-onset anorexia nervosa and related eating disorders. *Journal of Child Psychology and Psychiatry and Allied Disciplines*, 33, 281–300.

Lawrence, M. 1984: *The Anorexic Experience*. London: The Women's Press.

Lawrence, M. (ed.) 1987: *Fed Up and Hungry: Women, Oppression and Food*. London: The Women's Press.

Lazarides, L. 1999: *The Waterfall Diet*. London: BCA.

Le Grange, D., Stone, A.A., and Brownell, K.D. 1998: Eating disturbances in white and minority female dieters. *International Journal of Eating Disorders*, 24, 395–403.

Lean, M. 1997: Sibutramine: A review of clinical efficacy. *International Journal of Obesity*, 21 (Suppl. 1): S30–S36.

Lean, M.E.J., Han, T.S., and Morrison, C.E. 1995: Waist circumference as a measure for indicating need for weight management. *British Medical Journal*, 311, 158–61.

Lean, M.E.J., Han, T.S., and Seidall, J.C. 1998: Impairment of health and quality of life in people with large waist circumference. *Lancet*, 351, 853–6.

Leathwood, P. and Pollet, P. 1983: Diet-induced mood changes in normal populations. *Journal of Psychiatric Research*, 17, 147–54.

Lee, S. 1991: Anorexia nervosa in Hong Kong: A Chinese perspective. *Psychological Medicine*, 21, 703–12.

Lee, S., Chiu, H.F.K., and Chen, C.-N. 1989: Anorexia nervosa in Hong Kong: Why not more in Chinese? *British Journal of Psychiatry*, 154, 683–8.

Lee, S., Leung, T., Lee, A., Yu, H. et al. 1996: Body dissatisfaction among Chinese undergraduates and its implications for eating disorders in Hong Kong. *International Journal of Eating Disorders*, 20, 77–84.

Lepper, M., Sagotsky, G., Dafoe, J.L., and Greene, D. 1982: Consequences of superfluous social constraints: Effects on young children's social inferences and subsequent intrinsic interest. *Journal of Personality and Social Psychology*, 42, 51–65.

Lerner, R.M. and Gellert, E. 1969: Body build identification, preference and aversion in children. *Developmental Psychology*, 1, 456–62.

Lévi-Strauss, C. 1965: Le triangle culinaire. *L'Arc*, 26, 19–26 (English translation: The culinary triangle. *Partisan Review*, 33 (1966), 586–95).

Levine, M.J. 1997: *I Wish I Were Thin I Wish I Were Fat*. New York: Fireside.

Lieberman, H.R. 1989: Cognitive effects of various food constituents. In R. Shepherd (ed.), *Handbook of the Psychophysiology of Human Eating*, London: Wiley, 251–70.

Lieberman, H.R., Gabrieli, J.D.E., Nader, T., and Wurtman, R.J. 1990: Changes in mood, performance and memory induced by moderate doses of caffeine.

Lieberman, H.R., Spring, B., and Garfield, G.S. 1986: The behavioural effects of food constituents: Strategies used in studies of amino acids, protein, carbohydrate and caffeine. *Nutrition Reviews*, 44 (Suppl.), 61–70.

Lieberman, H.R., Wurtman, R.J., and Chew, B. 1986: Changes in mood after carbohydrate consumption among obese individuals. *American Journal of Clinical Nutrition*, 44, 772–8.

Lieberman, H.R., Wurtman, R.J., Garfield, G.S., Roberts, C.H., and Coviella, I.L. 1987: The effects of low doses of caffeine on human performance and mood. *Psychopharmacology*, 92, 308–12.

Lissner, L., Bengtsson, C., Lapidus, L., Larsson, B., Bengtsson, B., and Brownell, K. 1989: Body weight variability and mortality in the Gothenburg prospective studies of men and women. In P.B. Bjorntorp and S. Rossner (eds), *Obesity in Europe 88*, London: Libbey, 55–60.

Lissner, L. and Brownell, K.D. 1992: Weight cycling, mortality and cardiovascular disease: A review of epidemiologic findings. In P.B. Bjorntorp and B.N. Brostoff (eds), *Obesity*, Philadelphia: Lippincott, 653–61.

Lissner, L., Odell, P.M., D'Agostino, R.B., Stokes, J., Kreger, B.E., Belanger, A.J., and Brownell, K.D. 1991: Variability of body weight and health outcomes in the Framingham population. *New England Journal of Medicine*, 324, 1839–44.

Little, P. and Byrne, C.D. 2001: Abdominal obesity and the "hypertriglyceridaemic waist" phenotype. *British Medical Journal*, 322, 687–9.

Loke, W.H. and Meliska, C.J. 1984: Effects of caffeine use and ingestion on a protracted visual vigilance task. *Psychopharmacology*, 84, 454–7.

Loro, A.D. and Orleans, C.S. 1981: Binge eating in obesity: Preliminary findings and guidelines for behavioural analysis and treatment. *Addictive Behaviour*, 7, 155–66.

Lowe, C.F., Dowey, A., and Horne, P. 1998: Changing what children eat. In A. Murcott (ed.), *The Nation's Diet: The Social Science of Food Choice*, London: Longman, 57–80.

Lucas, A.R., Beard, C.M., O'Fallon, W.M., and Kurland, L.T. 1991: 50-year trends in the incidence of anorexia nervosa in Rochester, Minn.: A population-based study. *American Journal of Psychiatry*, 148, 917–22.

Lucas, A.R. and Soundy, T.J. 1993: The rise of bulimia nervosa. Ninth World Congress of Psychiatry, Rio de Janeiro, Brazil, June 6–12, Abstract 544, p. 139.

Ludwig, M.R. and Brownell, K.D. 1999: Lesbians, bisexual women, and body image: An investigation of gender roles and social group affiliation. *International Journal of Eating Disorders*, 25, 89–97.

Luebke, B.F. 1989: Out of focus: Images of women and men in newspaper photographs. *Sex Roles*, 20, 121–33.

Lynch, B. 1988: *The BBC Diet*. London: BBC Books.

Lytton, C. 1914: *Prisons and Prisoners*. London: Heinemann.

Macdiarmid, J.I. and Hetherington, M.M. 1995: Mood modulation by food: An exploration of affect and cravings in "chocolate addicts." *British Journal of Clinical Psychology*, 34, 129–38.

MacDougall, D.B. 1987: Effects of pigmentation, light scatter and illumination on food appearance and acceptance. In J. Solms, D.A. Booth, R.M. Pangborn, and O. Raunhardt (eds), *Food Acceptance and Nutrition*. London: Academic Press, 29–46.

Macintyre, S., Reilly, J., Miller, D., and Eldridge, J. 1998: Food choice, food scares and health: The role of the media. In A. Murcott (ed.), *The Nation's Diet: The Social Science of Food Choice*, London: Longman, 228–49.

Maddox, G.L., Back, K.W., and Liederman, V. 1968: Overweight as social deviance and disability, *Journal of Health and Social Behaviour*, 9, 287–98.

Maddox, G.L. and Liederman, V. 1969: Overweight as a social disability with medical implications. *Journal of Medical Education*, 44, 214–20.

Maes, H.H., Neale, M.C., and Eaves, L.J. 1997: Genetic and environmental factors in relative body weight and human adiposity. *Behavioural Genetics*, 27, 325–51.

Maimon, LA., Wang, L.W., Becker, M.H., Finlay, J., and Simonson, M. 1979: Attitudes toward obesity and the obese among health professionals. *Obesity Research*, 74, 331–6.

Mansfield, P.N. and Collard, J. 1988: *The Beginning of the Rest of your Life?* London: Macmillan.

Marlatt, G.A. and Gordon, J.R. 1985: *Relapse Prevention.* New York: Guilford Press.

Marshall, L. 1976: *The !Kung of Nyae Nyae.* Cambridge, MA: Harvard University Press.

Martz, D.M., Handley, K.B., and Eisler, R.M. 1995: The relationship between feminine gender roles stress, body image and eating disorders. *Psychology of Women Quarterly,* 19, 493–508.

Mason, E.E. 1987: Morbid obesity: Use of vertical banded gastroplasty. *Surgical Clinics of North America,* 67, 521–37.

Mattes, R.D. 1985: Gustation as a determinant of ingestion: Methodological issues. *American Journal of Sensory Studies,* 1, 275–90.

Mattes, R.D., Keumanyika, S.K., and Halpern, B.P. 1983: Salt taste responsiveness and preference among normotensive, prehypertensive and hypertensive adults. *Chemical Senses,* 8, 27–40.

Mattes, R.D. and Mela, D.J. 1986: Relationships between and among selected measures of sweet-taste preference and dietary intake. *Chemical Senses,* 11, 523–39.

Mazel, J. 1981: *The Beverly Hills Diet.* New York: MacMillan Publishing Co Inc.

McFarlane, T., Polivy, J., and Herman, C.P. 1998: Effects of false weight feedback on mood, self-evaluation, and food intake in restrained and unrestrained eaters. *Journal of Abnormal Psychology,* 107, 312–18.

McGuire, M.T., Wing, R.R., Klem, M.L., and Hill, J.O. 1999: Behavioral strategies of individuals who have maintained long term weight losses. *Obesity Research,* 7, 334–41.

McIntosh, E.N. 1995: *American Food Habits in Historical Perspective,* Westport, CT: Praeger.

McKensie, J.M. and Joyce, P.R. 1992: Hospitalization for anorexia nervosa. *International Journal of Eating Disorders,* 11, 235–41.

McReynolds, W.T. 1982: Towards a psychology of obesity: Review of research on the role of personality and level of adjustment. *International Journal of Eating Disorders,* 2, 37–57.

Meisel, R.L., Hays, T.C., del Paine, S.N., and Luttrell, V.R. 1990: Induction of obesity by group housing in female Syrian hamsters. *Physiology and Behavior,* 47, 815–17.

Mela, D.J. and Rogers, P.J. 1997: *Food, Eating and Obesity: The Psychobiological Basis of Appetite and Weight Control,* London: Chapman and Hall.

Mellbin, T. and Vuille, C. 1989: Further evidence of an association between psychosocial problems and increase in relative weight between 7 and 10 years of age. *Acta Paediatrica Scandinavica,* 78, 576–80.

Mennell, S. 1987: On the civilising of appetite. *Theory, Culture and Society,* 4, 373–403.

Mennell, S., Murcott, A., and van Otterloo, A.H. 1992: *The Sociology of Food: Eating, Diet and Culture.* London: Sage.

Michaud, C., Kahn, J.P., Musse, N., Burlet, C., Nicholas, J.P., and Majean, L. 1990: Relationships between a critical life event and eating behaviour in high school students. *Stress Medicine*, 6, 57–64.

Millett, K. 1969: *Sexual Politics*. London: Virago.

Mintel 1990: *Eggs. Market Intelligence*. London: Mintel.

Mintz, S.W. 1985: *Sweetness and Power: The Place of Sugar in Modern History*. New York: Viking.

Minuchin, S., Rosman, B.L., and Baker, L. 1978: The anorectic family. In *Psychosomatic Families: Anorexia Nervosa in Context*. Cambridge, MA: Harvard University Press.

Mishkind, M., Rodin, J., Silberstein, L., and Striegel-Moore, R. 1986: The embodiment of masculinity: Cultural, psychological and behavioural dimensions. *American Behavioural Scientist*, 29, 545–62.

Mitchell, J.E., Pyle, R.L., Eckert, E.D. et al. 1990: A comparison study of antidepressants and structured intensive group psychotherapy in the treatment of bulimia nervosa. *Archives of General Psychiatry*, 47, 149–57.

Moller, J.H., Taubert, K.A., Allen, H.D., Clark, E.B., and Lauer, R.M. 1994: Cardiovascular health and disease in children: Current status. *Circulation*, 89, 923–30.

Montague, C.T., Farooqi, I.S., Whitehead, J.P. et al. 1997: Congenital leptin deficiency is associated with severe early onset obesity in humans. *Nature*, 387, 903–8.

Mooney, L. and Brabant, S. 1987: Two martinis and a rested woman: "Liberation" in the Sunday comics. *Sex Roles*, 17, 409–20.

Morgan, H.G. and Russell, G.F.M. 1975: The value of family background in clinical features as predictors of long term outcome in anorexia nervosa: Four year follow up of 41 patients. *Psychological Medicine*, 5, 355–71.

Morgan, K. 1991: Women and the knife: Cosmetic surgery and the colonization of women's bodies. *Hypatia*, 6, 25–53.

Mori, D.L., Chaiken, S., and Pliner, P. 1987: Eating lightly and the self presentation of femininity. *Journal of Personality and Social Psychology*, 53, 693–702.

Morley, J.E., Levine, A.S., and Rowland, N.E. 1983: Stress induced eating. *Life Sciences*, 32, 2169–82.

Morris, A., Cooper, T., and Cooper, P.J. 1989: The changing shape of female fashion models. *International Journal of Eating Disorders*, 8, 593–6.

Mowrer, O.H. 1960: *Learning Theory and Behavior*. New York: John Wiley.

Muls, E., Kempen, K., Vansant, G., and Saris, W. 1995: Is weight cycling detrimental to health? A review of the literature in humans. *International Journal of Obesity*, 19 (Suppl. 3), S46–S50.

Mumford, D.B. 1993: Eating disorders in different cultures. *International Review of Psychiatry*, 5, 109–14.

Mumford, D.B., Whitehouse, A.M., and Choudry, I.Y. 1992: Survey of eating disorders in English Medium schools in Lahore, Pakistan. *International Journal of Eating Disorders*, 11, 173–84.

Mumford, D.B., Whitehouse, A.M., and Platts, M. 1991: Sociocultural correlates of eating disorders among Asian school girls in Bradford. *British Journal of Psychiatry*, 158, 222–8.

Munster, G. and Battig, K. 1975: Nicotine-induced hypophagia and hypodipsia in deprived and hypothalmically stimulated rats. *Psychopharmacologia*, 41, 211–17.

Murcott, A. 1982: On the social significance of the "cooked dinner" in South Wales. *Social Science Information*, 21, 677–95.

Murcott, A. 1983: Women's place: Cookbooks' images of technique and technology in the British kitchen. *Women's Studies International Forum*, 6, 33–9.

Murdock, G.P. and Provost, C. 1973: Factors in the division of labour by sex: A cross-cultural analysis. *Ethnology*, 12, 203–25.

Mvo, Z., Dick, J., and Steyn, K. 1999: Perceptions of overweight African women about acceptable body size of women and children. *Curationis*, 22, 27–31.

Myers, B.S. and Copplestone, T. 1985: *Landmarks of Western Art*. Middlesex: Newnes.

Nasser, M. 1986: Comparative study of the prevalence of abnormal eating attitudes among Arab female students of both London and Cairo universities. *Psychological Medicine*, 16, 621–5.

National Institutes of Health 1998: Clinical guidelines on the identification, evaluation, and treatment of overweight and obesity in adults – the evidence report. *Obesity Research*, 6 (Suppl. 2), 51–209S [published correction appears in *Obesity Research* 6, 464].

Neumark-Sztainer, D., Kaufmann, N.A., and Berry, E.M. 1995: Physical activity within community based weight control programme: Programme evaluation and predictors of stress. *Public Health Review*, 23, 237–51.

Newman, J. and Taylor, A. 1992: Effect of a means-end contingency on young children's food preferences. *Journal of Experimental Psychology*, 64, 200–16.

Newman, W.P., Freedman, D.S., Voors, A.W., Gard, P.D., Srinivasan, S.R., Cresanta, J.L., Williamson, G.D., Webber, L.S., and Berenson, G.S. 1986: Relation of serum lipoprotein levels and systolic blood pressure to early atherosclerosis: The Bogalusa Heart Study. *New England Journal of Medicine*, 314, 138–44.

NHS Centre for Reviews and Dissemination, University of York, 1997: *Systematic Review of Interventions in the Treatment and Prevention of Obesity*, York, UK.

Nicklas, T.A. 1995: Dietary studies of children and young adults (1973–1988): The Bogalusa heart study. *American Journal of Medical Science*, 310 (Suppl. 1), S101–S108.

Nielsen, S. 1990: The epidemiology of anorexia nervosa in Denmark from 1973 to 1987: A nationwide register study of psychiatric admission. *Acta Psychiatrica Scandinavica*, 81, 507–14.

Nielsen, S., Moller-Madsen, S., Isager, T., Jorgensen, J., Pagsberg, K., and Theander, S. 1998: Standardized mortality in eating disorders – a quantitative summary of previously published and new evidence. *Journal of Psychosomatic Research*, 44, 413–34.

Nuttall, F.Q. and Chasuk, R.M. 1998: Nutrition and the management of Type 2 diabetes. *Journal of Family Practice*, 47 (Suppl. 5), 545–53.

O'Donoghue, G., Treasure, J.L., and Russell, G.F.M. 1991: Eating disorders and motherhood. *Signpost* (newsletter for the Eating Disorders Association), April 1–5.

O'Kelly, L. 1994: Body talk. *The Guardian*, October 23, 30–2.

Ogden, C.L., Troiano, R.P., Briefel, R.R., Kuczmarski, R.J., Flegal, K.M., and Johnson, C.L. 1997: Prevalence of overweight among preschool children in the United States, 1971 through 1994. *Pediatrics*, 99, 11–17.

Ogden, J. 1992: *Fat Chance! The Myth of Dieting Explained*. London: Routledge.

Ogden, J. 1993: The measurement of restraint – confounding success and failure? *International Journal of Eating Disorders*, 13, 69–76.

Ogden, J. 1994: The effects of smoking cessation, restrained eating, and motivational states on food intake in the laboratory. *Health Psychology*, 13, 114–21.

Ogden, J. 1995: Cognitive and motivational consequence of dieting. *European Eating Disorders Review*, 24, 228–41.

Ogden, J. 1997: Diet as a vehicle for self control. In Lucy Yardley (ed.), *Material Discourses of Health and Illness*, London: Routledge, 199–216.

Ogden, J. 2000a: The correlates of long-term weight loss: A group comparison study of obesity. *International Journal of Obesity*, 24, 1018–25.

Ogden, J. 2000b: *Health Psychology: A Textbook*. 2nd edition. Buckingham, UK: Open University Press.

Ogden, J. 2002: *Health and the Construction of the Individual*. London: Routledge.

Ogden, J. and Awal, M., submitted: Obesity stereotypes: The role of body size and eating behaviour.

Ogden, J. and Chanana, A. 1998: Explaining the effect of ethnicity on weight concern: Finding a role for family values. *International Journal of Obesity*, 22, 641–7.

Ogden, J. and Elder, C. 1998: The role of family status and ethnic group on body image and eating behaviour. *International Journal of Eating Disorders*, 23, 309–15.

Ogden, J. and Evans, C. 1996: The problem with weighing: Effects on mood, self-esteem and body image. *International Journal of Obesity*, 20, 272–7.

Ogden, J. and Fox, P. 1994: An examination of the use of smoking for weight control in restrained and unrestrained eaters. *International Journal of Eating Disorders*, 16, 177–86.

Ogden, J. and Greville, L. 1993: Cognitive changes to preloading in restrained and unrestrained eaters as measured by the Stroop task. *International Journal of Eating Disorders*, 14, 185–95.

Ogden, J. and Mundray, K. 1996: The effect of the media on body satisfaction: The role of gender and size. *European Eating Disorders Review*, 4, 171–82.

Ogden, J. and Steward, J. 2000: The role of the mother daughter relationship in explaining weight concern. *International Journal of Eating Disorders*, 28, 78–83.

Ogden, J. and Taylor, C. 2000: Body size evaluation and body dissatisfaction within couples. *International Journal of Health Psychology*, 5, 25–32.

Ogden, J. and Thomas, D. 1999: The role of familial values in understanding the impact of social class on weight concern. *International Journal of Eating Disorders*, 25, 273–9.

Ogden, J. and Wardle, J. 1990: Control of eating and attributional style. *British Journal of Clinical Psychology*, 29, 445–6.

Ogden, J. and Wardle, J. 1991: Cognitive and emotional responses to food. *International Journal of Eating Disorders*, 10, 297–311.

Ogden, J. and Whyman, C. 1997: The effects of repeated weighing on psychological state. *European Eating Disorders Review*, 5, 121–30.

Ohlin, A. and Rossner, S. 1990: Maternal body weight development after pregnancy. *International Journal of Obesity*, 14, 159–73.

Ohlson, L.O., Larsson, B., Svardsudd, K., Welin, L., Eriksson, H., Wilhelmsen, L. et al. 1985: The influence of body fat distribution on the incidence of diabetes mellitus: 13.5 years follow up of the participants in the study of men born in 1913. *Diabetes*, 34, 1055–8.

Oliver, G. and Wardle, J. 1999: Perceived effects of stress on food choice. *Physiological Behaviour*, 66, 511–15.

Oliver, G. Wardle, J., and Gibson, E.L. 2000: Stress and food choice: A laboratory study. *Psychosomatic Medicine*, 62, 853–65.

Olivera, S.A., Ellison, R.C., Moore, L.L., Gillman, M.W., Garrahie, E.J., and Singer, M.R. 1992: Parent–child relationships in nutrient intake: The Framingham Children's Study. *American Journal of Clinical Nutrition*, 56, 593–8.

Olsen, L.C. and Mundt, M.H. 1986: Postpartum weight loss in a nurse-midwife practice. *Journal of Nurse-Midwifery*, 31, 177–81.

Oppenheimer, R., Howells, K., Palmer, R.L., and Chaloner, D. 1985: Adverse sexual experience in childhood and clinical eating disorders: A preliminary description. *Journal of Psychiatric Research*, 19, 357–61.

Orbach, S. 1978: *Fat is a Feminist Issue . . . How to Lose Weight Permanently – Without Dieting*. London: Arrow Books.

Orbach, S. 1986; 2nd edn 1993: *Hunger Strike: The Anorectic's Struggle as a Metaphor for our Age*. London: Faber and Faber.

Osler, M. and Schroll, M. 1997: Diet and mortality in a cohort of elderly people in a north European community. *International Journal of Epidemiology*, 26, 155.

Palazidou, E., Robinson, P., and Lishman, W.A. 1990: Neuroradiological and neuropsychological assessment in anorexia nervosa. *Psychological Medicine*, 20, 521–7.

Pangborn, R.M., Bos, K.E.O., and Stern, J.S. 1985: Dietary fat intake and taste responses to fat in milk by under, normal and overweight women. *Appetite*, 6, 25–40.

Pangborn, R.M. and Giovanni, M.E. 1984: Dietary intake of sweet foods and of dairy fats and resultant gustatory responses to sugar in lemonade and to fat in milk. *Appetite*, 5, 317–27.

Pangborn, R.M. and Pecore, S.D. 1982: Taste perception of sodium chloride in relation to dietary intake of salt. *American Journal of Clinical Nutrition*, 35, 510–20.

Parham, E.S., Astrom, M.F., and King, S.H. 1990: The association of pregnancy weight gain with the mother's postpartum weight. *Journal of American Dietetics Association*, 90, 550–4.

Patton, G.C. 1988: Mortality in eating disorders. *Psychological Medicine*, 18, 947–51.

Pavlou, K.N., Krey, S., and Steffee, W.P. 1989: Exercise as an adjunct to weight loss and maintenance in moderately obese subjects. *American Journal of Clinical Nutrition*, 49, 1115–23.

Paxton, S.J., Browning, C.J., and O'Connell, G. 1997: Predictors of exercise program participation in older women. *Psychology and Health*, 12, 543–52.

Paykel, E.S., Mueller, P.S., De La Vergne, P.M. 1973: Amitriptyline, weight gains and carbohydrate craving: A side effect. *British Journal of Psychiatry*, 123, 501–7.

Perri, M.G., Nezu, A.M., McKelvey, W.F., Shermer, R.L., Renjilian, D.A., and Viegener, B.J. 2001: Relapse prevention training and problem solving therapy in the long term management of obesity. *Journal of Consulting and Clinical Psychology*, 69, 722–6.

Pine, C.J. 1985: Anxiety and eating behavior in obese and non obese American Indians and White Americans. *Journal of Personality and Social Psychology*, 49, 774–80.

Piran, N., Kennedy, S., Garfinkel, P.E., and Owens, M. 1985: Affective disturbance in eating disorders. *Journal of Nervous Mental Disorders*, 173, 395–400.

Pliner, P., Chaiken, S., and Flett, C. 1990: Gender differences in concern with body weight and physical appearance over the life span. *Personality and Social Psychology Bulletin*, 16, 263–73.

Pliner, P. and Leowen, E.R. 1997: Temperament and food neophobia in children and their mothers. *Appetite*, 28, 239–54.

Polivy, J. and Herman, C.P. 1983: *Breaking the Diet Habit*. New York: Basic Books.

Polivy, J. and Herman, C.P. 1985: Dieting and bingeing. A causal analysis. *American Psychologist*, 40, 193–201.

Polivy, J.A. and Herman, C.P. 1989: Dietary restraint and binge eating: A response to Charnock. *British Journal of Clinical Psychology*, 28, 341–3.

Polivy, J. and Herman, C.P. 1992: Undieting: A program to help people stop dieting. *International Journal of Eating Disorders*, 11, 261–8.

Polivy, J. and Herman, C.P. 1999a: Distress and eating: Why do dieters overeat? *International Journal of Eating Disorders*, 26, 153–64.

Polivy, J. and Herman, C.P. 1999b: The effects of resolving to diet on restrained and unrestrained eaters: The "false hope syndrome." *International Journal of Eating Disorders*, 26, 434–47.

Polivy, J., Herman, C.P., and McFarlane, T. 1994: Effects of anxiety on eating: Does palatability moderate distress-induced overeating in dieters? *Journal of Abnormal Psychology*, 103, 505–10.

Polivy, J., Zeitlin, S.B., Herman, C.P., and Beal, A.L. 1994: Food restriction and binge eating: A study of former prisoners of war. *Journal of Abnormal Psychology*, 103, 409–11.

Pope, H.G. Jr, Hudson, J.I., and Yurgelun-Todd, D. 1984: Anorexia nervosa and bulimia among 300 suburban women shoppers. *American Journal of Psychiatry*, 141, 292–4.

Popper, R., Smits, G., Meiselman, H.L., and Hirsch, E. 1989: Eating in combat: A survey of US Marines. *Military Medicine*, 154, 619–23.

Povey, R., Conner, M., Sparks, P., James, R., and Shepherd, R. 2000: The theory of planned behaviour and healthy eating: Examining additive and moderating effects of social influence variables. *Psychology and Health*, 14, 991–1006.

Powell, D. and Khan, S. 1995: Racial differences in women's desire to be thin. *International Journal of Eating Disorders*, 17, 191–5.

Powell, K.E., Thompson, P.D., Coopersen, C.J., and Kendrick, J.S. 1987: Physical activity and the incidence of coronary heart disease. *Annual Review of Public Health*, 8, 253–87.

Prentice, A.M. 1995a: Alcohol and obesity. *International Journal of Obesity*, 19, S44–S51.

Prentice, A.M. 1995b: Are all calories equal? In R. Cottrell (ed.), *Weight Control: The Current Perspective*, London: Chapman and Hall.

Prentice, A. 1999: Aetiology of obesity I: Introduction. In *Obesity: The Report of the British Nutrition Foundation Task Force*. Oxford: Blackwell Science, 37–8.

Prentice, A.M., Black, A.E., Goldberg, G.R. et al. 1986: High levels of energy expenditure are in obese women. *British Medical Journal*, 292, 983–7.

Prentice, A.M., Black, A.E., Murgatroyd, P.R., Goldberg, G.R., and Coward, W.A. 1989: Metabolism or appetite: Questions of energy balance with particular reference to obesity. *Journal of Human Nutrition and Dietetics*, 2, 95–104.

Prentice, A.M. and Jebb, S.A. 1995: Obesity in Britain: Gluttony or sloth? *British Medical Journal*, 311, 437–9.

Prentice, A.M. and Paul, A.A. 2000: Fat and energy needs of children in developing countries. *American Journal of Clinical Nutrition*, 72 (Suppl. 5), 1253S–1265S.

Prescott-Clarke, P. and Primatesta, P. 1998: *Health Survey for England 1996*. London: HMSO.

Prochaska, J.O. and DiClemente, C.C. 1984: *The Transtheoretical Approach: Crossing Traditional Boundaries of Therapy*. Homewood, IL: Dow Jones Irwin.

Punch, M. 1977: *Progressive Retreat: a Sociological Study of Dartington Hall School*. Cambridge: Cambridge University Press.

Pyle, R.L. and Mitchell, J.E. 1986: The prevalence of bulimia in selected samples. *Adolescent Psychiatry*, 13, 241–52.

Pyle, R.L., Mitchell, J.E., Eckert, E.D., Halvorson, P.A., Neuman, P.A., and Goff, G.M. 1983: The incidence of bulimia in freshman college students. *International Journal of Eating Disorders*, 3, 45–51.

Raats, M.M., Shepherd, R., and Sparks, P. 1995: Including moral dimensions of choice within the structure of the theory of planned behavior. *Journal of Applied Social Psychology*, 25, 484–94.

Rand, C.S.W. and McGregor, A.M.C. 1991: Successful weight loss following obesity surgery and the perceived liability of morbid obesity. *International Journal of Obesity*, 15, 577–9.

Rastam, M. and Gillberg, C. 1991: The family background in anorexia nervosa: A population-based study. *Journal of the American Academy of Child and Adolescent Psychiatry*, 30, 283–9.

Rastam, M., Gillberg, C., and Garton, M. 1989: Anorexia nervosa in a Swedish urban region: A population-based study. *British Journal of Psychiatry*, 155, 642–6.

Ravussin, E. 1993: Energy metabolism in obesity. Studies in the Pima Indians. *Diabetes Care*, 16, 232–8.

Ravussin, E. and Bogardus, C. 1989: Relationship of genetics, age and physical activity to daily energy expenditure and fuel utilisation. *American Journal of Clinical Nutrition*, 49, 968–75.

Ravussin, E., Fontvielle, A.M., Swinburn, B.A., and Bogardus, C. 1993: Risk factors for the development of obesity. *Annals of NY Academy of Sciences*, 141–50.

Ravussin, E., Lilioja, S., Knowler, W.C. et al. 1988: Reduced rate of energy expenditure as a risk factor for body-weight gain. *New England Journal of Medicine*, 318, 467–72.

Regina, E.G., Smith, G.M., Keiper, C.G., and McKelvey, R.K. 1974: Effects of caffeine on alertness in simulated automobile driving. *Journal of Applied Psychology*, 59, 483–9.

Reiff, D.W. 1992: *Eating Disorders: Nutrition Therapy in the Recovery Process*. Aspen Publishers Inc.

Resnicow, K., Davis-Hearn, M., Smith, M., Baranowski, T., Lin, L.S., Baranowski, J., Doyle, C., and Wang, D.T. 1997: Social-cognitive predictors of fruit and vegetable intake in children. *Health Psychology*, 16, 272–6.

Riddle, P.K. 1980: Attitudes, beliefs, intentions and behaviours of men and women toward regular jogging. *Research Quarterly for Exercise and Sport*, 51, 663–74.

Rissanen, A.M., Heliovaara, M., Knekt, P., Reunanen, A., and Aromaa, A. 1991: Determinants of weight gain and overweight in adult Finns. *European Journal of Clinical Nutrition*, 45, 419–30.

Robbins, T.W. and Fray, P.J. 1980: Stress induced eating: Fact, fiction or misunderstanding. *Appetite*, 1, 103–33.

Roberts, A. 1992: Judges explain why anorexia must be treated. *The Times*, London, July 11.

Roberts, S.B., Savage, J., Coward, W.A., Chew, B., and Lucas, A. 1988: Energy expenditure and energy intake in infants born to lean and overweight mothers. *New England Journal of Medicine*, 318, 461–6.

Robinson, R.G., McHigh, P.R., and Folstein, M.F. 1975: Measurement of appetite disturbances in psychiatric disorder. *Journal of Psychiatric Research*, 12, 59–68.

Rodin, J., Bray, G.A., Atkinson, R.L., Dahms, W.T., Greenway, F.L., Hamilton, K., and Molitch, M. 1977: Predictors of successful weight loss in an outpatient obesity clinic. *International Journal of Obesity*, 1, 79–87.

Rogers, R.W. 1985: Attitude change and information integration in fear appeals. *Psychological Reports*, 56, 179–82.

Roncari, D.A., Kindler, S., and Hollenberg, C.H. 1986: Excessive proliferation of cultured adipocytes from massively obese persons. *Metabolism*, 35, 1–4.

Root, M.P.P. and Fallon, P. 1988: The incidence of victimization experiences in a bulimic sample. *Journal of Interpersonal Violence*, 3, 161–73.

Rosen, J.C. and Leitenberg, E. 1982: Bulimia nervosa: Treatment with exposure and response prevention. *Behaviour Therapy*, 13, 117–24.

Rosenfield, S.N. and Stevenson, J.S. 1988: Perception of daily stress and oral coping behaviors in normal, overweight and recovering alcoholic women. *Research in Nursing and Health*, 11, 165–74.

Ross, C.E. 1994: Overweight and depression. *Journal of Health and Social Behaviour*, 35, 63–78.

Rossner, S. 1984: Ideal body weight – for whom? *Acta Medica Scandinavica*, 216, 241–2.

Rossner, S., Sjostrom, L., Noak, R., Meinders, A.E., and Noseda, G. 2000: Weight loss, weight maintenance and improved cardiovascular risk factors after 2 years treatment with orlistat for obesity. *Obesity Research*, 8, 49–61.

Rothblum, E. 1990: Women and weight: Fad and fiction. *The Journal of Psychology*, 124, 5–24.

Rowland, N.E. and Antelman, S.M. 1976: Stress induced hyperphagia and obesity in rats: A possible model for understanding human obesity. *Science*, 191, 310–11.

Rowston, W.M. and Lacey, H.J. 1992: Stealing in bulimia nervosa. *International Journal of Social Psychiatry*, 38, 309–13.

Royal College of Psychiatrists 1992: Eating disorders. Council Report CR14, London.

Rozin, P. 1976: The selection of foods by rats, humans, and other animals. In J. Rosenblatt, R.A. Hinde, C. Beer, and E. Shaw (eds), *Advances in the Study of Behavior*, vol. 6, New York: Academic Press, 21–67.

Rozin, P. 1982: Human food selection: The interaction of biology, culture and individual experience. In L.M. Barker (ed.), *The Psychobiology of Human Food Selection*. Bridgeport, CT: AVI, 225–54.

Rozin, P. and Fallon, A. 1988: Body image, attitudes to weight, and misperception of figure preferences of the opposite sex: A comparison of men and women in two generations. *Journal of Abnormal Psychology*, 97, 342–5.

Rucker, C.E. and Cash, T. 1992: Body images, body size perceptions and eating behaviours among African-American and white college women. *International Journal of Eating Disorders*, 12, 291–9.

Ruderman, A.J. and Wilson, G.T. 1979: Weight, restraint, cognitions and counterregulation. *Behaviour Research and Therapy*, 17, 581–90.

Russell, G.F.M. 1970: Anorexia nervosa: Its identity as an illness and its treatment. In J.H. Price (ed.), *Modern Trends in Psychological Medicine*, London: Butterworths, 131–64.

Russell, G.F.M. 1979: Bulimia nervosa: An aminous variant of anorexia nervosa. *Psychological Medicine*, 9, 429–48.

Russell, G.F.M. 1995: Anorexia nervosa through time. In G. Szmukler, C. Dare, and J. Treasure (eds), *Handbook of Eating Disorders: Theory, Treatment and Research*, London: Wiley, 5–17.

Russell, G.F.M., Szmukler, G., Dare, C., and Eisler, I. 1987: An evaluation of family therapy in anorexia nervosa and bulimia nervosa. *Archives of General Psychiatry*, 44, 1047–56.

Russell, G.F.M. and Treasure, J.L. 1988: Intrauterine growth and neonatal weight gain in anorexia nervosa. *British Medical Journal*, 296, 1038.

Rutledge, T. and Linden, W. 1998: To eat or not to eat: Affective and physiological mechanisms in the stress-eating relationship. *Journal of Behavioural Medicine*, 21, 221–40.

Ryan, A.S., Craig, L.D., and Fin, S.C. 1992: Nutrient intakes and dietary patterns of older Americans: a national study. *Journal of Gerontology*, 47, M145–50.

Sandler, J. and Dare, C. 1970: The psychoanalytic concept of orality. *Journal of Psychosomatic Research*, 14, 211–22.

Saris, W.H., Astrup, A., Prentice, A.M., Zunft, H.J., Formiguera, X., Verboeket-van de Venne, W.P., Raben, A., Poppitt, S.D., Seppelt, B., Johnston, A., Vasilaras, T.H., and Keogh, G.F. 2000: Randomized controlled trial of changes in dietary carbohydrate/fat ratio and simple vs complex carbohydrates on body weight and blood lipids: The CARMEN study. The Carbohydrate Ratio Management in European National diets. *International Journal of Obesity and Related Metabolic Disorders*, 24, 1310–18.

Schachter, S. 1968: Obesity and eating. *Science*, 161, 751–6.

Schachter, S. and Gross, L. 1968: Manipulated time and eating behaviour. *Journal of Personality and Social Psychology*, 10, 98–106.

Schachter, S. and Rodin, J. 1974: *Obese Humans and Rats*. Potomac, MD: Erlbaum.

Schauberger, C.W., Rooney, B.L., and Brimer, L.M. 1992: Factors that influence weight loss in the puerperium. *Obstetrics and Gynecology*, 79, 424–92.

Schepank, H. 1992: Genetic determinants of anorexia nervosa: Results of studies in twins. In W. Herzog, H.C. Deter, and W. Vandereycken (eds), *The Course of Eating Disorders*, Berlin: Springer, 241–56.

Schifter, D.A. and Ajzen, I. 1985: Intention, perceived control, and weight loss: An application of the theory of planned behavior. *Journal of Personality and Social Psychology*, 49, 843–51.

Schilder, P. 1950: *The Image and Appearance of the Human Body*. New York: International Universities Press.

Schlettwein-Gsell, D., Barclay, D., Osler, M., and Trichopoulou, A. 1991: Dietary habits and attitudes. *European Journal of Clinical Nutrition*, 45 (Suppl. 3), 83–95.

284   References

Schmidt, U., Tiller, J., and Treasure, J. 1993: Setting the scene for eating disorders: Childhood care, classification and course of illness. *Psychological Medicine*, 23, 663–72.

Schneider, J. and Agras, W. 1987: Bulimia in males. A matched comparison with females. *International Journal of Eating Disorders*, 6, 235–42.

Schulz, L.O. and Schoeller, D.A. 1994: A compilation of total daily energy expenditure and body weights in healthy adults. *American Journal of Clinical Nutrition*, 60, 676–81.

Schwarzer, R. 1992: Self efficacy in the adoption and maintenance of health behaviours: Theoretical approaches and a new model. In R. Schwarzer (ed.), *Self Efficacy: Thought Control of Action*, Washington, DC: Hemisphere, 217–243.

Secord, P.F. and Jourard, S.M. 1953: The appraisal of body cathexis: Body cathexis and the self. *Journal of Consulting Psychology*, 17, 343–7.

Seid, R.P. 1994: Too close to the bone: The historical context for women's obsession with slenderness. In P. Fallon, M.A. Katzman, and S.C. Wooley (eds), *Feminist Perspectives on Eating Disorders*, New York: Guilford Press.

Selvini, M. 1988: Self starvation: The last synthesis on anorexia nervosa. In M. Selvini and M. Selvini Palazzoli (eds), *The work of Mara Selvini Palazzoli*, NJ: Jason Aronson Inc, 147–50.

Selvini Palazzoli, M. 1974: *Self Starvation: From the Intrapsychic to the Transpersonal Approach*. London: Chaucer.

Shepherd, R. 1988: Belief structure in relation to low-fat milk consumption. *Journal of Human Nutrition and Dietetics*, 1, 421–8.

Shepherd, R. 1989: Factors affecting food preferences and choice. In R. Shepherd (ed.), *Handbook of the Psychophysiology of Human Eating*, London: Wiley, 3–24.

Shepherd, R. and Farleigh, C.A. 1986a: Attitudes and personality related to salt intake. *Appetite*, 7, 343–54.

Shepherd, R. and Farleigh, C.A. 1986b: Preferences, attitudes and personality as determinants of salt intake. *Human Nutrition: Applied Nutrition*, 40A, 195–208.

Shepherd, R. and Farleigh, C.A. 1989: Sensory assessment of foods and the role of sensory attributes in determining food choice. In R. Shepherd (ed.), *Handbook of the Psychophysiology of Human Eating*, London: Wiley, 25–56.

Shepherd, R., Farleigh, C.A., and Land, D.G. 1984: The relationship between salt intake and preferences for different salt levels in soup. *Appetite*, 5, 281–90.

Shepherd, R. and Stockley, L. 1985: Fat consumption and attitudes towards food with a high fat content. *Human Nutrition: Applied Nutrition*, 39A, 431–42.

Shepherd, R. and Stockley, L. 1987: Nutrition knowledge, attitudes, and fat consumption. *Journal of the American Dietetic Association*, 87, 615–19.

Sherman, A.M., Bowen, D.J., Vitolins, M., Perri, M.G., Rosal, M.C., Sevick, M.A., and Ockene, J. 2000: Dietary adherence: Characteristics and interventions. *Control Clinical Trials*, 21, 206S–11S.

Shipman, W.G. and Plesset, M.R. 1963: Anxiety and depression in obese dieters. *Archives of General Psychiatry*, 8, 530–5.

Shute, J. 1992: *Life-size*. London: Mandarin.

Siever, M. 1994: Sexual orientation and gender as factors in socioculturally acquired vulnerability to body dissatisfaction and eating disorders. *Journal of Consulting and Clinical Psychology*, 62, 252–60.

Signorielli, N. 1989: Television and conceptions about sex roles: Maintaining conventionality and the status quo. *Sex Roles*, 21, 341–60.

Silverstein, B., Perdue, L., Peterson, B., and Kelly, E. 1986: The role of the mass media in promoting a thin standard of bodily attractiveness for women. *Sex Roles*, 14, 519–32.

Silverstein, B., Peterson, B., and Perdue, L. 1986: Some correlates of the thin standard of physical attractiveness of women. *International Journal of Eating Disorders*, 5, 898–905.

Silverstone, J.T. and Stunkard, A. 1968: The anorectic effect of dexamphetamine sulphate. *British Journal of Chemotherapy*, 33, 513–22.

Silverstone, T. and Kyriakides, M. 1982: Clinical pharmacology of appetite. In T. Silverstone (ed.), *Drugs and Appetite*, London: Academic Press, 93–123.

Sjostrom, L. 1980: Fat cells and body weight. In A.J. Stunkard (ed.), *Obesity*, Philadelphia: Saunders, 72–100.

Sjostrom, L., Rissanen, A., Andersen, T., Boldrin, M., Golay, A., Koppeschaar, H.P.F., and Krempf, M. 1998: Randomised placebo controlled trial of orlistat for weight loss and prevention of weight regain in obese patients. *Lancet*, 352, 167–72.

Slade, P.D. 1982: Towards a functional analysis of anorexia nervosa and bulimia nervosa. *British Journal of Clinical Psychology*, 21, 167–79.

Slade, P.D., Dewey, M.E., Newton, T., Brodie, D.A. et al. 1990: Development and validation of the the Body Satisfaction Scale (BSS). *Psychology and Health*, 4, 213–20.

Slade, P.D. and Russell, G.F.M. 1973: Awareness of body dimensions in anorexia nervosa: Cross sectional and longitudinal studies. *Psychological Medicine*, 3, 188–99.

Smart, L. and Wegner, D.M. 1999: Covering up what can't be seen: Concealable stigma and mental control. *Journal of Personality and Social Psychology*, 77, 474–86.

Smith, G. 1993: *Fibrenetics*. London: Fourth Estate.

Smith, G.S. and Kraus, J.F. 1988: Alcohol and residential, recreational, and occupational injuries: A review of the epidemiologic evidence. In L. Breslow, J.E. Fielding, and L.B. Lave (eds), *Annual Review of Public Health*, vol. 9, Palo Alto, CA: Annual Reviews.

Smith, L.M., Mullis, R.L., and Hill, W.E. 1995: Identity strivings within the mother daughter relationship. *Psychological Reports*, 76, 495–503.

Smolak, L., Levine, M., and Sullins, E. 1990: Are child sexual experiences related to eating-disordered attitudes and behaviours in a college sample? *International Journal of Eating Disorders*, 9, 167–78.

Snow, J.T. and Harris, M.B. 1986: An analysis of weight and diet content in five women's interest magazines. *The Journal of Obesity and Weight Regulation*, 5, 194–214.

Sobal, J. and Stunkard, A. 1989: Socio-economic status and obesity: A review of the literature. *Psychological Bulletin*, 105, 260–75.

Soley, L.C. and Kurzbard, G. 1986: Sex in advertising: A comparison of 1964 and 1984 magazine advertisements. *Journal of Advertising*, 15, 46–64.

Sparks, P., Conner, M., James, R., Shepherd, R., and Povey, R. 2001: Ambivalence about health-related behaviours: An exploration in the domain of food choice. *British Journal of Health Psychology*, 6, 53–68.

Sparks, P., Hedderley, D., and Shepherd, R. 1992: An investigation into the relationship between perceived control, attitude variability and the consumption of two common foods. *European Journal of Social Psychology*, 22, 55–71.

Sparks, P. and Shepherd, R. 1992: Self-identity and the theory of planned behavior: Assessing the role of identification with green consumerism. *Social Psychology Quarterly*, 55, 1388–99.

Spencer, J.A. and Fremouw, M.J. 1979: Binge eating as a function of restraint and weight classification. *Journal of Abnormal Psychology*, 88, 262–7.

Spillman, D. 1990: Survey of food and vitamin intake responses reported by university students experiencing stress. *Psychological Reports*, 66, 499–502.

Spitzer, L. and Rodin, J. 1981: Human eating behaviour: A critical review of studies in normal weight and overweight individuals. *Appetite*, 2, 293–329.

Staffieri, J.F. 1967: A study of social stereotype of body image in children. *Journal of Personality and Social Psychology*, 7, 101–4.

Starr Sered, S. 1988: Food and holiness: Cooking as a sacred act among middle eastern Jewish women. *Anthropological Quarterly*, 61, 129–39.

Steiger, H., Stotland, S., Ghadirian, A.M., and Whitehead, V. 1994: Controlled study of eating concerns and psychopathological traits in relative of eating disorders probands: Do familial traits exist? *International Journal of Eating Disorders*, 18, 107–18.

Steiger, H. and Zanko, M. 1990: Sexual traumata among eating-disordered, psychiatric, and normal female groups. *Journal of Interpersonal Violence*, 5, 74–86.

Stein, E.M., Stein, S., and Linn, M.W. 1985: Geriatric sweet tooth. A problem with tricyclics. *Journal of American Geriatric Society*, 33, 687–92.

Steptoe, A., Pollard, T.M., and Wardle, J. 1995: Development of a measure of the motives underlying the selection of food: The food choice questionnaire. *Appetite*, 25, 267–84.

Stern, J.S. 1984: Is obesity a disease of inactivity? In A.J. Stunkard and E. Stellar (eds), *Eating and Its Disorders*, New York: Raven Press.

Stewart, D.E., Robinson, G.E., Goldblock, D.S., and Wright, C. 1990: Infertility and eating disorders. *American Journal of Obstetrics and Gynecology*, 163, 1196–9.

Stice, E. 1998: Relations of restraint and negative affect to bulimic pathology: A longitudinal test of three competing models. *International Journal of Eating Disorders*, 23, 243–60.

Stice, E., Ozer, S., and Kees, M. 1997: Relation of dietary restraint to bulimic symptomatology: The effect of the criterion confounding the restraint scale. *Behaviour Research and Therapy*, 35, 145–52.

Stone, A.A. and Brownell, K.D. 1994: The stress-eating paradox: Multiple daily measurements in adult males and females. *Psychology and Health*, 9, 425–36.

Story, M., French, S., Resnick, M., and Blum, R. 1995: Ethnic/racial and socioeconomic differences in dieting behaviours and body image perceptions in adolescents. *International Journal of Eating Disorders*, 18, 173–9.

Striegel-Moore, H., Shrieber, B., Pike, M., Wifley, E., and Rodin, J. 1995: Drive for thinness in Black and white preadolescent girls. *International Journal of Eating Disorders*, 18, 59.

Striegel-Moore, R.H., Silberstein, L., and Rodin, J. 1986: Towards an understanding of risk factors for bulimia. *American Psychologist*, 41, 246–63.

Striegel-Moore, R.H., Tucker, N., and Hsu, J. 1990: Body image dissatisfaction and disordered eating in lesbian college students. *International Journal of Eating Disorders*, 9, 493–500.

Strober, M. and Katz, J. 1987: Depression in the eating disorders. A review of descriptive, family and biological findings. In D.M. Garner and P.E. Garfinkel (eds), *Diagnostic Issues in Anorexia Nervosa and Bulimia Nervosa*. New York: Brunner Mazel.

Strober, M., Lampert, C., Morrell, W., Burroughs, J., and Jacobs, C. 1990: A controlled family study of anorexia nervosa: Evidence of familial aggregation and lack of shared transmission with affective disorders. *International Journal of Eating Disorders*, 9, 239–53.

Strober, M., Morrell, W., Burroughs, J., Salkin, B., and Jacobs, C. 1985: A controlled family study of anorexia nervosa. *Journal of Psychiatric Research*, 19, 239–46.

Stuart, R.B. 1967: Behavioural control of overeating. *Behaviour Research and Therapy*, 5, 357–65.

Stuart, R.B. and Davis, B. 1972: *Slim Chance in a Fat World: Behavioural Control of Obesity*. Champaign, IL: Research Press.

Stunkard, A.J. 1958: The management of obesity. *New York State Journal of Medicine*, 58, 79–87.

Stunkard, A.J. 1984: The current status of treatment for obesity in adults. In A.J. Stunkard and E. Stellar (eds), *Eating and Its Disorders*, New York: Raven Press, 157–74.

Stunkard, A.J., Harris, J.R., Pedersen, N.L., and McClearn, G.E. 1990: A separated twin study of body mass index. *New England Journal of Medicine*, 322, 1483–7.

Stunkard, A.J. and Messick, S. 1985: The three factor eating questionnaire to measure dietary restraint, disinhibition and hunger. *Journal of Psychosomatic Research*, 29, 71–8.

Stunkard, A.J. and Penick, S.B. 1979: Behaviour modification in the treatment of obesity: The problem of maintaining weight loss. *Archives of General Psychiatry*, 36, 801–6.

Stunkard, A.J., Sorenson, T.I.A., Hanis, C., Teasdale, T.W., Chakraborty, R., Schull, W.J., and Schulsinger, F. 1986: An adoption study of human obesity. *New England Journal of Medicine*, 314, 193–8.

Stunkard, A.J., Sorensen, T., and Schulsinger, F. 1983: Use of the Danish adoption register for the study of obesity and thinness. In S. Kety (ed.), *The Genetics of Neurological and Psychiatric Disorders*, New York: Raven Press.

Stunkard, A.J., Stinnett, J.L., and Smoller, J.W. 1986: Psychological and social aspects of the surgical treatment of obesity. *American Journal of Psychiatry*, 143, 417–29.

Suematsu, H., Ishikawa, H., and Inaba, Y. 1986: Epidemiological studies on anorexia nervosa. *Shinshin-Igaku [Psychosomatic Medicine]*, 26, 53–8.

Sullivan, P.F. 1995: Mortality in anorexia nervosa. *American Journal of Psychiatry*, 152, 1073–4.

Sumner, A., Waller, G., Killick, S., and Elstein, M. 1993: Body image distortion in pregnancy: A pilot study of the effects of media images. *Journal of Reproductive and Infant Psychology*, 11, 203–8.

Sutton, S. 1998: Predicting and explaining intentions and behaviour: How well are we doing? *Journal of Applied Social Psychology*, 28, 1317–38.

Svendsen, O.L., Hassager, C., and Christiansen, C. 1994: Six months follow-up on exercise added to a short-term diet in overweight postmenopausal women – effects on body composition, resting metabolic rate, cardiovascular risk factors and bone. *International Journal of Obesity*, 18, 692–8.

Svensson, E., Persson, L., and Sjoberg, L. 1980: Mood effects of diazepam and caffeine. *Psychopharmacology*, 67, 73–80.

Syme, S.L., Marmot, M.G., Kagan, H., and Rhoads, G. 1975: Epidemiologic studies of CHD and stroke in Japanese men living in Japan, Hawaii and California. *American Journal of Epidemiology*, 102, 477–80.

Szmukler, G.I., Andrews, D., Kingston, K., Chen, L., Stargatt, R., and Stanley, R. 1992: Neuropsychological impairment in anorexia nervosa before and after refeeding. *Journal of Clinical and Experimental Neuropsychology*, 14, 347–352.

Szmukler, G., Dare, C., and Treasure, J. (eds) 1995: *Handbook of Eating Disorders: Theory, Treatment and Research*. London: Wiley.

Szmukler, G.I., McCance, C., McCrone, L., and Hunter, D. 1986: Anorexia nervosa: A psychiatric case register study from Aberdeen. *Psychological Medicine*, 16, 49–58.

Szmukler, G.I. and Patton, G. 1995: Sociocultural models of eating disorders. In G. Szmukler, C. Dare, and J. Treasure (eds), *Handbook of Eating Disorders: Theory, Treatment and Research*, London: Wiley, 177–92.

Szmukler, G.I. and Tantam, J. 1984: Anorexia nervosa: Starvation dependence. *British Journal of Medical Psychology*, 57, 303–10.

Taylor, C.B., Fortmann, S.P., Flora, J. et al. 1991: Effect of long term community health education on body mass index. *American Journal of Epidemiology*, 134, 235–49.

Theander, S. 1970: Anorexia nervosa: A psychiatric investigation of 94 female patients. *Acta Psychiatrica Scandinavica*, Suppl. 214.

Thompson, J.K. 1990: Body image disturbance: Assessment and treatment. Elmsford, NY: Pergamon.

Thompson, J.P., Palmer, R.L., and Petersen, S.A. 1988: Is there a metabolic component to counterregulation? *International Journal of Eating Disorders*, 7, 307–19.

Thompson, M., Zanna, M., and Griffin, D. 1995: Let's not be indifferent about (attitudinal) ambivalence. In R.E. Perry and J.A. Krosnick (eds), *Attitude Strength: Antecedents and Consequences*, Hillsdale, NJ: Erlbaum, 361–86.

Thornton, B., Leo, R., and Alberg, K. 1991: Gender role typing, the superwomen ideal and the potential for eating disorders. *Sex Roles*, 25, 469–84.

Tiggemann, M. and Pennington, B. 1990: The development of gender differences in body-size dissatisfaction. *Australian Psychologist*, 25, 306–13.

Tiggemann, M. and Rothblum, E.D. 1988: Gender differences in social consequences of perceived overweight in the United States and Australia. *Sex Roles*, 18, 75–86.

Todhunter, E.N. 1973: Food habits, food faddism and nutrition. In M. Rechcigl (ed.), *Food, Nutrition and Health: World Review of Nutrition and Dietetics*, 16, 186–317. Basel: Karger.

Toner, B.B., Garfinkel, P., and Garner, D. 1988: Affective and anxiety disorders in the longterm follow-up of anorexia nervosa. *International Journal of Psychiatric Medicine*, 18, 357–64.

Torgerson, J.S. and Sjostrom, L. 2001: The Swedish Obese Subjects (SOS) study – rationale and results. *International Journal of Obesity*, 35, S2–S4.

Touyz, S.W., Kopec-Schrader, E.M., and Beumont, P.J.V. 1993: Anorexia nervosa in males. *Australian and New Zealand Journal of Psychiatry*, 27, 512–17.

Treasure, J.L. and Holland, A.J. 1989: Genetic vulnerability to eating disorders: Evidence from twin and family studies. In H. Remschmidt and M.H. Schmidt (eds), *Anorexia Nervosa*, Toronto: Hogrefe and Huber, 59–68.

Treasure, J. and Holland, A. 1995: Genetic factors in eating disorders. In G. Szmukler, C. Dare, and J. Treasure (eds), *Handbook of Eating Disorders: Theory, Treatment and Research*, London: Wiley, 65–81.

Treasure, J. and Szmukler, G.I. 1995: Medical complications of chronic anorexia nervosa. In G. Szmukler, C. Dare, and J. Treasure (eds), *Handbook of Eating Disorders: Theory, Treatment and Research*, London: Wiley, 197–220.

Treasure, J., Todd, G., and Szmukler, G.I. 1995: The inpatient treatment of anorexia nervosa. In G. Szmukler, C. Dare, and J. Treasure (eds), *Handbook of Eating Disorders: Theory, Treatment and Research*, London: Wiley, 275–91.

Trenchard, E. and Silverstone, J.T. 1983: Naloxone reduces the food intake of human volunteers. *Appetite*, 4, 43–50.

Trichopoulou, A., Kouris-Blaza, A., Wahlqvist, M.L. et al. 1995: Diet and overall survival in elderly people. *British Medical Journal*, 311, 1457.

Truswell, A.S. 1999: *ABC of Nutrition*. 3rd edition. London: BMJ Books.

Tuomisto, T., Hetherington, M.M., Morris, M.F., Tuomisto, M.T., Turjanmaa, V., and Lappalainen, R. 1999: Psychological and physiological characteristics of sweet food "addiction." *International Journal of Eating Disorders*, 25, 169–75.

Tuorila, H. 1987: Selection of milks with varying fat contents and related overall liking attitudes norms and intentions. *Appetite*, 8, 1–14.

Tuorila-Ollikainen, H., Lahteenmaki, L., and Salovaara, H. 1986: Attitudes, norms, intentions and hedonic responses in the selection of low salt bread in a longitudinal choice experiment. *Appetite*, 7, 127–39.

Twigg, J. 1983: Vegetarianism and the meanings of meat. In A. Murcott (ed.), *The Sociology of Food and Eating: Essays on the Sociological Significance of Food*. Aldershot, UK: Gower.

Twigg, S. 1997: *The Kensington Diet*. London: Bantam Books.

US Department of Agriculture 1999: Continuing Survey of Food Intakes by Individuals 1994–96.

US Department of Health and Human Services (USDHHS) 1990: *The Health Benefits of Smoking Cessation: A Report of the Surgeon General*. Rockville, MD: USDHHS.

Van Dale, D., Saris, W.H.M., and ten Hoor, F. 1990: Weight maintenance and resting metabolic rate 18–40 months after a diet/exercise treatment. *International Journal of Obesity*, 14, 347–60.

van Elderen, T., Maes, S., and van den Broek, Y. 1994: Effects of a health education programme with telephone follow-up during cardiac rehabilitation. *British Journal of Clinical Psychology*, 33, 367–78.

Van Otterloo, A.H. and Van Ogtrop, J. 1989: The regime of plenty, fat and sweet: Talking with mothers on food and health. Amsterdam: VU-Uitgeverij.

Van Strien, T. 1999: Success and failure in the measurement of restraint: Notes and data. *International Journal of Eating Disorders*, 25, 441–9.

Van Strien, T., Cleven, A., and Schippers, G. 2000: Restraint, tendency to overeating and ice cream consumption. *International Journal of Eating Disorders*, 28, 333–8.

Van Strien, T., Frijters, J.E.R., Bergers, G.P.A., and Defares, P.B. 1986: The Dutch eating behaviour questionnaire for assessment of restrained, emotional and external eating behaviour. *International Journal of Eating Disorders*, 5, 747–55.

Vendsborg, T.B., Bech, P., and Rafaelson, O.J. 1976: Lithium treatment and weight gain. *Acta Psychiatrica Scandinavica*, 53, 139–47.

Viner, K. 1997: The new plastic feminism. *The Guardian*, London, July 4, 5.

Wadden, T.A. 1993: Treatment of obesity by moderate and severe calorie restriction: Results of clinical research trials. *Annals of Internal Medicine*, 119, 688–93.

Wadden, T.A., Foster, G.D., Wang, J., Pierson, R.N., Yang, M.U., Moreland, K., Stunkard, A.J., and Van Itallie, T.B. 1992: Clinical correlates of short and long term weight loss. *American Journal of Clinical Nutrition*, 56, 271S–274S.

Wadden, T.A. and Stunkard, A.J. 1985: Social and psychological consequences of obesity. *Annals of Internal Medicine*, 103, 1062–7.

Wadden, T.A., Stunkard, A.J., and Smoller, W.S. 1986: Dieting and depression: A methodological study. *Journal of Consulting and Clinical Psychology*, 64, 869–71.

Wadden, T.A., Van Itallie, T.B., and Blackburn, G.L. 1990: Responsible and irresponsible use of very-low-calorie diets in the treatment of obesity. *Journal of the American Medical Association*, 263, 83–5.

Waller, G., Hamilton, K., and Shaw, J. 1992: Media influences on body size estimation in eating disordered and comparison subjects. *British Review of Bulimia and Anorexia Nervosa*, 6, 81–7.

Wardle, J. 1980: Dietary restraint and binge eating. *Behaviour Analysis and Modification*, 4, 201–9.

Wardle, J. 1995: Parental influences on children's diets. *Proceedings of the Nutrition Society*, 54, 747–58.

Wardle, J. and Beales, S. 1986: Restraint, body image and food attitudes in children from 12 to 18 years. *Appetite*, 7, 209–17.

Wardle, J. and Beales, S. 1988: Control and loss of control over eating: An experimental investigation. *Journal of Abnormal Psychology*, 97, 35–40.

Wardle, J., Bindra, R., Fairclough, B., and Westcombe, A. 1993: Culture and body image: Body perception and weight concern in young Asian and Caucasian British women. *Journal of Community and Applied Social Psychology*, 3, 173–81.

Wardle, J. and Marsland, L. 1990: Adolescent concerns about weight and eating: A social developmental perspective. *Journal of Psychosomatic Research*, 34, 377–91.

Wardle, J., Steptoe, A., Bellisle, F., Davou, B., Reschke, K., Lappalainen, R., and Fredrikson, M. 1997: Health dietary practices among European students. *Health Psychology*, 16, 443–50.

Wardle, J., Steptoe, A., Oliver, G., and Lipsey, Z. 2000: Stress, dietary restraint and food intake. *Journal of Psychosomatic Research*, 48, 195–202.

Wardle, J., Volz, C., and Golding, C. 1995: Social variation in attitudes to obesity in children. *International Journal of Obesity*, 19, 562–9.

Warren, C. and Cooper, P.J. 1988: Psychological effects of dieting. *British Journal of Clinical Psychology*, 27, 269–70.

Wegner, D.M. 1994: Ironic processes of mental control. *Psychological Review*, 101, 34–52.

Wegner, D.M., Erber, R., and Zanakos, S. 1993: Ironic processes in the mental control of mood and mood related thought. *Journal of Personality and Social Psychology*, 65, 1093–4.

Wegner, D.M., Schneider, D.J., Cater, S.R. III, and White, T.L. 1987: Paradoxical effects of thought suppression. *Journal of Personality and Social Psychology*, 53, 5–13.

Wegner, D.M., Shortt, J.W., Blake, A.W., and Page, M.S. 1999: The suppression of exciting thoughts. *Journal of Personality and Social Psychology*, 58, 409–18.

Weise, H.J.C., Wilson, J.F., Jones, R.A., and Neises, M. 1992: Obesity stigma reduction in medical students. *International Journal of Obesity*, 16, 859–68.

Weiss, E. 1980: Perceived self infliction and evaluation of obese and handicapped persons. *Perceptual and Motor Skills*, 50, 1268.

Wenzlaff, R.M. and Wegner, D.M. 2000: Thought suppression. *Annual Review of Psychology*, 51, 59–91.

Westenhoefer, J. 1991: Dietary restraint and disinhibition: Is restraint a homogenous construct? *Appetite*, 16, 45–55.

Westenhoefer, J., Broeckmann, P., Munch, A.K., and Pudel, V. 1994: Cognitive control of eating behaviour and the disinhibition effect. *Appetite*, 23, 27–41.

Westenhoefer, J., Stunkard, A.J., and Pudel, V. 1999: Validation of the flexible and rigid control dimensions of dietary restraint. *International Journal of Eating Disorders*, 26, 53–64.

Whitaker, A., Davies, M., Shaffer, D., Johnson, J., Abrams, B., Walsh, T., and Kalikow, K. 1989: The struggle to be thin: A survey of anorexic and bulimic symptoms in a non-referred adolescent population. *Psychological Medicine*, 19, 143–63.

Willenbring, M.S., Levine, A.S., and Morley, J.E. 1986: Stress-induced eating and food preference in humans: A pilot study. *International Journal of Eating Disorders*, 5, 855–64.

Willett, W.C., Manson, J.E., Stampfer, M.J., Colditz, G.A., Rosner, B., Speizer, F.E. et al. 1995: Weight, weight change, and coronary heart disease in women: Risk within the "normal" weight range. *Journal of the American Medical Association*, 273, 461–5.

Willi, J., Giacometti, G., and Limacher, B. 1990: Update on the epidemiology of anorexia nervosa in a defined region of Switzerland. *American Journal of Psychiatry*, 147, 1514–17.

Willi, J. and Grossman, S. 1983: Epidemiology of anorexia nervosa in a defined region of Switzerland. *American Journal of Psychiatry*, 140, 564–7.

Williams, G.C., Grow, V.M., Freedman, Z.R., Ryan, R.M., and Deci, E.L. 1996: Motivational predictors of weight loss and weight loss maintenance. *Journal of Personality and Social Psychology*, 70, 115–26.

Williams, P. and King, M. 1987: The "epidemic" of anorexia nervosa: Another medical myth? *Lancet*, i, 205–7.

Williamson, D.F., Madans, J., Anda, R.F., Kleinman, J.C., Kahn, H.S., and Byers, T. 1993: Recreational physical activity and 10 year weight change in a US national cohort. *International Journal of Obesity*, 17, 279–86.

Williamson, I. 1999: Why are gay men a high risk group for eating disturbance? *European Eating Disorders Review*, 7, 1–4.

Wilson, C.A. 1973: Food and drink in Britain. Harmondsworth, UK: Penguin.

Wilson, G.T. 1989: The treatment of bulimia nervosa: A cognitive-social learning analysis. In A.J. Stunkard and A. Baum (eds), *Perspectives in Behavioral Medicine: Eating, Sleeping and Sex*. Hillsdale, NJ: Lawrence Erlbaum.

Wilson, G.T. 1995: Behavioral treatment of obesity: Thirty years and counting. *Advances in Behavioural Research Therapy*, 16, 31–75.

Wilson, G.T., Rossiter, E., Kleifield, E.I., and Lindholm, L. 1986: Cognitive-behavioural treatment of bulimia nervosa: A controlled evaluation. *Behaviour Research and Therapy*, 24, 277–88.

Wing, R. 1993: Behavioural treatments for obesity. *Diabetes Care*, 16, 193–9.

Wing, R.R., Epstein, L.H., Marcus, M.D., and Kupfer, D.J. 1984: Mood changes in behavioral weight loss programs. *Journal of Psychosomatic Research*, 28, 189–96.

Wing, R.R., Goldstein, M.G., Acton, K.J., Birch, L.L., Jakicic, J.M., Sallis, J.F. Jr, Smith-West, D., Jeffery, R.W., and Surwit, R.S. 2001: Behavioral science research in diabetes: Lifestyle changes related to obesity, eating behavior, and physical activity. *Diabetes Care*, 24, 117–23.

Wing, R.R., Koeske, R., Epstein, L.H., Norwalk, M.P., Gooding, W., and Becker, D. 1987: Long term effects of modest weight loss in Type 2 diabetic patients. *Archives of Internal Medicine*, 147, 1749–53.

Wolf, N. 1990: *The Beauty Myth: How Images of Beauty are Used Against Women*. London: Vintage.

Wong, M.L., Koh, D., Lee, M.H., and Fong, Y.T. 1997: Two year follow up of a behavioural weight control programme for adolescents in Singapore: Predictors of long term weight loss. *Annals of Academic Medicine Singapore*, 26, 147–53.

Wooley, O.W. and Wooley, S.C. 1982: The Beverly Hills eating disorder: The mass marketing of an eating disorder. *International Journal of Eating Disorders*, 1, 57–69.

Wooley, O.W., Wooley, S.C., and Dunham, R.B. 1972: Can calories be perceived and do they affect hunger in obese and non obese humans? *Journal of Comparative and Physiological Psychology*, 80, 250–8.

Wooley, O.K., Wooley, S.C., and Dyrenforth, S.R. 1979: Obesity and women: A neglected feminist topic. *Women's Studies International Quarterly*, 2, 67–79.

Wooley, S.C. and Garner, D.M. 1994: Dietary treatments for obesity are ineffective. *British Medical Journal*, 309, 655–6.

Wooley, S.C. and Wooley, O.W. 1984: Should obesity be treated at all ? In A.J. Stunkard, and E. Stellar (eds), *Eating and Its Disorders*, New York: Raven Press, 185–92.

World Health Organization 1994: *World Health Statistics Annual*. Geneva: WHO.

World Health Organization 1998: Obesity: Preventing and managing the global epidemic. In *Geneva: World Health Organization*, Report of a WHO Consultation on Obesity, Geneva, June 3–5, 1997.

Wyrwicka, W. 1984: Anorexia nervosa as a case of complex instrumental conditioning. *Experimental Neurology*, 84, 579–89.

Yap, P.M. 1951: Mental disease peculiar to certain cultures: A survey of comparative psychiatry. *Journal of Mental Science*, 97, 313–27.

Yudkin, J. 1956: Man's choice of food. *Lancet*, i, 654–49.

Zhang, Y., Proenca, R., Maffei, M., Barone, M., Lepold, L., and Friedman, J.M. 1994: Positional cloning of the mouse obese gene and its human homologue. *Nature*, 372, 425–32.

Zilber, N., Schufman, N., and Lerner, Y. 1989: Mortality among psychiatric patients: The groups at risk. *Acta Psychiatrica Scandinavica*, 79, 248–56.

Index